THE CLASSROOM SOCIETY:
The Construction of Educational Experience

CROOM HELM CURRICULUM POLICY AND RESEARCH SERIES
Edited by William Reid, Colin Richards and Ian Westbury

EVALUATING CURRICULUM PROPOSALS
A CRITICAL GUIDE
Digby C. Anderson

THE CLASSROOM SOCIETY:

The Construction of Educational Experience

HERBERT A. THELEN

A HALSTED PRESS BOOK

Croom Helm London

John Wiley & Sons
New York — Toronto

© 1981 Herbert A. Thelen
Croom Helm Ltd, 2-10 St John's Road, London SW11

British Library Cataloguing in Publication Data

Thelen, Herbert A.
   The classroom society.
   1. Teacher-student relationships
   2. Teachers — Great Britain
   3. Students — Great Britain
   I. Title
   371.102   LB1033

   ISBN 0-7099-2402-X

Published in the U.S.A. and Canada
by Halsted Press, a division of
John Wiley & Sons, Inc., New York

Library of Congress Cataloging in Publication Data

Thelen, Herbert Arnold, 1913-
   The classroom society.
   'A Halsted Press book.'
   Includes index.
   1. School management and organization — United States.   2. School
environment — United States.   3. Classroom management — United States.
4. Teacher-student relationships.   I. Title.
LB2806.T53   1981   371.2'00973   81-6453 AACR2

   ISBN 0-470-27222-8

Reproduced from copy supplied
Printed and bound in Great Britain
by Billing and Sons Limited
Guildford, London, Oxford, Worcester

Contents

Foreword

Few writers can be found today who address themselves to the fundamental questions of education. What makes a school educative? How
do we know when a school educates its students? What do we mean
when we use phrases like 'an educated society'? Perhaps these questions, and people who could address them, were not important in
times when economic growth seemed to lead to limitless future possibilities and when the public purse could afford not only to maintain,
but also to increase the scale of educational provision. In such times
'progress' could be seen as making more opportunities available to
more people and not as hinging on a sense of the quality of those
opportunities or the value of what they led to. In such a world
administrators and politicians could put aside big questions and
concentrate on problems of space, scheduling, teacher recruitment,
organization and funding; professional educators could devote themselves to limited and specialized areas of study and research — in the
case of teachers, to specific subject-matters of the curriculum and in
the case of academics, to the pleasures that come either from explorations of psychology, sociology, philosophy and other disciplines as
they apply to education or from the lure of 'curriculum development'.
'Problems' could be limited and specialized and issues of ultimate
significance postponed to another day.

The big questions of education are, however, always with us and, in
times like the present, they begin anew to claim and even demand our
attention. Social policies focusing on the distribution of social goods
give way to policies that attend to social investment: that shift of
priorities, in turn, requires us to ask what kind of a social order we
want to invest in. There is a need to deliberate about the consequences
of the ever increasing flow of social concerns and knowledge areas
pressing for places in the curriculum. We need to ask what knowledge, and what *kind* of knowledge, is of most worth? And there is a
newly-emerging concern for a 'leadership' within education that
articulates visions of futures — radical perhaps — that are different
from the past but, which at the same time, conserve that which is most
crucial to man's nature. Most important, there is a need to put
together the fragmentary insights and perspectives that are the

hallmark of the recent past of education into a coherent, but fresh whole.

The Classroom Society: The Construction of Educational Experience shows one way by which these tasks of the present can be ventured. In this book Herbert A. Thelen draws on a long experience of observing and seeking to understand how men and women go about building their futures together in order to offer a set of reflections on what this uniquely human work means for education. As he follows his questions about human nature and man's social work and explores a conception of education and educating that flows from his conclusions about this human work, he develops a timeless agenda for both social and educational philosophy and institution-building. It is an agenda for public deliberation and academic inquiry to which deep issues are central and in which the pursuit of wise policies is the core concern.

The vision of what might be offered by this book challenges the very forms of most contemporary discussion about education. It asks us to embed our sense of education in our appreciation of what our societies might become and what our schools might offer our children and youth. It shows how unimportant are so many of the starting points of contemporary discussion and debate as it invites us to confront our aspirations for ourselves, for our fellow citizens, and for our children, our legatees. It asks us to consider whether we really believe that the teaching of basic skills of literacy and numeracy is the most important task of the schools. It challenges the assumption that conformity is a value to hold foremost in our minds as we think about where our orders are headed. It asks what spirit should animate institution-building and national development.

Thelen builds his challenge to the ways so much of educational thought is conducted from two starting-points. He draws upon a sure grasp, based on observation, psychological inquiry, and his own experience of institution-building, of what men and women can do together when their human energies are released by challenging and appropriate circumstances. He draws upon an equally sure sense of what man seeks and what he values in himself, in others, in relationships and in community. Starting from these enduring principles — and they are those upon which any vision of education must be built — he leads us from values like 'quest' and 'community', 'authenticity', 'productivity' and 'legitimacy' to the implications of these values for how we should frame and answer *the* critical questions about our schools. How close are they to our sense of what they might be? What does it mean to seek improvement of schools if we want them to become microcosms of an authentically human world? What is the relation between school and society — now and in the future we are seeking together? How might our ends be realized by thinking about old and new models of education? And, finally, how might we assess the extent of our achievement, how might we judge our enterprise?

We welcome this volume to the *Curriculum Policy and Research Series*. It is a demanding book because it goes to the heart of so many issues and so many of our problems. It is a rewarding book because it invites us to ask what we want, and to venture a path that will lead to the realization of these wants. And it is a practical book because it shows how big questions become simpler as they become *our* questions, and can only be answered as we answer them for ourselves in ways that reflect our needs and our aspirations. It shows how we might begin such a quest, formulate our own sense of what is educative, and then share that insight with others.

Ian Westbury
University of Illinois at Urbana-Champaign
William A. Reid
University of Birmingham
EDITORS

Preface

Classrooms, like other social enterprises, vary over a wide range on almost any dimension you choose: morale, caring , achievement, creativity, sullenness, etc. As a wild guess I'd say that the upper three-fourths of the spectrum of classes is generally considered good enough to get by. A lot of the lowest quarter get by too, although nobody is very happy about it. The remainder doesn't get by, not because it is so much worse but because some ethnic, religious, parental, ideological or taxpayer group gets mad enough to blow the whistle. This often results in some cosmetic political maneuvering which masquerades as 'educational change,' 'increased opportunity,' 'education for excellence,' 'continuous-progress education,' etc. (The rhetorical possibilities are virtually unlimited.)

In addition to judging a particular school against other schools in the area, one can judge it against a thought-out conception (or model) of a good (i.e. educative) school. One can try to imagine a school whose way of life capitalizes on what is known about inquiry, community, personal motives, role conflicts, cooperative work, school subjects and social systems in general. Compared to this conceived school, all existing schools will be found wanting in at least some important respects.

There are two ways to think about this imaginary school. In one view, it is a utopia — all its practices are ideal. It demonstrates what a school should be like after it has arrived. The other view is that what makes the conceived school educative is not that it has arrived but that it is making intelligent progress. Students and teachers cooperatively strive to do the best they can with the resources they have; and it is participation in this thoughtful joint effort rather than in demonstration of a perfect model that educates. Education is achieved through thoughtful, determined and usually only partially successful coping with realities that make a difference in the educatee's life. Education is not achieved by learning to make the 'right' responses in a variety of situations that have little psychic claim on the student. (Such achievement may be defended as an essential component of socialization, however doubtful its educational value. Good educative process includes whatever socialization is necessary, but processes of

1

socialization may have little or no educational value.)

This book is concerned with improving the educational quality of two major parts of the enterprise: the way of life of students in classrooms and the policy-making efforts of adults interested in or responsible for education. I think that much of the same thinking applies not only to both these kinds of activities but also, with small changes in details, to the improvement of life in offices, industries, families and other personal-social transactions. In other words, this book attempts to get down to fundamentals.

Among the fundamentals is the existence of a generalized set of expectations — the cultural archetype — for what schools and other societal enterprises should be like. These expectations exert strong pressures and to improve schools one must find some way to work with rather than against them (Chapter 1).

Another fundamental is our understanding of the sort of thinking required in order to educate students and improve enterprises like education (Chapter 2).

Another fundamental is the way in which sophisticated thinking becomes effective to improve education as it contributes to the national culture-changing and culture-maintaining dialogue (Chapter 3).

The effectiveness of the contribution depends on characteristics of the interactive social system, and I suggest five criteria for a dialectical system that can best generate and use comprehension-seeking contributions (Chapter 4).

Having this much idea of the social system and processes through which improvement is sought, we next consider how we may conceptualize the 'way of life' to be changed — as being, most fundamentally, adaptive, participative and transcendental (Chapter 5).

But change has direction and significance only as it affects the present and potential values of the enterprise. Hence we must identify and define education-relevant values — authenticity, legitimacy and productivity — that are useful in specifying goals for each moment in the operation (Chapter 6).

As we move in on the teacher's role, we see that, although his goal is the education of each child in the room, what he really contends with is the whole group of students. We consider that this group has most of the properties of a small society; and the teacher's most fundamental function is to monitor the quality of life in this society. The term 'society' is a catch-all for a number of ways the group can exist: as individuals, as a psyche-group or a socio-group, as task or project groups. Each of these operating structures has its own special functions in facilitating the educative growth of students (Chapter 7).

Having some understanding of the processes and functions in which the teacher must participate and intervene, we get 'practical,' and look at the teacher's role as classroom manager (Chapter 8).

Next comes the teacher's role as educator: his ways of selecting and setting up learning activities in an educative sequence. I present a generalized scenario of such inquiry-oriented teaching and I explain the teacher's decisions and reasoning at each step of the model. I intend that this model will be thought of as a sort of 'resource unit,' out of which a large family of small but educative scenarios — all emphasizing inquiry processes in the classroom-community — can be generated (Chapter 9).

But many other models are possible, depending on what starting concepts you emphasize. Different school subjects, in so far as they are true knowledge 'disciplines,' start with their own concepts. I illustrate this proliferation by generating six 'models' for art education (Chapter 10).

Finally, we need continual feedback to inform and correct our action; we must continually assess the state of the enterprise. I select what I consider to be the most salient indices of quality in our educational system: self-realizing learning by individuals; classroom self-development into an effective inquiry-oriented milieu; the state of the informally and formally organized school organization as a dialectical system; the coordination of local school effort with national educational thrusts; and the basic conception of desired educative change in all parts of the system from technicist to humane orientations.

The acknowledgements to be given for this book, which sums up 40 years in education, could most pleasantly go on and on. My ideas have grown through a variety of exciting and utterly engrossing activities, and their listing may help the reader gain some sense of what is behind this book. My ideas of inquiry began with my work for a masters in physical chemistry with E. D. Eastman, at Berkeley. My first employment was as analytical chemist at Shell Chemical Co., Pittsburg, California. Next came my preparation as a high-school science teacher, under L. F. Foster, and my participation as a teacher in the Evaluation Staff's activities in the Eight-year Study. Contacts in this study with R. W. Tyler, Hilda Taba and others led me to doctoral work at the University of Chicago. There I was enthralled with Dewey and Lewin; and I conducted a study comparing freshman chemistry classes (at Oklahoma A and M College) which planned their own experiments with those that just followed the manual. During my long membership in the Education Department at Chicago I was centrally involved in developing T-group training with the National Training Laboratories (R. Lippitt, L. Bradford, K. Benne, A. Zander, D. Cartwright, J. French, *et al.*). My students and I conducted research there and at home on group 'emotionality' (taking off from W. Bion). I reworked T-group ideas into the development of citizen neighborhood action in the Hyde Park-Kenwood Community Conference (T. Wright, J. Abrahamson). A year spent working with managers, teachers, and social-workers from seven countries for the purpose of seeing how to raise productivity directed my thoughts toward cultural factors (Office of European Economic Cooperation, Paris). Back home again, I helped invent a training program which would apply our developing ideas to the preparation of elementary-school teachers (with J. Getzels, P. W. Jackson and K. Rehage). Then there was a year at the Center for Advanced Study in the Behavioral Sciences, where, among other things, this book was started 19 years ago. Also about this time we did a major study, reported in Chapter 7, on 'teachability grouping.' Finally there were two other major researches; one, under NIMH auspices, on learning activities and systems to help disadvantaged students; and the other, under Spencer Foundation sponsorship, to study classroom ethos (Chapters 1 and 6). For the last several years, I have continued in action- and therapeutic-oriented seminars, graduate classes, doctoral studies and consultation — to assimilate, experiment with and give shape to the thinking in this fifth version of the book.

Herbert A. Thelen
Chicago
1980

Note

I would like to stress at the outset that the use of the male gender throughout when referring to the teacher and pupil is merely for clarity and in no way reflects on female members of these groups.

1   The Cultural Archetype: Education's Guardian Angel

What Everyone Knows

One thing most citizens of Western countries have and share is their experiences at the receiving end of teaching. During their formative years they have accommodated to an array of teaching styles, personalities and demands. They have talked over their classroom experiences with friends and parents. As a result of this common experience and discussion of it, practically everybody 'knows' what teachers do and what teaching 'is.'

Teachers call the class to order. They tell the students what to do. They assign work. They demand, hear and correct recitations. They pass judgment on students, encouraging some and discouraging others. Listening to students is a sign of friendliness; being strict with students is a token of scholarship. Familial dignity carries over into classrooms, and teachers are to comport themselves within the boundaries of morality publicly professed by school authorities and parents. Methodologically, the essential (if not priceless) ingredients of teaching are the textbook, the question and answer session and the evaluation — which might more accurately be characterized as the sacred text, the daily catechism and the year-end confirmation to certify the true or sincere believers (and give them As).

I shall refer to this coherent, traditional, unquestioned set of expectations as the cultural archetype. A man may study teaching empirically and education philosophically to his heart's content, but he can never quite eradicate nor can his practices very far depart from the great expectations of this cultural archetype. Like the image of mother, this 'understanding' of teaching is built into our culture simply by virtue of common and prolonged experience. It acts as a force to restrain change and to secure order. It is at once the guardian and avenging angel of every classroom.

On the basis of similarity of attitudes, one could hypothesize that the cultural archetype may descend pretty directly from the pedagogue: 'Among the Greeks and Romans, the pedagogue was originally a slave who attended the younger children of his master, and conducted them to school, to the theater, etc., combining in many cases instruction with guardianship.'[1] In that model, the teacher stands *in loco parentis*; he is an adjunct member of the household, hired by parents (and therefore inferior in status to them). His power over children is 'official,' that of a civil servant, a prerogative of office rather than a consequence of education: his authority is legitimated by certification rather than by wisdom; and his objectives derive from social-class aspirations rather than from the needs of individual children.

These cultural expectations are as 'real' in teaching as are IQs, developmental phases, sex, subject matter and achievement; but their 'meaning' varies among individuals and groups. People accept the expectations as part of the natural order; but, like gravity and sex, they do not necessarily like them. For some, the archetype means opportunity and a secure place in society; for others it means alienation and denial. Moreover, the great expectations do not constitute a specific job description and they may give rise to kaleidoscopic permutations of teacher behaviors. The enduring and compelling force of the cultural archetype resides not in specific stipulations and prohibitions; it is instead the spirit or ethos inherent in the pattern. Regardless of their reason or merit in other frames of reference, practices that violate this spirit seldom last more than two or three years.

The archetype of schooling is maintained and elaborated by national cultures. The ethos of schools is part and parcel of the ethos of society, and therefore changes in the larger society, whether due to drift, catastrophe or plan, are paralleled by changes in the way of life of the small society of the classroom.

As institutional organizations, schools tend to reflect the same sorts of ethnic tolerance, orientation to authority, aspiration for achievement and principles of social self-control that are characteristic of middle-class offices, shops, clubs and bureaucracy in general. Schools are confronted with the same choices and options that represent the growing edge and diversity of the culture. Society's uncertain and ambiguous expectations about the deprivation and privilege of various groups tends to govern their position in school. Efforts to 'equalize opportunities' among diverse students or to redistribute educational resources in accordance with need have about the same success as similar welfare efforts in other parts of society. The belief, paramount in the 1920s, that schools can be innovators and leaders in solving racial, economic, political and social problems strikes us today as quaint.

What all this says is that to change the schools in any fundamental way — toward meaningful inquiry rather than superficial 'achievement,' toward realization of individual potentials, toward cooperative, mutually enriching learning rather than individual scrambling for credentials — will require corresponding changes in the cultural milieu. The real target for basic changes in the attitudes and intentions of schools is the subcultural system of education — the pattern of expectations, attitudes and aspirations that dominate the dialogue among participants in the educational enterprise both in and out of school.

It seems appropriate, therefore, to start our analysis by identifying just what the archetype does and does not stipulate.

How Students Perceive Their Classes

Since classrooms are the heart of the educational enterprise, let us see in more detail how the cultural archetype is reflected in the expectations of students. While these expectations differ among community subcultures, a recent study has attempted to discern more fundamental themes that seem to be held in common among contrasting schools in the Midwest of the United States.[2]

In this study, students were given a list of 24 statements suggesting what they might expect classrooms to be like. They rank-ordered these statements to describe a particular class they were in. The students were all eleventh graders, the classes sampled most of the school subjects and the schools were college-preparatory, rural-traditional, high-level vocational, inner-city and interest-oriented. Altogether, 900 students reported from 49 classrooms. It is evident from the findings that each of these schools has its own pattern of expectations, and that the patterns suggest somewhat different classroom dynamics. Nevertheless, looking beneath these differences, there are some common tendencies and it seems reasonable to suppose that these tendencies, which hold regardless of local variations, may be attributed to the more general cultural archetype of education.

The items fell into four clusters which ranged from 'most characteristic' to 'least characteristic.' There is no way to tell from these data whether 'least characteristic' means weakly present or actually rejected or suppressed. What we know for sure is that relative to the other items the least characteristic are just that. On the basis of other information, especially from observation of classrooms and from interviews with the school principals, we believe that the least characteristic items are actually rejected; and that they could not coexist with the most characteristic items: in other words, the two extremes are mutually exclusive within the cultural archetype — although, as we shall insist later, not within an adequate theory of education.

The expectations held most commonly to be characteristic of classrooms remind one of parental admonitions throughout the land and across generations. Successful students expect to 'feel like contributing to activities,' to 'think new thoughts of their own,' to 'learn some things that will be useful in other situations,' to 'face up to problems and solve them' and, to a lesser extent, to 'accomplish a great deal.' Most students rate these features as characteristic also of their imagined ideal classroom. In contrast, unsuccessful (dissatisfied, low-achieving) students tend to see these items as rather uncharacteristic. Such students appear to live outside the mainstream of education.

The next cluster of items, quite but not most characteristic, describe the image of teaching that generally characterizes classroom pedagogy: that one 'understands and meets task requirements,' that 'he gets feedback as to how well he is doing,' that 'tasks are arranged in a smooth sequence,' that the group is 'given reasons for what it does,' and that 'attention is directed to the "significant aspects" of tasks.' The picture shows the teacher as task-director, corrector and cajoler; and it shows students as laborers rather than workers (see Chapter 7).

In comparison with their ideal classrooms, students typically see these features as too dominant in their actual classrooms (by five to nine ranks out of the 24). The most satisfied students, however, tend to idealize those items which describe most clearly what teachers do. This is very much in line with what we found and reported several years earlier as the 'survival' factor[3]:

> This factor is contributed to by all the scores through which a child says how well he likes things — teachers methods of working, goals, other students, and so on. It is also contributed to by scores which, taken together, give a picture of conformity: the student is high on everything that is expected of him, no matter what. This liking is accompanied by rather low-level work and by lack of emotional involvement. There is rejection of fight and flight and of all but muted expressions of feeling. We cannot help but wonder if this factor does not portray successful adjustment to the demands of typical classrooms.[3]

Next most characteristic is the third cluster of items. They are in the middle, possibly ho-hum range, even though individual classes may be much higher or lower than the average. We labelled the theme 'group maintenance' and characterized it as follows: The theme in brief is that the class has some difficulties that are characteristic of almost any group; that it would like to be rid of them; that it wishes the informal (interpersonal, friendship) structure were more support-ive and the group more cohesive. Students would like more say in shaping their lives and teachers wish they could be freer of the role of disciplinarian. Perhaps the most striking (but understandable) aspect is the wishful rejection of the inevitable process problems of working together and dealing with societal issues (e.g. racial, social class) that all groups have to contend with.

As might be expected, these qualities of the member role differenti-ate between the satisfied students and the achievers. The satisfieds are optimists: they perceive more that the class is a good group and that students help each other, and they perceive, less than do the achievers that it has problems of working together and that it is troubled by societal issues. They also perceive less that one can be the sort of person he wants to be — which adds to our suspicion that being satisfied is primarily a mechanism of successful 'adjustment.' The achievers see and want less of 'good group process' and they are less aware of decision-making by students. Like the satisfieds, their ideals include more helping and less social friction. Achievers feel less effective as classroom members than do the satisfieds.

The fourth cluster contains seven items that are rated from some-what uncharacteristic to the least characteristic of the 24.

The theme appears to be of 'dialectical processes' of the sort called for by American ideology and its democratic way of life. (We will explain the importance of this cluster to effective school improvement in Chapter 4.) Since this theme is strongly rejected, it is evident that classroom life is not perceived as an exercise in living up to our pro-fessed politicoideological sentiments.

Let us show how these rejected items go together. We begin with the democratic political ideal: that the society 'capitalizes on diversity of individual backgrounds' and that 'persons contribute their special skills for the benefit of the community.' Society can utilize diversity provided that it is unified in 'common shared purposes.' Wisdom is sought as 'individuals clarify their own personal experiences,' partly through 'rapping with each other' and partly through 'challenging each other.' Participation in the dialectic is involving and one has a sense of 'excitement.'

Of these seven items, students are generally well satisfied with the uncharacteristic status of four: capitalizing on diversity of individual backgrounds, having shared group purposes that guide classroom behavior, clarifying private personal experience and rapping with each other. With respect to the remaining items, students and teachers would like considerably more excitement (by 15 and 13 ranks, respectively) and more utilization of individual resources or special skills (by eight and 14 ranks, respectively). The students, who probably read 'challenging each other' as 'attacking each other', are satisfied with its low rank; but the teachers, reading 'challenge' as 'stimulation' would like to upgrade it by eleven ranks. In short, the wish is that the classroom would be less dull, the students could have the sort of self-esteem and sense of first-class citizenship that comes from contributing and that interpersonal transactions would be more stimulating (from the teacher's point of view).

Our four themes, then, are about expectations of the student's role, the teacher's technical functions, group maintenance and democratic dialectics. The pattern of these thematic ingredients, organized by the underlying ethos of society, gives us one account of the cultural archetype of education which we must know, appreciate and cope with. Let us review this pattern briefly, to see what suggestions it offers about the educational problems we shall have to face up to.

The first theme specifies highly valued characteristics of the student's role. It presents the popular understanding of how students must participate if they are to 'get an education.' But as we look at the next three themes, the expectations of the first theme begin to look more sentimental than realistic. Most disquieting is the impact of the fourth theme: the rejection of those dialectical processes of social interaction that are usually thought necessary for students to seek identity, find personal meaning in experience and learn to be effective participants in society. The rejection of these processes would seem to limit very seriously the opportunity of students to 'become educated.'

The relatively high position of the second theme — the lesson-supervising teacher — suggests that 'training' (in the sense of learning to make acceptable responses in prescribed situations set up and supervised by a more powerful adult) is a more accurate label than 'education' for what goes on in classrooms. Finally, the indifferent position of the group-maintenance theme suggests that there is only accidental connection between the experiences of students in and out of the classrooms — that learning to live effectively in the classroom may or may not contribute significantly — if at all — to effective living in the larger society.

How the Archetype Thwarts Educational Growth

For a person to learn a new competence such as interpreting data, typing, critiquing stories, a number of things have to happen in a sequence such that each event builds on past events and anticipates next events. The function of the teacher is to facilitate the occurrence of each necessary event at the time that the learner 'needs' it or is 'ready' for it. The teacher may also encourage the competence-learning sequence to begin by providing a challenging environment, along with the resources of know-how, experimental opportunities and emotional support that the student will need to meet the challenge.

Obviously, whatever the required sequence is, one may expect that the cultural archetype would selectively reinforce some facilitative behaviors of the teacher and inhibit others. This would mean that the required sequence could not be fully realized. Some phases or aspects would be glossed over or omitted; unnecessary rituals might be introduced; the sequence might be terminated before completion. Thus we have noted above that the archetype tends to reinforce technical exercises and to suppress dialectical quests for meaning.

Let us now present a reasonable learning scenario and then consider how the archetype's expectations would block certain needed facilitations by the teacher. Let us imagine that the learner is confronted with some stress which invites growth in, let us say, more sophisticated ways of historical thinking. A number of responses are logically possible: he may refuse the invitation. He can rationalize away the whole state of affairs; he can collapse the distinctive problem-elements to familiar worn-out dictums: 'This is something I've often seen — so what's new?' He can respond selectively, keeping a steady eye on his own self-interests and ignoring the rest.

In a stress situation, then, we can undertake problem-solving that will relieve the situation or deal with the stress at its source. We can also go into emotion-avoidant mechanisms, run away from the situation, fight it, become dependent on other people to see us through, etc. We can even follow our impulses to act out, discharging our tensions directly, unknowingly, unawarely into the environment, in the hope that we can get rid of our burden and restore our equanimity.

We may try a range of avoidant techniques before we finally accept the stress as a fact to be dealt with — and learned from. In that case, we 'grow,' developing some new kind or quality of relationship, some more precise cognitive differentiation, some special skill in dealing with particular objects. Ideally, these performances would initially be sufficiently undeveloped that nothing would have to be unlearned. (It is much easier to learn in a field where one is totally ignorant than where one is certain of things that are not so.)

The usual state of readiness for growth is one of diffuse situational anxiety. The individual is restless, he has some sort of concern that he cannot quite nail down. This concern may be pleasant or unpleasant: something is felt to be enticing or inappropriate in the situation — if he could only decide what it is. There is some feeling that what he knows and lives by — what he depends on to see him through situations of this sort — may not be quite adequate; his attitudes might turn out to be inappropriate to his real interests, or his present expectation may be a mite untrustworthy.

He recognizes his state of doubt and it is accompanied by a new sensitivity to elements which he has not reacted to in the past. He feels that the situation is peculiar and that to try to run away from it would violate the expectations he holds of his own behavior. He recognizes that he is 'not the sort of chap' who would fake out. The whole person is involved and concerned and he may, if this state is prolonged, develop a variety of symptoms — ulcers, fidgeting, a rash, impulsive behavior, a neurotic world view, etc.

The next step is a focussing of concern. The tension no longer appears to be a diffuse property of the whole organism — it tends instead to get located somewhere in the cognitive domain or in the domain of relationships. He begins to try to diagnose, but without really expecting to reach clear conclusions. During this period he accumulates impressions from friends (in psyche-groups): he communicates his own feeling and gets reactions to it; he gets some sympathy from other people which legitimates his concern even though he is still not quite sure what it is that he is concerned about. He gets many new inputs of attitude because his sensitivity keeps him on the alert, and he picks up all sorts of sensations that he normally would not. He may have a rich fantasy and dream life, replete with imagery — and he may not know why. But all this begins to relieve the strain in the total organism so that it can continue to function more or less as usual in other areas. Through these explorations the strain becomes localized.

Now comes a period of experimentation. Up until now, he has been accumulating impressions and sensitivities; but now he begins to experiment, to formulate themes and alternatives. He tries, playfully, to find out what might happen were he to do thus and so. He talks to his friends, not so much for comfort as for challenge. He has a sense of stumbling over modes of action that might be useful in his present situation.

The required playfulness is possible only on the plane of unreality on which one does not play 'for keeps.' This means that a lot of exploration or experimentation can be undertaken without making any binding commitment. He operates in the subjunctive: if I were to do so and so, what might happen?

In addition to exploring possible attitudes, ideas and actions, he may also explore reference groups. If he changes in some way, who will be his new friends and enemies? In what social strata will his life now tend to be directed? This sort of concern is felt (because it is internalized as part of socialization) even though it may not be articulated in language.

I think this plastic period ends in the discernment of the pattern of a whole dramatic episode — and this pattern is felt to be the prototype for similar situations. He has penetrated and comprehended the present troublesome confrontation and has developed ideas that will greatly increase his power to comprehend further situations of the same genre. He has managed to perceive in an initially broad, diffuse, unfocussed problematic situation a prototype for a class or family of situations and he has had some reinforcing success in coping with the first instance of this type.

I think that at this point growth and development may (temporarily) become ends in themselves. A period that physiologists have called *allometric assimilation* is ushered in. It is a snowballing period during which the more skill or competence the person has the more input from the environment he can accept and process — with further growth of skill or competence. He revels in the new skill or interest; it preempts energy from other activities. At this phase the work feels so rewarding and pleasantly challenging that he would gladly sacrifice other usually rewarding activities (such as dinner) in order to keep at it. This sort of untrammeled growth can occur as long as there is a supply of nutrients, energy, relationships, money or other material easily available in the environment. But once these are used up or available only with difficulty, a new stage begins in which the consuming interest is brought under control by the whole system — by other parts of his personality, by the duties of life that he has to attend to and even by the expectations of society itself. At this point further development of competence is no longer an end in itself. Preoccupation with it drops off. The sense of proportion within the whole organism is reestablished. The new competence now joins the armamentarium of past competences to contribute to the further adaptation of the individual to his life circumstances. During this incorporation within the organism there may be considerable stress and strain and some part of this input might very readily act like a new confrontation and herald the beginning of the next sequence of growth activities.

After this comes a mature 'steady state,' habituation and institutionalization. (You can also refer to neural pathways and cell assemblies.) There may be development of greater efficiency or smoothness of operation, but no more major reorganizations are expected. New discoveries tend less to result from speculative leaps and more from having sufficiently thought out and detailed information that the individual can immediately sense any novel or unexpected elements in the scene. Having a mature developed prototype for coping, plus the requisite skill, does not in itself mean the end of creativity. It only means being more ready to push deeper with more significant questions.

The scenario of competence growth just presented illustrates the sort of 'model' a teacher needs in order to identify activities to be facilitated. In later chapters we shall be concerned with policies to guide facilitative effort, but for the present let us discern the obstacles to facilitation that are built into the archetype. There are many ways to hinder growth and when I list them I am appalled at how well they coincide with much present classroom practice.

The teacher, of course, can only invite and reinforce tendencies toward growth. He cannot make growth happen unless it is 'ready' to occur anyway. The teacher can augment and nurture the child's readiness by confronting him with affective stimuli, impressions or sensations. It helps if the stimuli are of the proper complexity, with proper timing, and coded for interpenetration of the child's worldview.

One archetype-reinforced way to hinder the possibility of growth is to have the child confronted, not by a slice of the real world of blocks, birds or things that excite, but only by the teacher. And hence the world can be known to the child only as it filters through the teacher's nervous system. Such a confrontation, however nice the teacher may be, tends to boil down to some version of 'Kiddies, guess what I have in mind.'

When we get to the second phase, assuming that growth has begun, it seems quite clear to me that the encouragement of the right to have fun and to speculate playfully requires someone who is warm and permissive. It requires a milieu which encourages the child not to count the cost or consequences of what he sounds like he is saying. A small group of friends is often helpful at this point.

Since the archetype is indifferent to such social facilitation, the teacher may just skip this phase entirely. After the teacher has aroused the children, he can lead them into a series of questions and answers which he has programmed to allow the children no room for explorations of their own. And if he is especially enamored of his pedagogical prerogatives he may oversee the program in such a way that he conveys to the students his feeling that their ideas are no good. If a child were bright enough to have ideas worth considering, he should be the teacher. Since he isn't, he doesn't. If he wants to chatter, let him do it outside the classroom. It is quite easy to kill growth at this point.

During the plastic period, the dominant function is experimentation and exploration. There is continuous seeking for alternatives which can be followed — at least in thought — to their bitter end, in order to see where they will go. This is a good time for conscious planned investigation in simulated or role-played situations. All possible points of view and all angles are *a propos*. You do not simply ask, for example, 'What is justice to a man who lacks money?' without at the same time adding, 'and to a rich merchant in the same town.'

For authentic experimentation during this period, the usual criteria of failure must be suspended. The only thing that can be wrong in a genuine experiment is one's expectations or preconceptions. One may guess wrong in one's prediction of what will happen. The only real failure is not learning from the experience.

This is where the archetype's suppression of dialectical processes is fatal to growth. The teacher is very likely simply to give one right answer, and to insist that it is right and that no alternative makes sense. The teacher shapes the child's overt behavior as in teaching pigeons to play ping-pong. He gives no reason why anything is right beyond 'because I say so'; and if the child wants more explanation or more basis of authority than that, then the teacher may mock or shame him. Just to twist the dagger a little more, the adult may tie the child up in guilt, alleging that, however the teacher may respond to the child, it hurts the adult more than the child; but, never mind, it is all for the child's own good — at the adult's expense.

During the period beyond the plastic period, skill develops for its own sake. The teacher would help by picking up cues from the child as to what the skills 'mean' to the child and how this meaning can be enhanced and reality-tested through practice. Thus the teacher tries to help the child see how his new proficiency can be utilized advantageously in many situations. In *Education and the Human Quest*,[4] I suggested that this is a period for hunting through the community in order to locate settings in which the child can practice this new exciting, engrossing and preoccupying competence. It is ridiculous to think that the school can provide the whole range of experiences that are at the cutting edge of development for all kids. Children should be invited (and supervised) in planning their own projects, taking field trips and making up plays — preferably engaging in activities that have a product so that the children can mentally connect means to ends and can become aware of their new productive strengths.

But such joint inquiry, which progresses through the children's contribution of their special skills, calls for a social technology to which the archetype is blind. Thus the teacher is likely to circumvent these curricular possibilities ·by assigning problems or practice exercises in which children apply verbal formulas given by the teacher — who then judges their responses to be 'right' or 'wrong.'

When it comes to getting the new growth incorporated into the youngster's total system, I think the child himself has to discover the limitations of his new competence, not through cut ·and dried 'application exercises' but rather through new purposive undertakings that have real-life consequences for him. But since the cultural archetype makes little provision for the differentiation of instruction to suit individual imperatives, it is difficult for the student to bring his new potential powers under control, to arrive at closure as he finds the language to explain his competence, indicate its importance, name its potential values and costs and formulate his hopes for it.

We have seen, then, that the archetype actively blocks some necessary activities (e.g. dialectical quest for meaning) but that it is merely ignorant of and therefore unable to utilize other activities (e.g. individualized courses of action). Among other important questions to which the archetype is indifferent are the following. Does the role of the student change as a result of learning? If the learner really has developed new strengths then should he not be given more responsibility in the classroom? Should that new strength not mean something to society? Would the fact that he is now more adequate and more competent not mean that in some way he can take on more responsibility and get more reward?

When I see a class which is just as dependent on the teacher at the end of the semester as it was in the beginning for information, plans, judgements, etc., I wonder what kind of growth really occurred. I conclude that to facilitate the growth of a child we must regard every increment of his growth as a new strength to be capitalized on by him in his adventures on the way to successful living.

The Collapse of Innovations: A 'Natural History'

We have so far been considering the archetypical pattern of expectations for classrooms. The expectations are both descriptive and prescriptive. They forecast their own fulfilment. Over time, any school, however novel or experimental, tends to drift toward the archetype's basic assumptions about what school is like and should be like. To maintain a school that deviates from this prescription calls for constant vigilance, active thought, tireless replanning, and a clear set of guiding principles and commitments. This required pattern of behaviors, stimulated through dialectical interaction (Chapter 4), amounts to a different way of life, an alternative or even a counterarchetype which can be maintained against the norm only by holding the line in each and every decision, however trivial it may seem. A great 24-hour-a-day expenditure of energy is required, and the minute the staff relaxes and gets comfortable, the innovative features will erode and the way of life will collapse or regress to the archetype.

This is not to say that the archetype resists all changes in practice. The problem is not so much with the novel procedures as it is with what the novelty of the procedures is taken to mean about the school's ethos, intentions or culture. In general, schools may safely experiment with techniques as long as they are seen to represent alternatives within the prescribed lifestyle. That is, new procedures are likely to be approved in order to increase efficiency but not to enhance quality of education.

The further a school is from the assumptions of the archetype, the more unstable it tends to be and the more susceptible it is to spontaneous changing. The changes tend to follow a sort of 'natural history.' A far-out school such as a parent-run 'humane' cooperative-progressive school tends (if it survives long enough) to become more manage-

ment-oriented and to resort to legislative rather than concensual decision-making. Over time, it becomes increasingly bureaucratic, gradually coming to resemble a factory, with emphasis on standard techniques of instruction and management. Its inflexibility makes it
unresponsive to changes which inevitably come sooner or later to the
neighborhood. Instead of developing the necessary flexibility, the
school goes the other way and become ghettoized. This natural history
of entropic degradation — the 'vulgar collapse' of distinctive-
ness — is worth examining in more detail.

Consider a far-out progressive school. It is likely to have been
founded by three or four persons who are members of a larger group
of activists. They feel very strongly that society and its schools are
'inhumane.' The innovative team is angry and is passionately determined to make their new school 'different.' They are, however, not
very clear about operating details and methods. Their conceptual
equipment tends to boil down to desires for permissiveness, first-hand
activity (conducted visibly out in the community) and each child
'doing his thing.'

Children from a range of social classes and cultural backgrounds
are selected for the student body, which numbers between ten and 40
and spans the elementary-school years. At first there is much discussion among parents and teachers about what they want to do and
how to go about doing it; but after the initial enthusiasm wears off
these discussions are felt to be unproductive and emotionally disrup-
tive, and the teachers rely more and more on catch-as-catch-can conversations with each other.

As time goes by, the teachers become aware of their differing interpretations of 'humaneness,' 'permissiveness' and 'responsibility.'
There grows an uncomfortable sense of ideological or philosophical
disunity, which they suppress temporarily through solidarity-
generating projects and field trips, and through the necessity of
maintaining a united front to the community. But it is difficult for
them to balance their internal forces for unbridled 'openness' (e.g.
intellectual and emotional anarchy) against the social-organizational
requirements for cooperation in common purpose. How can the
school be an organized mini-society with planned activities and at the
same time an open community with voluntary participation in emergent creative activities?

The inner processes required to solve this problem are dialectical,
and we shall have much to say about them. But for the time being, let
us note that they call for capabilities which the faculty and parents do

not have; and they do not have them because both their exercise and their outcomes would violate the cultural expectations. Hence the school cannot develop a strong organizational identity or common self-image; and it cannot maintain the force of its original inspiration in the face of the suspicions, indifference and hostility of the community. One storefront school in Chicago, for example, was padlocked by the police simply because it 'didn't look like a school.' The suspicions of the constabulary were aroused by a friendly gesture from an overabundantly endowed twelve-year-old female student.

In order to survive, our progressive school will probably fall back on the kind of 'democratic' decision-making we are all familiar with from clubs, staff meetings and Robert's Rules of Order. The faculty now engages in much discussion to clarify its purposes. Individuals initiate proposals, some of which are seriously studied by the faculty and, when reviewed favorably, are implemented by suitable departments, grade groups or committees. Changes are expected, and the school is open to suggestions from many sources.

The principal is good-natured, self-confident and protective of the school. As manager, he is skillful and reasonably unobtrusive. As spokesman, he is persuasive and modest. Relationships among the faculty are collegial and supportive.

The school aims to operate through consent of the governed, including pupils. This requires that the 'governed' participate in decision-making. It is found that decisions are reached most effectively in decentralized groups that are smaller and more homogeneous than the organization as a whole. Hence school-wide discussion turns from attention to goals to the task of working out a rational scheme of organization that can provide guidelines for routine delegation of responsibilities. Discussion of overall purposes is short-circuited and ceases. As Rapaport shows, the parts ultimately lose their sense of the wholeness of the organization and tend to devote themselves — by default perhaps — to their own preservation and enhancement. Teachers increasingly identify much more strongly with their subject fields than with the school as an organization. The faculty as a group loses interest in long-range planning and policy-making; and it becomes incapable of implementing school-wide objectives for learning.

Throughout these shifts the school is reasonably stable; but its accomplishments are those of individual teachers who tend to get promoted out of the school within a few years. With the loss of these natural leaders, the school lacks the people it needs effectively to induct new teachers into its unique spirit and the school loses its elan. The sense of educational mission which the procedures were developed to serve gets lost in the shuffle. School practices become institutionalized as ends in themselves and they gradually acquire the status of sacred rituals.

The school's functions have now become those of a factory: to process the throughput of raw materials (students) and convert them into a uniform product (certified). The nonuniformity of the input materials requires that they be sorted, sifted and shunted into different 'tracks' which run at different speeds. Grouping for this purpose usually turns out to separate students by race, economic condition and intelligence.

By now, the principal has become a priestly director. Communication is top-down and the panoply of bureaucracy is everywhere evident, simple and uncomplicated. The organization is highly structured. Procedures are detailed in thick, seldom-revised handbooks. The authority for squelching deviation from the orthodox is the record of the orthodox. Directives can change the procedures but not the spirit of the enterprise. They can upgrade requirements but not standards, ceremonies but not cohesiveness, individual choices but not autonomy.

Unresponsive to individual 'whim,' hard-nosed, rational, unchanging and run by a firm hand, the school offers the kind of security parents can understand. It is also enough like the school they went to that they can be assured the younger generation is getting as much — but no more — than they got. Moreover, this is a comfortable school to work in. Most of the teachers came through schools like this and its attractions helped decide them for teaching as a career.

The bureaucratic school very well satisfies the cultural expectations. Its ethos and management are similar to those of factories, businesses, governments and welfare agencies. There is some gap between the American dream and the organized way of life but this discrepancy is expected and accepted within the culture.

We have been considering the way in which cultural expectations and culturally suppressed dialectical capabilities practically guarantee the demise of radical schools and the drift of democratic schools into bureaucracy. One further characteristic of cultural expectations remains to be considered: the perversions that occur when the attempt is made to maintain the bureaucratic school in the face of drastic changes in the community.

To understand what happens we need a bit of history. For example the cultural archetype of American high schools developed during their formative period, say from 1824 to 1870. During this period, the clientele was mostly middle-class, and it is this sector that internalized the expectations and handed them down. The major change in schools during the last 30 years has been their opening up to lower-class minorities. These minorities have not internalized the middle-class expectations, but they understand that such expectations (whatever they are) will dominate the schools just as they dominate all other institutions in the official or productive society. To the poor, as well as to the community as a whole, the middle-class school is the major device for socializing *all* our children into the productive society. Hence its middle-class nature must be maintained. And an impossible situation develops: the attempt to enforce the middle-class school way of life in a non-middle-class student body. The prototype for the school that results is the inner-city ghetto school.

Because teaching and administrative procedures deny under-the-nose realities, they have to be imposed and maintained by force. The faculty orientation becomes authoritarian, legalistic, literal-minded and necessarily preoccupied with law and order.

The student beneficiaries have little part in the operations except, perhaps, to bend at the hips. The quality of interpersonal relationships — not the instructional procedures — violate the archetype. The school is attacked by militants, minority leaders and humanitarians of all stripes. The major concern of the faculty is self-protection and the major preoccupation of the principal is suspicion of the faculty's loyalty.

The school is nonprofessional. Faculty discussion centers on wages, hours, race and discipline — plus the more colorful and covertly gratifying escapades of the students. Students are segregated by 'educability,' which is to be fostered by mating IQ with docility, and there is little pretense of teaching the lowest group. The major division of the students is into two kinds of characters: those who fit the *management* procedures and those who do not. It is presumed that these latter will be intractable in the larger society, and so the school teaches them that there is not now, nor ever will be, any significant place for them in the productive society.

The ghetto school is an artificial society. It would fall apart in a minute if the imposing forces (e.g. threats of punishment) were withdrawn. Actual physical force is used enough to establish its presence, but the major effort is to head off and prevent incidents that would require the use of physical force. This calls for spies, infiltration, ambiguous promises and, above all, for 'not letting anyone get away with anything.'

In this authoritarian school, there simply is not enough energy available to do anything new: the whole outfit is too dispirited, hopeless and defensive. About the only prospect for change admissable in the archetype is a massive administrative transfusion. The new bosses come in and change the routines to other routines; but they finally place their broken lances alongside those of their predecessors, who found out rather more than they wanted to know about the difficulties of resurrection by fiat. As for the public, it excludes the ghetto school from the educational archetype and relocates it within its expectations of housing, jobs and health for the poor: 'It isn't as bad as it was and, anyway, these things take time.'

In summary, the state of the school is somewhere between formal democracy and informal bureaucracy. The school is quite flexible within this narrow sociopolitical range. We may now add these new findings to help round out the earlier impressions about roles, functions, maintenance and dialectical processes in the small society of the classroom.

Projection: Tomorrow's Schools

The cultural archetype is a spirit or ethos. It exerts itself through classroom practices. The practices are by no means the same in all classrooms. Classrooms differ markedly in teacher style, room arrangement, richness of materials, amount of homework and so on. The similarities are in the bureaucratic-democratic orientation of practically all classrooms to labor rather than to work, to a given or preset curriculum rather than to an emergent one, to 'meanings' learned as badges of social class rather than as personal equipment for richer living, etc. The collapse of progressive schools to this common cultural denominator is a denigration more of spirit than of *modus operandi*.

There are certain changes that the archetype actually invites. These are changes in techniques of managing and instructing students; and the school authorities intend these changes to make schooling more efficient and/or beneficial to undergroups. Such changes are incited by hopes of profit by entrepreneurs, by political pressures of minority leaders, by cries for help from classroom teachers, by liberals seeking a more even distribution of society's benefits, etc. (The changes are usually opposed by taxpayer groups, however.) Adoption of these archetypically approved changes by schools adds up to a sort of drift with little awareness of long-range consequences. Over a period of several years, these political, economic and ideological accommodations may produce a pattern of operations that is radically different in procedures even though its spirit or ethos is unchanged.

In order to clarify the sort of changes schools seem to be drifting into, I tried to project the four themes identified from our students' perceptions into the school of tomorrow — say circa 2000 AD. Needless to say, I offer it as a tongue-in-cheek fantasy, not as a firm prediction.

Assuming a stable society, and in the absence of any counterforce such as the vigorous development of professionalism in education, the school of AD 2000 will look something like this.

When the students enter the building on the first day of the new year they step on to a moving rubber sidewalk which transports them quietly and efficiently to the intake office. Here they are sent to small booths in which they are presented with a machine-programmed test which requires them to answer by pushing buttons. The responses to the test are fed directly into a computer. By the time the students have finished the test a slot opens and a card issues out; on the card is printed the student's schedule of courses for the semester. The student goes to his first class and sits in a leather armchair facing a large television screen. The other students in the class have been selected to be with him — the groups are homogeneous with respect to their predicted ability to push the buttons on the television program at the same rate. The program flashes on the television screen. It begins with a welcome, some patriotic music and a very short inspirational address by a teenage idol. He exhorts the students to study hard, refers to the importance of education and then is quickly displaced by an animated and musical cartoon in full color extolling the virtues of English. After ten minutes of this a teacher appears on the rostrum, introduces himself and the students to each other. He explains that he is there to give individual attention to any student who needs it at any time. The teacher is in effect to be an educational consultant, but he will also be available for more personal discussion. The students are then sent to their offices which they will have during the day and which turn out to be nicely appointed work cubicles. The central features of each cubicle are a television screen with a series of buttons in front of it and a desk at whose side is a locker. When the student presses the right button the necessary equipment appears in the locker so that he will have a tray full of chemical equipment laid out for each day's work in chemistry, a tray with the necessary mathematical texts and tools for the subject and so on. What goes on in the cubicle primarily is learning, directed by the program which appears on the television screen. As the student complies with each instruction — by manipulating a piece of chemical glassware or doing a computation in a mathematics problem or parsing a sentence — he indicates that he has accomplished his task by pushing a button, and the next instruction emerges. At the end of each work session there is a short test whose questions are flashed on the screen one at a time and the student indicates his answers. The results are automatically wired into the computer, which corrects its own program for the next day's instruction, making it simpler or harder or adding more steps or fewer as the student's aptitude seems to require. Thus the curriculum is continually adjusted by feedbacks from the student's own performance in the preceding lesson.

During the 40 minutes before lunch, the students are sent out for physical education whose games are freely chosen — after 15 minutes of body-building calisthenics.

A feature of the school of the future is the instant availability of any help whenever the student needs it. In both the work cubicle and the simulation room the student can phone any one of a number of people for advice or consultation about this work. If he would like to discuss something that is bothering him on a more personal level he can wander into any one of several offices located conveniently throughout the building. These offices are comfortably furnished with upholstered chairs and the student is served a little milk or juice, made to feel comfortable, and invited to say whatever is on his mind.

There is considerable concern in the school for the identification of talented and elite types. These are identified very readily, of course, by the computers. They run the student government. Since these people are expected to be the leaders of the new society, they must learn, along with everything else, how to deal with follower types. They are therefore assigned by the computers to students whose work is failing or who are not making expected responses and make it their business to call on such laggards, talk with them and through friendly persuasion convince them of the importance of doing their part by conforming to the program requirements. Since the student officers, as the coming elite, will eventually control society, they are trained to operate the computers, to write new programs for special purposes and to make effective use of a variety of communication media. As leaders they must have prophetic vision and value commitments, so they are placed in charge of the inspirational side of school life and in their hands is the planning and management of the huge biweekly festival celebrations. These celebrations usually include an athletic contest, barbecue, a torchlight parade and then an inspirational program. The high point is a dignified ceremony in which diplomas are handed out to the students who have earned them since the last festival.

A word should be said about these diplomas. Since each student is encouraged to move at his own rate, thus taking account of individual differences, he may have completed enough work for the diploma at any time. (This depends somewhat on the entrance requirements of the college he is steered toward.) In each student's life there comes that glad moment when on completion of one of his examinations the computer hands him back a blue slip on which is written, 'Congratulations. You have now earned your high school diploma and it will be presented to you with full ceremony during the next school festival.'

So much then for the life of the students in this school. The school, while physically isolated from the immediate community and its trivial preoccupations, is nevertheless in close contact with the national curriculum bureau in Washington. This agency is connected by teletype to the curriculum computer in each school. As new facts are established by the committee, they are quickly inserted into the local courses of study. Another national bureau in Washington collates statistics collected by the newly created Department of Education and Manpower, from manufacturer's associations, labor unions and so on. Forecasts of the manpower needs of the nation are fed back into the intake computers at the school in order to steer able students into whichever kinds of studies the national welfare seems to require. Similarly, there is feedback from the schools: as each student is launched in a program of preparation for a role which will utilize his special talents this information is tabulated in Washington so that the school systems of the country do not oversubscribe their quotas.

Our little fantasy can be viewed with approval or revulsion. One might feel that the school is a friendly considerate place in which the student's welfare is put first, in which every problem is treated as a reasonable difficulty, in which there are no problem children but only students with distorted perceptions of the world. It is a school in which there is very little waste of students' time, in which the programs are automatically geared to capability, in which curricula are always up to date and in which the necessary manpower and leadership of the country is prepared.

The school should have a good chance to survive because it expresses and is reinforced by the cultural archetype. Thus the new school assumes that test-measured 'achievement' is equivalent to education. The school uses ever-advancing technology to structure activities and to program individuals through them, without concern for what it all 'means' to the student. The school makes no attempt to relate social experience in the school to the need to learn social effectiveness for use outside school. By reducing the social system of the school to a crowd support-system for prescribed verbal learnings, the school cannot provide for the dialectical processes of adaptation and growth.

I have tried to project into the fantasy some additional antieducative notions: emphasis on the manpower goal at the expense of individual development reduces the possibility of emergent discovery and exploration by individuals; the criterion of 'meaningfulness for each individual' becomes a phrase to be mouthed only on ceremonial occasions. The increasing standardization of content in courses and examinations produces, as the first condition of academic survival, conformity to a detailed set of specifications fixed by outsiders who do not know the children, the community or the school situation. A simple logical proposition emerges: the more detailed the specifications, the more persons will be found who do not fit. Hence the development of differentiated ability tracks, adjustment groups and of the personnel services they require. It is seen that maladjustment is to be dealt with by making special adjustments in a variety of groups created for the purpose rather than by building a community such that each person is cared for sufficiently that he can learn to act on his own behalf. Passing examinations and pleasing teacher rather than learning to cope more adequately with the world becomes the goal of education; and kids learn that there is no place in the world for them except whatever place adults give to them.

The Child's Real Education

It is easy to critique the necessarily fragmentary descriptions of classrooms given to us by experts, reporters, teachers or even by our own children. We imagine how we would feel in the kind of place just described, and then we explain our comfort or discomfort in terms of lofty generalizations about 'education.' But when we wish to assess the education a child really gets in school, our fundamental question should be, 'What situations in school are felt by the child as dramatic, and how does the child learn to cope with and reach conclusions about these dramatic situations?' Or, in more currently fashionable 'cognitive' terms, 'What are the problems that the child formulates and copes with, and what conclusions does he draw from his efforts to cope?'

In classrooms dominated by the demand that the student learn information because the teacher says he must, the dramatic problem for the child is how to understand this arbitrary-seeming, contextless and artificial demand in such a way that he can get enough reward to keep him going. The successful student is rewarded by his virtuous acquiescence in the assumption that the game is worth the candle, that it is more valuable than the other things he might have done with his time and effort. He knows that if he can win the game, he will gain respect, envy, freedom from parental nagging and status in the peer group. He doesn't worry about whether the things he learns are worth learning, because that would destroy the game. It is the fact and amount, not the content of achievement that matters.

Since none of these gamesmanship understandings are officially intended or even recognized, the series of dramatic episodes through which they develop is called the 'hidden' curriculum; and what is learned willy-nilly and often ignorantly or falsely from the hidden curriculum is generally more influential in shaping the life and society of the future than is what is learned from the official, expertly supervised, information-oriented curriculum. The child becomes what he understands, not what he merely knows. He substitutes unexamined cultural archetypes or doctrines, transmitted through the hidden curriculum, for creative and analytical thought about the lessons to be learned from each situation.

Succeeding chapters will show what would be involved in the reconceptualization of school education that we so sorely need.

Summary

We begin by viewing some of the hard but elusive, often intangible realities of the cultural archetypical school. We find that four major themes emerge from the way students perceive their classrooms: the eager-beaver student role, the orientation of the teacher to technical functions, the indifference to social context and the suppression (or, at least, denigration) of growth-producing interactive processes. We then present a scenario for student learning and consider the points at which the archetype would be antifacilitative, an obstacle to growth. We further note that the expectations of the cultural archetype act as a strong pressure to make schools conform to a political-social pattern somewhere between formal democracy (e.g. Robert's Rules) and informal bureaucracy (e.g. limited negotiation). Then, just for fun, we imagine what future schools would be like if this same archetype continues to operate (and the society is stable) into the year 2000.

We point out that all the above is pretty conjectural (which is not to say that it is unsound) and that, for an assessment of education as growth of capabilities of individuals, we would have to go phenomenological, asking about the real problems that each child actually works on and about the conclusions he reaches from this effort.

Notes

1. *The Century Dictionary of the English Language* (The Century Company, New York, 1889), p. 4351.
2. A full account of this study is given in H. A. Thelen *et al.*, *The Educational Ethos of the Midwestern High School* (Department of Education, University of Chicago, 1974, mimeograph). This study was partially supported by the Spencer Foundation for two years. A shorter account, with implications for legal education, is H. A. Thelen, 'The Educativeness of Classrooms,' *Paideia*, vol. 1, no. 1 (March 1975), pp. 4-9.
3. H. A. Thelen, *Classroom Grouping for Teachability* (Wiley, New York, 1967), p. 71.
4. H. A. Thelen, *Education and the Human Quest* (Harper, New York, 1960), Chapter 6.

2 Educational Policies: The System of Costs and Benefits

How one judges descriptions of real or conjectural classrooms depends ultimately on how one specifies what education is for. Whatever else it may be for, there is general agreement that 'learning' is central and that the fundamental myth about 'education' that distinguishes it from other child-serving agencies is its commitment to learning and to utilizing knowledge as the major means for helping children grow up properly. In practice this means that class time in the elementary school and class groups in the secondary school are distributed among school 'subjects' and the matter or content of school subjects is mostly written 'knowledge,' which, for one reason or another, students are supposed to learn.

One's learning may be for the purpose of 'knowing' the multiplication table up to the nines, 'the' major events of the Civil War, a statement of the kinetic-molecular theory, the English equivalents of the French words in a story or the rule that students are to do what teachers tell them to. If the knowing is not seasoned with a liberal dash of understanding and comprehension then, as far as the students can make out, what adults call 'knowledge' is simply bits of information to be accumulated, recalled and verbalized in response to such button-pushing demands as, 'Recite the multiplication table,' 'What major event of the Civil War occurred on April 9, 1865?' and, 'Who are students supposed to obey in the classroom?'

Some knowledge known in this 'low-level' way is harmless or even beneficial. It may be easier to retrieve 'facts' from one's head than from a book; and of course, the really awesome hoard of a whiz kid may be worth big money on a TV quiz show. Many curriculum makers believe fervently that knowledge must be memorized as information before more sophisticated operations of understanding and utilization are possible. On the negative side, we note that 'knowing' of this sort, which has been shrewdly characterized as 'accumulation of a verbal repertoire,'[1] tends to involve taking unexamined assumptions for granted. A great part of 'what everyone knows' about education, which I earlier referred to as the cultural archetype of education, does indeed get in the way of serious efforts to rethink education.

Of course, there are those who stoutly defend 'what everyone is supposed to know.' Fundamentalists in religion, education or subject-matter 'disciplines' believe that certain books, traditions or myths are given to man by some higher authority; and that for a person to question such gifts is a sign that he rejects not only the super authority but, even worse, its earthly surrogate (teachers) as well. Fundamentalists place a high premium on knowing as unquestioned acceptance of ideas, partly because they believe that in his humble estate the common man should submit to the gods of tradition, aristocracy, scholarship, religion, test-making, wealth and, sometimes, school administration. When one sees 'rote' learning riding tall in the classroom saddle, one is tempted to guess that the nonexamination of knowledge is an obeisance to the teacher as god-surrogate; or that the material is so utterly common or profane that it isn't worth thinking about; or that education is conceived in the terms popular around the turn of the century, as exercizing of the mental muscles or 'faculties.'

A person who accumulates a lot of 'mere' knowledge or bits of information has, potentially, a great many answers. But he does not know what the questions are to which he has answers. Thus, he has the cart of learning before the horse of need. By contrast, learning in the situations of 'real life' responds to some sort of internal demand or challenge which will be satisfied as knowledge is learned, thus 'clearing the slate' and restoring readiness to embark on further, possibly more mature, adventures. The development of challenge, its satisfaction through the experience of gaining and using knowledge and the assimilation of the experience in new understanding has about it the quality of high drama.

To understand means to 'see' relationships between causes and effects, intentions and actions, attitudes and needs, environment and opportunity, self and others, man and God, dreams and wishes, parts and wholes. Each new understanding answers to particular needs in particular situations; and each responds to a very fundamental human drive: to find order in one's experience of otherwise chaotic, undifferentiated, kaleidoscopic events in one's past, present and future world. A person who apprehends the world as an orderly (i.e. rational and understandable) place can project the benefits and costs of what he is thinking of doing; he can use intelligence in the pursuit of purposes. A person who cannot see dependable relationships, and therefore orderliness and predictibility, is destined always to be at the mercy of someone else who, through more acute intelligence or power, can see or impose order (his brand) on situations; these are the persons who set the rules of the game.

The fact that the need for understanding is universal in no way guarantees the dependability, truth or utility of understandings. For some purposes, such as to understand why I prefer Bach (J.S.) to Bock (beer), the reward is in the fun of speculating, not in the accuracy of the conclusion. But when an understanding is to be acted on, with real-world consequences, then its dependability — as well as our reasons for believing it to be dependable — are of the utmost importance.

The great mass of understandings people live by — the cultural propositions that affect their conduct, security and growth in every-day situations — cannot be confirmed as logically true or scientif-ically valid. Their authority must be based on other considerations; and prominent among these are our intuitive experience-based prescriptive assumptions about morals, values and purposes. An example: for a person to be an educator he must count among his bases for action the understanding that children are educable and that they can improve their capabilities through the use of their intel-ligence. This understanding smacks of faith more than of empirically demonstrable truth, and there are certainly occasional cases which seem to refute it. But many teachers sense intuitively that decisions made in accordance with this faith produce more moral, humane and, in the long run, educative action than do decisions which deny this faith.

Understandings may remain as unexpressed, deeply internalized bases of action; or they may be formulated explicitly in statements. If we wish to claim that an understanding is true, dependable, useful or valuable, then we must express it in words or acts and show that these outward manifestations meet certain generally agreed rules or criteria. When we claim truth, the rules are in the domain of logic and rationality. For 'dependability,' the rules are in the domain of empiri-cal science; for usefulness, it is the strategy of action that must be specified; for value, what matters is the moral consequences which follow when the understanding is acted on.

The Quest for Educational Policies

To cope with the myriad questions that we must somehow come to terms with calls for a kind of thinking that goes beyond knowing and understanding. This additional kind of thought is what my favorite

Century dictionary (1889) labels *comprehension* and defines (in part) as follows:

> To take into the mind; grasp by the understanding; understand the force, nature, or character of; conceive; know sufficiently for a given purpose; specifically, to understand in one of the higher degrees of completeness: as to *comprehend* an allusion, a word, or a person.[2]

With a little tinkering, this definition specifies what is most needed in educational policy:

> To *comprehend* the educative enterprise at all levels from the nation to the classroom; to *conceive* of the character of education as a dialectical process which is to be *understood in the higher degree of completeness* of an educative system; and which is to be *known sufficiently for the purposes* of generating an instructional model for the use of teachers and an assessment model for the use of policy-makers.

The state of an individual's understanding of 'education' determines which of several approaches to improving instruction he will select. At the lowest level of understanding, he is uncertain about what he is doing, why he is doing it and how to tell how well he does it. About all this chap can do is shop around for something to imitate. At a higher level of understanding, he recognizes that he has problems and wishes he could eliminate them. He looks for some formula that works in management or psychiatry or elsewhere, and he substitutes it for that part of his instructional practice that he now sees was at fault. This method in effect tries to identify and replace a few faulty parts of the whole system with something magical and up-to-date. To the observer, such improvements look like fads, and they usually last about three years; examples are 'language laboratories' and 'cooperative schools.' At a higher level of understanding, there is the chap who sees the relationships among the various procedures and activities of a unit or lesson and also tries to pick up cues during the operation to help him plan the next step more responsively. Since he knows what he is doing, he can utilize all sorts of input-cues: scientific findings, pupil complaints, new ways to organize the class, new kinds of audio-visual materials and so on. Finally, at the highest level of understanding is the person who not only understands his classroom as an educative social system but also comprehends its relationships to other systems that overlap: families, community, political, societal, philosophical. This is the only one of the four whose practices and policies can respond to societal purposes and values, to middle-range (i.e. 10-20-years) expectations of the future, and to the state of public morality.

To gain a clearer notion of what is involved in raising the level of understanding a notch or two, let us examine a widespread innovation of some years ago, which operated somewhere between our second and third levels.

One of the really striking feats of the psychological laboratory was B. F. Skinner's discovery of how to teach pigeons to play ping-pong.[3] He followed a simple plan: every time the pigeon moved in the right direction, such as accidentally bumping into the ball, Skinner gave the bird some grain; and the bird, being hungry, happily ate it. Over time the pigeon tended to repeat more and more frequently the movements that had been thus 'rewarded' in the past. As these performances became established in the pigeon's repertoire, the grain began to appear only when two or more movements were linked in the proper sequence. Ultimately the experimenter's fantastic ingenuity and (following Tolman's famous observation about successful rat experimenters) Skinner's ability 'to think like a pigeon' got the bird to play ping-pong.

The principles of 'operant conditioning' which Skinner so beautifully demonstrated with pigeons became the authority for a revolutionary new pedagogical method called 'programed learning' (with one *m*). A complex learning task, such as solving quadratic equations, was broken down into a sequence of several hundred 'frames.' Each frame presented a bit of information, a question and several answers to choose from. If the student chose the right answer he was told to go on to the next frame. The questions were very carefully worded with all sorts of hints (called 'prompts'), so that the student seldom chose the wrong answer. Thus his 'learning' was 'error-free' and he was 'rewarded' by 'continuous success.' Each student could go at his own rate — and this was labelled 'individualization.' The teacher was 'freed' to give help to students 'at the times they needed it' — if they asked for it, that is. Otherwise the teacher merely administered the programs and the tests and recorded the results.

But in moving from the domain of laboratory animal training to the classroom-social-educational domain, something got lost. Nobody ever figured out a very convincing way to break down complex learning tasks into tiny component performances which, through proper sequencing, would get linked up. In fact, in some experiments students 'learned' just as well when the items were presented in random order as when they were in sequence. Continuous 'success' was not rewarding enough to counter the intense boredom that developed after a few weeks, so teachers had to figure out 'motivating devices,' such as going back to regular teaching — relegating the 'programs' to the role of conventional workbooks. The students who needed help often did not care to identify themselves in front of their classmates. Some students, when quizzed after completing a section of the program, were unable to say what the section was about, even though they had successfully answered the questions.

These observations raise a host of fundamental questions. Is it miseducative to teach the student that, contrary to his own experience, the answers to all questions are 'right' or 'wrong'? How does this square with our experience of 'maybe' and 'possibly'? Does docilely working through preset programs help or hinder the development of capability to program oneself? Can frame-by-frame accumulation of fragments of information produce insight into principles? What are the implications of ignoring all human competencies except those shared with pigeons? How do the programmers know that the content of their programs is appropriate to 'the' child, and what child do they have in mind?

But hold on a minute! All these questions assume that classrooms are supposed to be educative, but whose idea of 'educative' are we talking about? Our questions reflect only one of several possible views. How can we be sure that our (or anybody's) assumptions about education are right? Perhaps programed learning assumes a view of education far different from ours? Or maybe it views education as only incidental to some other purpose that is considered more compelling. For instance, teachers who liked programed learning said that it provided a clear structure for learning tasks and thus made *classroom management* and discipline easier; after all you 'have to manage a class before you can teach it.' They also said (but not to parents) that programs call only on 'lower-level' abilities and therefore disabled and lower-class students from less educated families can successfully complete the work and eventually graduate. This claim immediately took program technology out of the educational realm and located it squarely in the middle of the important issue of equal opportunity and equal benefits for all.

In 1954 the US Supreme Court ruled that educational opportunities of blacks could never equal that of whites until the schools were racially 'integrated.' This was a heartening decision for blacks, but since then a question has emerged: when we concentrate on opportunity, do we mean opportunity to succeed or opportunity to fail? What good, so the question runs, is 'equal' opportunity that does not secure equal benefits? When benefits are equal, then members of both races are equally likely to enter and graduate from high school. Any classroom technology which seems to promise that result is tremendously appealing to a political leadership. At the present time, with minorities becoming politically potent, the modern versions of programed learning (e.g. various forms of 'continuous-progress learning') are clearly the wave of the foreseeable future, and it will probably be at least a decade before the 'equal benefits' of high-school graduation will be generally comprehended as being far from equal. The 'benefits' of a diploma are not conferred by the diploma itself but by the system into which the diploma is supposed to provide entry; and this larger society has been protected from making the necessary reductions in discrimination by the sentimental illusion that the diploma would take care of everything.

It appears that the quest for understanding and educational policies based on that understanding is fed by experience and is theoretically without end. Yet at some point we must assume that our understanding is sufficiently advanced that we can act. When, then, is understanding adequate? We shall see that this depends on the number and kinds of questions we must answer and on how good the answers have to be.

The Cost-benefit Balance

Comprehensive understanding of the kind needed for 'policy' is sufficiently achieved when enough questions have been well-enough answered that a humane person can act confidently and live comfortably with the results. Confidence rests on a coherent pattern of understandings and, in policy matters (e.g. behavior-deciding situations), the pattern is organized by the key proposition that *every act has both costs and benefits*, advantages and disadvantages. This seemingly simple-minded proposition spawns all sorts of further questions. For example, what acts are we talking about? Are we interested in costs and benefits over the short range, the long range or both? How short is the 'short range,' and how long is the 'long range'? Is a particular cost or benefit direct or indirect? How direct is 'direct' and how indirect is 'indirect'? Who are the people whose costs and benefits are to be calculated? Why these people? Who are we leaving out? (This really swings once you get the hang of it!)

These questions are, of course, to be answered separately for each of the alternative courses of action or policies that one can formulate in response to the dramatic or problematic situation. The conventional practice is to conduct 'thought experiments' in which one tries to imagine that each alternative, in turn, has been adopted; one concocts a 'scenario' for what will happen; and one studies the scenario to assess the consequences for the various participants. In this analysis one draws on one's own and others' knowledge and experience with similar alternatives.

The most difficult step for the decision-maker is the final one: making the decision. Presumably a second obvious principle now comes into play: *select the alternative which represents the most favorable balance between benefits and costs.* But is the most favorable or optimum balance one in which costs are least, or benefits greatest, or the difference between the two largest? Shall we opt for heavy short-range costs for the sake of greater long-range benefits? Will the short-range benefits be sufficiently compelling that action will become self-sustaining? One sees that the 'favorable' balance depends on many details of the imagined scenario or projected strategy of action that the decision will set in motion.

Whatever the strategy is, it will be more congenial to some people than to others. There is the strong probability that one group will get most of the benefits and another group will pay most of the costs. There is, in other words, a fine line between exploitation and fairness; and finding that fine line may call for lengthy negotiation — and new learning — among the disputants. Thus the problem of defining the favorable balance moves into the domain of rights and privileges, justice and morality. In contract negotiations, for example, the quest for the just distribution of costs and benefits may be cumbersome, inept and expensive; negotiation itself has its own costs and benefits. But at least the quest is possible because the protagonists can meet face to face and keep at it until they agree that the solution they have found is the best obtainable with the resources that are available to them.

But what about classrooms? What costs and benefits are generated by the teacher's managerial and instructional strategies? And by the official and hidden curricula? Is good test or examination achievement a benefit? For whom? What about bad test achievement? At least achievement tests provide some sort of data even if we have little understanding of their meaning in the overall system. But what about less measurable variables such as self-esteem or anxiety? It is often thought that some amount of some kind of anxiety is beneficial to learning; but at what point does additional anxiety become a cost instead of a benefit? How would you strike the balance between costs and benefits to the student, teacher and society in an information-oriented curriculum or in programed learning as compared, let us say, to an inquiry-oriented curriculum or an 'open' classroom?

If the information-oriented curriculum is specified by societal tradition or by some distant curriculum committee (possibly dead) or by the school authorities (likewise), what sort of negotiations are open to students? If we don't think there should be such negotiations because students are too 'immature,' etc., then how are justice and equity to be achieved? Do we assume that these have nothing to do with education? Should students and/or their parents hold the teacher accountable for an equitable balance between pupil costs and benefits? Would that be fair to the teacher? Is is possible that the form of the school — its organizational structure, procedures and expectations — is such that these sorts of negotiations are impossible? This appears to be the position of proponents of 'deschooling' and of 'independent' schools, which are usually run cooperatively by teachers and parents. Yet the typically short life of these independent schools — usually one to three years — suggests that maybe these, too, can't hack it: that the deeper problem is with the nature of society and of the expectations and cultural archetypical controls that it imposes on all organized public enterprises.

You see what happens in the search for understanding: a relatively trivial scientific project gets embedded in philosophical concepts of man and society.

To comprehend means to see how each act or incident or idea is embedded in, connected to, or part of some larger whole; it means seeking or *creating* the context, point of view or pattern of circumstances within which the item 'makes sense.' And the sense it makes is a property of the relationship, not of the item *per se*. I have been using the words 'domain' or 'realm' to stand for the context within which an idea is examined or understood. Another word for it is 'system,' as in social system, system of knowledge, system of government, transportation system, personality system, political system and so on through all the identifiable functions and purposes of society.

A system or domain is generated by some point of view. The point of view may be organized around the idea of a technological function such as transportation or communication; or a societal enterprise such as politics or economics or education; or a basic concept such as justice or quantum theory. Every system implies its own purposes, concerns and perennial questions; its own methods for investigating the world and assimilating ideas about it; and its own propositions about roles, occupations or positions in society which are especially interested in it, have special responsibilities to it and are specially affected by the consequences of its development.

When we say that the educational enterprise is embedded in several systems, we mean that its operation is conceived to be affected by the resources, boundaries, environments, management and purposes of several overlapping systems.[5] And the benefits and costs must be calculated from the different standpoints of each of these systems and must be included in the projection of the favorable balance.

These notions apply very neatly to the history of the American educational enterprise. The Founding Fathers thought that education was important, and their ideas of education were part of a larger system of ideas about democratic or, at least, nontyrannical government. Their system of political ideology produced the system of policy which is codified and institutionalized, by fiat, in the Constitution. This system of legalized policy was interpreted by states and local groups as they created the organizational system of the schools. The schools, as active human social enterprises, then took their place along with other such enterprises within the larger personal-economic-social system of the community. One is struck by the number of domains through which the original quasiphilosophical inspiration had to pass in order to become operational and institutional: from philosophy to law to government to community. In each of these passages the original inspiration has been modified and an additional load of legal, political and social expectations and archetypes has been added. At each step, new benefits and costs were seen and these helped shape the evolving enterprise. As more and more determinants get stirred into the equation, the influence of any one of them became relatively less. Thus, the original compelling philosophical inspiration for education has become less and less influential on operations — to the point where it is now necessary to distinguish between 'schooling' and 'education.' Moreover, any new purely educational idea has very little likelihood of making much difference. To change the schools would mean to change the political, legal, governmental and social systems (among others); it is clear why change is seldom successfully initiated from inside schools. On the other hand, as the political, legal, governmental and social systems respond to war, depression, and other major upheavals, the schools also change; and a good case could be made for the proposition that they change in whatever way results in their paying the costs of protecting the present distribution of benefits in the other systems.

Plainly, striking the favorable balance is complicated. Not only must we see the proposed operation within several quite different support systems, we must also adjudicate the claims of these systems: their readiness for growth, their values for different groups of participants, the short- and long-range costs and benefits to their operation. To our comprehension of the part-whole relationships within each system we must add a higher order of comprehension, the way these systems operate together in some more inclusive system. Ultimately this more inclusive system has to be the humane society, but in any particular decision situation we are not interested in all the details of this ultimate system but rather the details identified as salient within the smaller systems. Thus the general conception of the humane society provides the frame of reference for constructing a system more sketchy than the whole humane system but more inclusive than the original component systems. It is in terms of this system, created especially for each decision or policy-making need, that the favorable balance is uniquely determined. This is our goal here.

Summary

We state that how one judges a school depends on one's beliefs as to the purposes which the school should serve; and that one generally agreed purpose is to help students utilize knowledge to live more effectively. In the archetypal school, this purpose is interpreted to call for the student's acquisition of specified information. We argue that this is inadequate, and suggest that the knowledge goal should be comprehension. In this case, the aim of curriculum construction would be the furtherance of comprehension-seeking inquiry. We recommend also that these same sorts of thinking should dominate our investigation of education. We present several levels of understanding as a way to suggest the kind of enquiry we have in mind. We use efforts to apply programed learning to classrooms as an illustration of how the quest for comprehension is connected to practice. We see that the scope of inquiry expands to ever-larger systems. Finally, we employ the notion of the cost-benefit balance to emphasize that the object of our inquiry has to be conceived as a socio-cultural-educational system; and also to enable us to know when comprehension is robust enough that action can safely begin.

Notes

1. E. J. Green, *The Learning Process and Programmed Instruction* (Holt, Rinehart and Winston, New York, 1962).

2. *The Century Dictionary of the English Language* (The Century Company, New York, 1889), p. 1154.

3. B. F. Skinner, *The Behavior of Organisms* (Appleton-Century-Crofts, New York, 1938).

4. B. F. Skinner, 'The Science of Learning and the Art of Teaching,' *Harvard Educational Review*, vol. 24, no. 2 (1954), pp. 86-97.

5. These are the five basic considerations that the scientist believes must be kept in mind when thinking about the meaning of a system. C. West Churchman develops them lucidly in *The Systems Approach* (Dell, New York, 1968). For exciting speculations connecting philosophy to 'systems,' see also C. West Churchman, *The Design of Inquiring Systems* (Basic Books, New York, 1971).

3 Dialogue: The Vehicle of Educational Change

National Dialogues

Changes in societal enterprises are produced, maintained and transmitted through people talking to people, both directly and via media. Through talking, ideas are reworked in new syntheses, interpretations and determinations. These emergent processes are embedded in the lush, seemingly unorganized and random dialogue of a nation. This dialogue shapes the mood of a country at election time, consolidates its conscience, marshalls its resources in war, celebrates the myth of progress through technology and confirms the mystique of its way of life.

These operations of dialogue have as their central element the groping for agreement among attitudes, hopes, sentiments and expectations. Dialogue is a unifying process. What sort of unity, with what benefits and costs, do our present national dialogues develop? The answer depends on the nature of the dialogue: and a one-word reply is that they are basically reactive or accommodative. In our cultures, agreements are sought to give the individual confidence that he understands 'what is going on.' We seek to put our thoughts and feelings into words, and to confirm them against similar efforts by others. This is informal theory-building, and it is psychologically important and valuable, especially when in the process people have a good laugh or cry together. In the reactive development of public opinion, the will of the people becomes influential in a backhanded way. Power elites and various pressure groups manufacture quasievents such as demonstrations, proposed deals with Russia, rumors about cutting welfare or imposing oil tariffs, suggestions about education for the handicapped, etc. With proper management of the media these dramatic inputs get before the public. There is then a period of reactive discussion spurred, perhaps, by feedback from real or alleged opinion polls. The entrepreneurs assess the dialogue, weigh the estimated costs and benefits (to them) and decide whether to go ahead. The assumption of those in power is that it is the public's job, not theirs, to show cause why they should not proceed on their own authority or on the basis of a presumed 'mandate' conferred by an election. At no point is there discussion of policy and long-range objectives, or a candid appraisal of present and eventual costs to the public.

There are, however, additional things that the national dialogue might accomplish and that many of its participants try hard to make it accomplish. What I have in mind is the benefits that depend on *active* rather than reactive agreements. The prime example would be arriving at national purposes and commitments based on shared comprehension of at least a minimum set of properties of a decent and viable society. Such dialogue would formulate the national will, not merely to squelch or cheer on initiatives but to strive for sound social policy and for personal self-realization through participation. It would nourish the humane-social system which we call community and which, in the opinion of many social philosophers, is in the most dire peril. They see that the old preindustrial community fell victim to the Industrial Revolution. They feel that our problems of waste, conservation, pollution, energy and so on, are now so interrelated that only a strong united resolve can save us; and that the fundamental precondition is that we restore our sense of, and loyalty to, our human community.[1] It is only now, as we try tentatively to generate this sense, that we begin to appreciate what the trade-off of community for technological benefits has cost us.

The present situation is that since we have plenty of dialogue throughout society the problem must be how to improve its quality so that its potentials for education, community-building and policy-making can be better realized. In this chapter we shall see what sort of discipline would be involved in these improvements and we shall be especially interested in implications for education.

The Dialogic Pool

Forty years ago, Dewey pinned considerable hope on the invention and spread of communications technology.[2] National TV, radio, movies, conferences, associations, journals, bureaucratic networks and all the rest certainly do provide the tools for the development of effective dialogue at national level, but they have not noticeably augmented active dialogue. The crucial ingredient in such dialogue cannot be captured by information technology; it is the voluntary, autonomous, active and reconstructive assimilation by each person not of words and pictures, but of understanding. National communication technologies make plenty of input available to local communities, but this input is of no avail except as persons, through local dialogue, search out its private and public implications for their joint action.

It is true that people watch TV, read books and try to influence legislation. Scientists and practitioners find out things, publish them and sometimes speak about them on talk shows. Different people do these things in different amounts, and nobody does all of them. And, as we attempt to keep track of this marvelously lush unorganized talk, we see that things happen. Presidents and prime ministers send up trial balloons. Newspapers, TV, and articles in journals register reactions. Personages take positions, offer rationales, demonstrate 'logic.' Legislation is, or is not, passed. Discussion of all sorts goes on in many local, associational and national settings, and among loosely or tightly knit formal and informal groups; and what happens is a byproduct of this public, more or less popular discussion. Scientific findings, local wisdom and reformist prophecies make a difference only as they are taken up in the widespread dialogue. The problem of 'dissemination' is the problem of introducing ideas into the dialogue and keeping them there long enough (and in such a way) that they are assimilated into (or become meaningful in) the thinking of people whose informed action is needed to produce adaptive change.

To clarify the sense of this haphazard public dialogue, I offer, with well-merited diffidence, the allegory of the dialogic pool. This contains and is composed of the expressed concerns, ideas, metaphors, slogans, recollections of the past, opinions, scientific findings and popular know-how that constitute the content of public discussion. It is into this pool that scientists, for example, toss their findings. The findings make a small eddy and then, mayhap, sink without a trace (on to a library shelf from which they may or may not ever be exhumed); or they get scooped out of the pool, worked over and thrown back in a new more manageable form — a report of an application, a novel they stimulated. Perhaps they float under the nose of some politician who is fishing for a good vote-getting issue; and he refers to them in a torrential speech which provokes a nation-wide flood of reaction.

It is the existence of this pool, with its dialogic crosscurrents, bleaching action and dissolving and aggregating powers that injects the outcomes of individual experiences into 'society.' There may be any number of little input streams from the various specialized communities (scientific, economic, welfare), down which they float their wisdom in elegant little packages; but unless the tide is running in the pool, the packages just accumulate like delta sand doing no good and, worse, blocking navigation upstream, in the pursuit of public interests, to the source of knowledge.

In all this fishing out, working over, throwing back and recycling of ideas, there is a continual sorting process. Some notions are in the pool for a day, others for years. These latter grow like coral reefs, associating to themselves other relevant thoughts. In the large pool they form small floating islands of established concerns; and from time to time some islands are beached and others are in the middle of the maelstrom. These ever-changing but always identifiable islands are land-marks (sea-marks?) in the dialogic pool.

Such permanent islands are the premises of the dialogue, the moorings for the deeper questions that float in and out of active concern. There is no final answer to these questions — that is why they are perennial; but their existence and continual reinterpretation over the centuries forms, orients and charts the history of human communities.

We educators must become adept, after local screening and formulation, at getting our better ideas into the national pooled discourse. Further, we must develop the habit of fishing in the pool, skillfully extracting intriguing ideas and working them over with our partners in action. But the most difficult and essential requirement is that we discern among the islands of the pool an agenda for continuing, long-range educational dialogue; and, even more, that we see this educational dialogue as integral to the total economic, political and spiritual dialogue of society. As we develop these capabilities, we shall learn that changes in the operation of schools and training programs are inevitable by-products of professional dialogue and that action is the social consummation of ideas rather than a separate end in itself.

A Musical Model

Participation in educative dialogue will call for discipline. The dialogue will be constructed from the same elements as garden-variety discussion: skills, attitudes, 'sets,' knowledge and techniques; but what will make it effective is the incorporation of these components within the serious pursuit of personal-professional missions. An individual cannot develop this capability by himself, although solitary meditation is necessary to it. The capability does not develop through 'fellowship,' although this relationship may facilitate it. Similarly, participating in 'ideological' protest, raising one's family life to the level of art, cooperating in service to the community and writing books like this do provide useful experiential input but may or may not be exercises in educational discipline.

The difference between the old and new dialogues may be conveyed most cogently by an analogy. Let us compare four string instrumentalists individually practising their scales and passages versus playing as a quartet. In both cases, the operation occurs in the same room at the same time; the players are affected by each other's behavior; each privately 'gets something out of it'; much of the 'content' of performance is the same. The obvious difference is that the quartet makes music and the individualists do not.

In a beginning quartet, effort is coordinated through the written score, which programs a sequence of external demands that each player must meet; and individuals are typically anxious about creditably getting over the tough spots. (This is like teacherdominated recitation.) But as professional discipline develops, the score becomes only a set of familiar guide-posts — objective existential cues — and the authority for coordinating effort becomes a shared *feeling* of the quality to strive for, along with a shared *intention* to attain this quality as well as possible. Each person's performance begins to be 'disciplined' by awareness connected to two senses: the sense of *context* and the sense of *form*.

Context is multidimensional: one is aware of the other players and appreciates their acceptance of each other's efforts to contribute; one is aware of many ideas and assumes their relevance to the group's intention; one is aware of present effort as part of a stream of remembrance and anticipation; one is aware of one's own progress toward greater effectiveness in the total situation. It is these contextual awarenesses that make contributions significant in the quasipublic 'life space,' that unify individual acts and that relate parts to the whole and the individual to society.

Form is also multidimensional: one is aware of the elements and components of performance and of the unique way in which they are combined; one sees how the united effect is produced by the subtle interplay of instrumental techniques as they produce an identifiable sequence of melodic figures and harmonic modes. One has a deep sense of the internal logic of the piece, enabling each player to anticipate not only what 'must' come next but also the general characteristics of subsequent movements. This sensed form is more than understanding; it is also commitment. Certain melodic patterns must be completed or responded to in formally appropriate ways; and the fact of a particular harmony creates imperatives for the manner of its continuance, resolution or displacement. The sense and awareness of form clarifies and reinforces expectations even as they emerge, gives dialogue its authority and thrust, enables individual intelligence to guide individual contribution and makes the structure of public dialogue resonate with the internal structure of the group's mood and common experience.

Finally, in the overall performance there is continual interplay between context and form, and it is this interplay that makes each performance unique. Even the same piece of music, let alone different pieces, never comes out the same way twice. The context may be dominated by fellowship and the group's playing celebrates this relationship. (The beer flows freely and performers have been known to play a fly crawling up the staff.) Or the circumstances may conduce to serious musical intention; the quartet 'knows' within a few minutes that this is going to be a truly memorable evening of music. Yet again, some new insight into the form of the piece or some new technical proficiency may place the performance within a new context of intention, relationship and aspiration. In different contexts the same form is interpreted or executed with different qualities of expressiveness, and with different meaning to the players.

Discipline, then, is not merely proficiency in skills, aesthetic appreciation, knowledge of requirements, etc. It is also meditative awareness of these elements, and anticipation of their potentially significant 'conjoint' consequences; and it is the voluntary commitment of each participant to utilize his awareness intelligently to shape his performance and insight toward the evolving end of comprehension.

Anatomy of Dialogue

During the conversion of undisciplined discussion to dialogue, four features need to be singled out for special attention. The competencies involved in these features vary markedly from one person to the next; and that is not only 'normal' but is a potential source of strength for the development of the dialectic — and for the education of its participants.

The Experiential Universe

Experiences of its members are the community's direct contacts with existential reality, the world of people, acts, emotions and materials. One's experience is not defined by the job that one holds, although job descriptions suggest something about one's opportunities for different sorts of experience. But the distinction between '20 years of experience' and 'one year of experience repeated 20 times' is worth making. The unique properties of experience are given by the personal-social context of a person's life. Two persons in 'identical' job-situations experience it differently.

A number of implications flow from this simple, obvious and often-ignored fact.

First, since the uniqueness of experience in seemingly similar jobs is the ultimate source of creativity for the enterprise, we must learn to respect each other's experiences. If we do not, we shall cut off the enterprise from the most salient inputs that it desperately needs.

Second, all further processes of awareness, theorizing and application are limited and biased by one's experience — or, more precisely, by how one's experience is 'internalized.' That is, each person, through experiencing, develops what appear to the observer to be 'basic assumptions' about the nature, meaning, utility, processes and expectations of education. These basic assumptions may operate intuitively, being quite 'unavailable' under normal circumstances to the person's awareness; in this case we theorize their existence to the extent necessary to account for consistencies observed within the person's style of life.

More pointedly, regardless of what he says, each person acts *as if* he has a theory or rationale of experience. These typically hidden rationales determine the quality of further experience; they generate selective 'resistance,' 'distortion,' or insensitivity to new stimuli — as well as 'openness' and reaching out. In many persons, — in schools, for example — these unaware rationales seem like built-in variations of the cultural archetype. All variations embody some different insight or creative approach, although considerable digging may be required to uncover the germinal contribution.[3]

The Quest for Awareness: Educational Relevance

With awareness, life becomes an altogether different ball game because the person is transmuted from involuntary reactor to autonomous actor. Without awareness, intelligence and self-direction are not possible and education reduces to training.

It is on the level of awareness, somewhere between the levels of experiencing and theorizing, that the problems of education come into the starkest focus. Each specialty — research, teaching, administration — not only attends to some of the raw materials of experience; it also deliberately shuts out other aspects, often overriding the clamor of its own intuitions. Awareness is a kind of knowledge, and knowledge destroys innocence.[4] What are the things that we dare not, in our various jobs, be aware of? What are the humane intuitions we have to suppress because knowledge is too confounding or even painful? A partial list would include: the researcher whose concepts restrict 'mastery' to specific performances; the teacher who feels that he can 'keep order' only by sacrificing his concern for individual pupils; the teacher-trainer who settles for grinding out technicians because his students are too 'immature' for educational philosophy; the theorists and leaders who join with publishers to convince teachers that 'going at one's own rate' is all there is to individualization; the bureaucrats and policy-makers who allow reports of research to persuade them that inner-city schools should be treated with 'benign neglect' or that racial integration can be produced merely by bussing; the teachers who willingly go along with upper-status parents who insist on segregation through 'ability grouping' — and the thousand and one other instances in which the criterion of *plausibility* displaces trust in one's own continuously examined experience.

Peoples' awarenesses differ, then, by virtue of different experiential content, subconscious and expedient patterns of defense, job specifications of what is 'relevant' and skills attuned to realizing some kinds of awarenesses but not others — as when the teacher's vocabulary for describing pupils is so limited that he can sort them out only as 'bright' or 'dull.' Awarenesses articulated by the various participants are the manifest content of dialogue; and acceptance of the fact of their differences enables the group to seek greater public reason and greater private meaning.

The Organization of Awareness: Theory and Neurosis

Man is a pattern-seeking animal. Inconsistency and conflict among his awarenesses is painful — which helps explain the all too frequent abortion of awarenesses that one senses would not, if allowed to fructify, 'fit' into one's already more consciously developed pattern. Abortion protects the claim of innocence.

The name for selecting, suppressing and distorting awareness to protect a preconceived pattern of thought is *neurosis*. The neurosis most prevalent in education — practically an occupational disease — is suppression and distortion of humane educational intuition by the sacred, culturally reinforced pattern of practices which we call *schooling*. But apart from strong, publicly exerted social and political expectations, there is an additional special reason for the neurosis of our profession: our experience with the teaching-learning process is so multidimensional as to defy comprehensive understanding. We intuit this multidimensionality: we sense that we are, *in fact*, regardless of the rhetoric of curriculum model-makers, dealing with 'whole' children and classroom 'microsocieties'; that as we talk to a child we are also responding in some way to his parents and community; that when we give a grade we are at one and the same time acknowledging past performance, encouraging or dissuading from further pursuits, assessing 'growth' and rewarding or punishing service to our aspirations. In this bewildering complexity are inextricably mingled past, present and future; experience, awareness and theory; and thought, feeling and action. It is no wonder that we seek simplistic, scientifically authorized theories and then legitimate them with passionately defended ideology.

Yet each simple theory or Procrustean concept *does* contain some piece of the truth. Our neurosis is not in having limited theories but in trying uncritically to make too much of our experience fit them — and in ignoring the experiences that do not. The ideal educator would 'know' the competing theories and their ideologies, and then would disregard them. He would assimilate each as the embodiment of a form, design or mode of thought and action; and these forms would become a repertoire of templates, a propositional inventory for constructing appropriate strategies of conduct in each situation.

The Unifying Principle: Humane Concerns

The continual quest for comprehension is the essence of dialogue. The required realizations are hard for individuals to come by, especially in the thermal immediacy of actionoriented interpersonal exchange; and once gained, they may be discouraging or even frustrating. Given this additional aggravation, how can a group find a 'sense of meeting' or a warrant for action amidst the indigestible welter of heterogeneous, incongruent, unexamined idiosyncratic inputs?

Diversity can be accepted and utilized only to the extent that it can be ordered by means of a unifying principle. I believe that the unifying principle that can make individuality of response a source of strength rather than a perpetuation of chaos is the love that is manifested through humane concerns. The qualities of humaneness are compassion and enlightenment. Concern without compassion is empty and concern without enlightenment is futile. 'Humane' studies in philosophy, theology literature and cultural anthropology can be seen as attempts to identify and explicate the perennial concerns of man and society. It seems to me that the quality of education might and should be characterized by its manner of participation in dialogue by virtue of its humane concerns.

We turn now to some of the considerations involved in managing constructive dialogue.

Summary

Having seen something of the realities to be coped with and the kind of thinking that will be required, we turn to the social processes of dialogue through which thinking is stimulated and made consequential. Nation-wide dialogic processes continually rework our culture and its expectations for education and other enterprises. I suggest that to develop comprehension-seeking inquiry we shall need to self-manage our local dialogue in such a way that its humane potentials (of enlightenment and caring) will be optimized. Under such conditions individual participants will be able to conceptualize education-relevant experiences and generate useful higher-order concepts, sound theories and humane concerns.

Notes

1. A consistently interesting forum for dialogue along these lines is the journal *Fields Within Fields*, founded and edited by Julius Stulman (World Institute Council, United Nations Plaza, New York, 10017).

2. John Dewey, *The Public and Its Problems* (Holt, New York, 1927).

3. C. Argyris and D. Schon, *Theory in Practice* (Jossey-Bass, San Francisco, 1974).

4. And results in expulsion from the Garden of Eden. For a catalogue of important research findings that teachers reject in order to protect their innocence, see B. S. Bloom, 'Innocence in Education,' *School Review*, vol. 80, no. 3 (1972), pp. 333-54.

4 Dialectics: Joint Policy-making and Educative Teaching

We have seen (Chapter 2) that what appears at first blush to be a simple rational decision to 'apply' operant conditioning to classrooms is not simple at all. The benefits and costs seen by the administrator or educator may be quite different from, and even opposite to, those perceived by the harried teacher; and these in turn are not the same as those hoped for by politicians, employers, textbook publishers, scientists and others. These 'others' ultimately expand to take in everyone who pays taxes for schools and everyone including the unborn who will be affected by the 'education' our people receive. But since only a small fraction of these legitimate interests can be known, let alone responded to, our policy decisions will always involve a lot of guessing. Therefore we need to ask how guess-decisions can be made intelligently. Are there certain qualities characteristic of processes that lead to the best obtainable policies? If we could produce these qualities in our decision-making dialogue, would they guarantee good outcomes?

To an educator or theologian, concerned with the growth of individuals into mature, humane, capable (etc.) people, the answer would be, 'Let everyone act as wisely, responsibly and decently as he can in all situations and the rest will follow.' This may ultimately be true, and it is certainly desirable; but it also calls for a range of information, a degree of self-confidence and a clarity of purpose that has to be learned, reinterpreted or confirmed afresh in every problematic situation. These learnings come from reality-based comprehension-seeking dialogue with others and, for the dialogue to be fruitful, the participants must construct it consciously, according to shared understandings of its architectural principles. These principles are not doctrines and they are not prescriptions; they are informed apprehensions of how the full resources of diverse individuals can be brought to bear in the joint search for wisdom. Such principles are internalized within one's character, but they still have to be learned. The settings most conducive to this learning are the settings in which such learnings are needed; and these in turn include all the situations in which one makes decisions about how to act or

51

about what must be done. Since what one does changes the realities others must cope with, all decisions for action have a social-moral component. The educated man, if not the technologist, recognizes that in his actions and decisions he is helping to shape the classroom, the community, the society and the destiny of man. He discovers that new ways of thinking about himself are added to the old self-interested ways, and he is aware of a new kind of significance in his life, namely that of his constructive contribution to the good of society. He sees himself contributing to the functions required to maintain the viability of the enterprises in which he participates; these functions include planning, decision-making, vigilance, caring, producing and communicating. In different situations he operates in the roles of parent, teacher, consumer, voter and others besides.

The enlightened person and the participant in societal functions come together and become one at all the moments of decision-making. At such times, two sorts of dialogue occur simultaneously: the *internal private dialogue*, which we call thinking and which includes weighing, creating, forecasting and evaluating; and the *external, public, observable dialogue*, which includes planning, goal-setting, agreeing, assessing and formulating policies for action. When such dialogue is effective, the internal and external forms provide counterpoint to each other: they mutually stimulate each others' development; and they receive benefits from each other. It is thus that personal morality becomes public morality and that objective facts become personal insights. The joint action of these internal and interactive dialogic processes is the *means* of comprehension. The special adjective for this quality of mutuality of inner and outer processes is *dialectical*.

In view of the necessity of dialectical processes in all aspects of living, it is not surprising that they have been studied from many points of view. The inner dialogue among 'dialects' has also been conceived as occurring among the individual's 'overlapping group memberships'[1] and among the person's inner 'selves.'[2] Philosophers have struggled with the nature of the process and have been struck with its various characteristics of disputatiousness, logical structure, fallacies, self-generative conflicts which lead to new 'syntheses' and so on. Argyris[3] gets at it from the standpoint of reconciling and integrating one's 'espoused' or articulated theories of action with one's 'theories-of-use,' which one acts on without awareness. Some psychologists find the 'constructive handling of conflict'[4] to be the most fundamental aspect. One is certainly justified in concluding that the dialectical process is complex, inclusive and possessed of multiple perspectives; it is a comprehending system, a 'whole' made of interdependent 'parts.' And it is generally to be fundamental to the adaptive development, tranquillity and education of persons, organizations and societies.

We are concerned with the sense in which the term fits the processes of mutually stimulating inner and outer dialogue and produces personal comprehension along with social-educational policy. We shall begin our inquiry with dialectic's linguistic partner, dialect.

Personal Dialect and Community of Discourse

An individual's dialect is his 'way of talking,' his 'manner of speaking,' his 'mode of expression' and it tends to be similar to that of others raised in the same community. In the United States, we normally can distinguish among the dialects of Westerners, Southerners, urbanites, and ruralites — although the 'national standardized' dialect of the television networks is gradually ironing out regional differences.

> Speakers are usually conscious that a certain dialect belongs to them; they feel it as their own, in opposition to others; they feel united in a common sentimental bond with all other speakers of the same dialect; and this inner, deep linguistic consciousness has a strong influence both on their lives and on their language.[5]

In short, an individual's dialect, including its connected inner habits ideas and sentiments, constitutes his 'personal culture' — his orientation to the world, his framework of assumptions about reality and values, his ways of organizing knowledge and, probably, the bases for his identity.

A person's dialect emerges from a community of discourse in which he participates. Linguists are concerned with geographical communities whose dialects are most deeply internalized within the person. But it is also useful to recognize other, more limited and specialized communities of discourse which a person joins not by the accident of birth but by years of learning. I refer to the scientific, religious, legal, business, educational, political and other functional communities, each with its own common pattern of 'habits, ideas and sentiments' which 'discipline' the lives of its members. Dialects are uniquely organized and utilized by and in each personality. In dramatic or problematic circumstances, these patterns are resources to be drawn on, selected from, combined or otherwise brought to bear on the situation. Each pattern contributes to the evolving created rationale of 'habits, ideas and sentiments' which will legitimate the action to be taken. The 'inner dialogue' referred to earlier is the process of 'integrating' each person's different dialects into a new synthesis designed to guide action in a situation.

All of this goes on inside a person; and when two persons interact in the same problematic situation, each is engaged in inner dialogue. For productive interaction, their inner dialogues must be sufficiently parallel that they can assimilate inputs from each other and yet sufficiently independent that their own special personal resources can generate new initiatives. For them to reach agreement on a policy or action, each must reach the same conclusion from his own inner dialogue and, because the inner dialogues are unique, each will comprehend this common conclusion somewhat differently. It follows that, as they cooperate on the agreed course of action, something about their manners of execution is bound to generate further dramatic confrontations for each other and thus stimulate more comprehension-seeking, policy revision and action implementation.

Criteria for Effective Dialectical Systems

The incongruent dialects of participants must be brought together in interplay which not only challenges and develops each but also arrives at sound policies to govern their action. Whether and how well this dialectical interaction occurs depends on the setting and the situation — in other words, on certain features of the social-action system. Five criteria appear to distinguish effective from noneffective dialectical systems, whether they be oriented to action, learning or policy-making. These criteria are as follows.

(1) Inclusiveness: does the system systematically identify and include the people-resources it needs at each phase of its inquiry?
(2) Adaptability: does the system continually adapt its own organization to face the challenges it discovers for itself?
(3) Vitality: does the system manage its inner dialectic in such a way as to maintain the level of energy it needs for creative production?
(4) Internalization: do the members understand how the system

operates (and their functions in it) sufficiently to ensure voluntary and zestful cooperation?

(5) Equanimity: can the system, under stress, muster sufficient know-how, imagination and guts to convert the inevitable and necessary dialectical conflict into sound conjoint policy?

Let us now develop these criteria somewhat further, together with their implications for educational policy-making.

Inclusiveness

Theoretically, the educative system includes the classroom, school, neighborhood, community and, more selectively via TV, the nation and the world. But in practice the educator must begin by deciding what function and activity he wishes to facilitate and then he must ask what demands (for skills, information, motivation, etc.) will have to be met. Finally he is ready to consider what people will be needed both to operate the activity and to give the operators the necessary support and encouragement. Definition of function, as everybody knows but seldom takes to heart, must precede definition of organizational structure.

Who, then, should be included in the system?

One answer is: all those whose interdependent or interlocking action produces and constitutes the activity under consideration. This suggests there could be as many ways of drawing up the system as there are distinguishable kinds of activity (e.g. one system for reading, another for character development, another for sex education).

Another answer is: all those who for any reason have a publicly recognized interest in the activity. This would include audiences, by-standers, parent groups, legislatures, financial supporters, politicians, media, curriculum-makers, scholars, etc. These persons are more remote from the action but, if goaded, may take a hand in it.

Another answer is: all those persons, whether real or imagined, that each participant identifies with; the persons who shape his attitudes and world view, and those whose approval he seeks as he participates in the system. These persons — reference groups and ego-ideals — are carried about in the member's head, and his notion of what they would think and do is an important factor in shaping the meaning and quality of his experience in the activity.

In any real system, all three answers are operative. For policy-making, the scope of inclusiveness is the range and variety of knowledge-dialects required for comprehension. This range corresponds to the range of roles required to generate the dialects: the citizen (institutional) concerned with the well-being of the larger social system; the practitioner (productive), competent to provide know-how for coping with problems; and the 'interperson', concerned with group cohesion and morale. These fundamental roles proliferate in many specializations; and in action-projects the list might well include concerned citizens, experts, 'gate-keepers,' sponsors and representatives of each identifiable group which feels that its welfare is at stake. For school improvement, the recognizable stake-holders include students, teachers, administration, support personnel and, depending on the topic under consideration, appropriate resource people from the community.

Adaptability

Is the system's repertoire of organizational modes adequate for effective utilization of its own resources? The wording of the question is fancier than the idea behind it. There are times when what has to be done can be best accomplished by individuals working separately from each other. There are other times when the most effective organization would be a twosome or dyad; or a small group of friends who choose each other; or a working committee or team, put together to get a job done; or a large, formally managed legislative assembly or audience — as when the entire class is led by the teacher. Then, too, there are many specially organized communication devices such as role-playing, panel discussion, group interview, 'listening teams.' Each has its special utility.

If the activity is dramatic, with a beginning, middle and end and with a plot, form and message, then at different times during the drama each of these kinds of organizations may be most effective and should, therefore, be employed. Moreover, each form of organization puts the person in a different role; it brings out or activates a different 'self'; and all these selves, each with its own special province, must be 'integrated' within the whole person or way of life. The roles of friend, cooperative producer, legislator, critic and bystander all have their most facilitative settings and, conversely, each setting is best utilized through production of the appropriate role.

Vitality

For a system to operate effectively, it must have sufficient vitality in all its parts. Participants must be 'motivated,' 'involved' or 'turned on' enough to overcome the vicissitudes of frustration and inadequacy.

The vitality of the system can be understood as a byproduct of its dialectical processes, in which case its social organization would be understood as a structural form for channeling individual tensions into productive enterprise. In policy-making, the built-in arrangement for vitalizing or activating members is their exposure to and participation in overlapping dialogues. Not only must the citizen and producer roles seek reconciliation; so also must the producer and interperson and the citizen and interperson — and all three dialogues have to be assimilated within each participant's personal culture. The source of vitality is the active need of individuals to find consistency within their own thoughts and attitudes; and this need is engendered by deliberately arranging for inputs which are 'potentially' cooperative, because they are addressed to the same purpose, but which nevertheless stem from different ways of approaching the purpose. In a sense, the reconciliation which the individual must find is between two or more subcultures or dialects as conveyed by persons competent to represent them.

The consistency, controversy or conflict emerging from overlap of different approaches should be distinguished from the more intense but less significant conflict arising from inconsistent elements within one approach. The former arises when an adolescent girl talks first to a minister and then to a doctor about sex; her sense of conflict may escalate to the level of moral issues. On the other hand, if she talks to two doctors and one advises that the pill is harmful whereas the other says it is safe, the inconsistency is intensely felt because it is at the practical level of deciding between mutually exclusive alternatives for action. But the inconsistency can be resolved at its own level by getting more evidence of the same kind, and very little reconstruction within the girl's mind is called for. Both kinds of inconsistency activate the girl's thought and affective processes, but the former dialectical kind has real consequences for ultimately changing the whole system of society, whereas the latter does not go beyond itself.

Thus the vitality of a system is generated in and flows from the private psychic quest of its members as they attempt to 'integrate' their various role rationales. Psychologists make the point more vividly by speaking about a person's various 'selves.' In different theories or mythologies there are different selves corresponding to the various ways of slicing life into its component functions. But, however the selves are defined, they get into controversy with each other, negotiate and try to 'get it all together' in a mutual-assistance pact. Negotiation is inside the person but it produces his overt activity in the real external world. His conscious awareness of his overt activity (and its consequences) gives new input to his inner negotiations. It provides new 'content' to chew on and it reality-tests tentative settlements on the way to conclusion.

When the various internal selves are having a bad time working out their conflicts, controversies, etc., they may be helped by incorporating some other person's selves around their internal conference table. Thus in a personal-decision situation we ask ourselves what certain imagined people such as our father, an old friend, Baron Munchausen or Lincoln 'would have done'; and we also consider this from the standpoint of real people, physically present, with whom we identify in the interactive group.

In this view, the face-to-face group is the public meeting-place for reflections of the various selves of all the participants; and discussion in a vital group is only the external interpersonal aspect of intrapersonal negotiations among internal selves. Each person increases his strength by assimilating some of the public reflected selves (or 'others') into his own negotiating team. Thus, in similar vein, friends are frequently thought of as extensions of the self.

The particular selves who will be available for incorporation and participation in the life of another depend upon the purposes and organization of the activity. Hence to encompass, as one must, the full reach of a person's potentials, the entire repertoire of organizational forms and activities must be drawn upon.

I conclude that a group or system is 'vital' to the extent that discussion of its issues and concerns constitutes the externalized aspect of the inner negotiations among the selves of the members. It follows that the most appropriate organization at any given time is the one that most effectively brings 'on stage,' and supports, whichever selves and 'others' are most salient to the inner negotiations of participants.

Internalization

The more fully a person perceives, understands and incorporates into his own mentality a system of which he is a part the better he can work with it and modify it to increase his — and therefore its — effectiveness. This process of incorporating the external world within oneself is *internalization*.[6]

For a person to internalize a system, his knowledge must go way beyond descriptive information and characterization. We have, for example, graduate students who 'know' more about a department than their professors; but they cannot 'work with it.' Theirs is the sort of understanding-cum-estrangement most of us have about national politics, the economy, society, other ethnic groups, literature, etc. We cannot with any confidence or conviction 'put ourselves in the picture' — or build a picture around us.

To internalize a classroom or other system, an individual must participate in its functions so that he can get the first-hand data which he needs; think about it, so that he can intuit its pattern and be able to predict how the system would react to things he might do; and, ultimately, assimilate these understandings within his own way of life so well that he more or less spontaneously produces mature behavior. At this happy point of mastery and autonomy we would say that he had got it all together: conception, intuition and practice.

A man with internalized understanding appears to do the appropriate thing intuitively, just as a great artist or practitioner performs superbly when he simply does what he 'feels' is right. But in fairness to these people we must appreciate that their 'natural' intuitions underwent a great deal of arduous training. Central in this preparation was the purposive direction of *consciousness*. Consciously sought and examined experience is the method of incorporating the world within the self. A person is not 'intuitive' because he remembers all the details — that just makes him a scholar — so much as because he has forgotten them, remembering only their essential form or pattern. *This* is the substance of intuition. With it one can easily recall, reconstruct or even seemingly 'make up' the details; without it, every decision is a laborious, rational, technical computerized act which can never be fully authentic.

Participants internalize their policy-making system when they consciously participate in planning, decision-making, evaluating, etc. For more of their 'selves' are then activated and, as they negotiate internally, they seek more diverse and comprehensive input. We shall see that, because of the dominant role of consciousness, a great amount of knowledge is going to be acquired. The kinds and amounts will depend on how particularly and fully the person in his situation 'needs' to understand the system. When, as in the educative classroom, the system is set up to exemplify, simulate, carry out and confront a vast array of human-social-civilizing functions, then learning subject matter is part of the process of internalizing the system; and it is in this wise that the 'content' of 'subjects' can contribute to increased personal autonomy and competence within the system.

The use of consciousness to examine one's experience is a fairly sophisticated undertaking; but it is the essence of the humane, educated way of life. I call the process sophisticated because it proceeds most effectively through forms or kinds of discourse which must be learned. The function of such discourse is explanation, orientation, prediction and judgment — the so-called 'higher mental processes' through which what otherwise would be mere information takes on the cloth of knowledge and, at times, the splendid raiment of wisdom.

The classroom or other system develops through the internalization within each person of observed and shared activity. The way that the activity is internalized influences the way in which the person participates in the next activity. When a person's activity is interdependent with that of other persons, their differing internalizations lead to frictions and discrepancies which, through reason and dialectical discourse, can generate readiness for further joint activity.

Equanimity

The dynamic that drives social systems is the quest for reconciliation of two opposing tendencies. One tendency is for the system to fly apart as each individual maximizes his autonomy to 'do his thing.' Opposed to this is the tendency to seek security and predictability in common agreements and understandings of the culture and way of life of the group. The optimum reconciliation of these centrifugal and centripetal tendencies would be signified by agreements that structure a secure and predictable social order and at the same time define action fields within which each individual can make personally significant choices. The equanimity of the group is the quality of the balances or trade-offs achieved between these two pursuits within and by the system.

For much policy-making, the dialects and roles to be included in the group are those of practitioner, theorist and empiricist. The concern and responsibility of the theorist is with universal propositions: the framework of assumptions and, by implication, values, that are to be adopted by the group and that will give it its identity. Once agreed upon, these become the authority for group functioning and for individual self-discipline. The theorist is the purest representative and conveyor of the group's centripetal tendencies. In sharp contrast, the concern and responsibility of the practitioner is to find better ways to do his thing in his own local and idiosyncratic situation. Practitioners continually confront the group with diverse inputs and demands; they best convey the individualistic or centrifugal tendencies of the system. In order to resolve the conflict between these opposing tendencies, the group has to find some compelling and accessible authority that can mediate between the propositions of the theorists and the 'needs' of the practitioners. This authority is nature itself: the way the world 'is,' as distinct from the way the theorist encapsulates it or the practitioner selectively perceives it. Hence the empiricist is needed. We can see that the theorist needs the empiricist's help to convince the others that his propositions do indeed illuminate existential reality. The practitioner likewise needs the empiricist's help to convince others that his accounts and allegations about his experience are dependable, that is, that they are in line with what has already been established about similar classes of situations and phenomena. The opposing forces are conciliated by confident agreement that what is to be done (empirical) has a chance to be done because the practitioners see it as a better means to their goals; and that it will be socially and humanely significant because it reflects propositions that (theoretically) should capture enduring long-range values and aspirations.

In dealing with these oppositions which are both within and between persons, every group nurtures its own ethos, spirit, 'basic assumption emotionality culture' (Bion) or daemon; it is almost tangible. On the one hand, there may be petulance, short-temperedness, scratchiness, condescension and emotional contagion; individual efforts get side-tracked and forward no apparent intention. On the other hand, there is constructiveness, responsiveness, pattern-seeking and openness; individuals can be polarized by controversy at 10.0 a.m. and be singing close harmony by lunch time.

In this latter case, the dialogue is productive and the spirit of the group is characterized by equanimity. As usual, my *Century Dictionary of the English Language* spells out what I have in mind better than I can:

> *equanimity.* Evenness of mind or temper; calmness or firmness, especially under conditions adapted to excite great emotion; a state of resistance to [contagion of] elation, depression, anger, etc.

> This watch over a man's self, and the command of his temper, I take to be the greatest of human perfections . . . I do not know how to express this habit of mind, except you will let me call it *equanimity. Tatler*

> When selfishness has given way to generosity, and perfect love has cast out fear — then all this shows itself in that equipoise of soul

which we call good temper or *equanimity*. J. F. Clarke, *Self-culture*, 287

Out of an *equanimous* civility to his many friends. Eikon Basilike

The attitudinal component of equanimity is good will, expressed by members and imputed to each other. The creative component of equanimity is playfulness, which explores ideas through constructive fantasy. The threat-reducing component of equanimity is defusing through humor, objectivity and experimental-mindedness. The adaptive component of equanimity is receptivity to, and deliberative utilization of, all sorts of contributions; it is the ability to capitalize on diversity. The security-giving component is trustworthy relationships between means and ends and short- and long-range goals; it is also likely to include respect for the system's own history. And the supportive component is the assumption that everyone is a first-class citizen having the same humane concerns and entitled to the same rights and privileges as everyone else in the system.

Maintenance and enhancement of equanimity is effected by the dialogic skills of the participants and therefore all members must share responsibility for their joint endeavor. Three sorts of action seem especially conducive to equanimity.

The first action is generative and dialectical: to confront the mood of the group with its opposite, usually through some version of the query, 'So what?' Thus, when members get into the safe rut of endlessly piling description on description, one asks, 'So what does that show, or what may we learn from all this?' When a person has given a long repetitious ramblelogue about some situation, one asks, 'What do you *feel* about it?' Or, 'What do you think will happen next?' Or, 'What ought he to have done?' After the group has been giving itself catharsis and now wonders whether to do it all over again, one asks, 'So what are some of the causes of this feeling?' Or, 'How do you suppose the situation got so bad?' When a group of teachers has been complaining about a child or principal, theorizing about what is wrong with him, the voice of reason asks, 'What is there about *us* that makes us get so upset by his behavior?' When someone offers a solution too soon and tries to push it through, one asks, 'What are the alternatives?' If the discussion is limping along with nobody daring to propose anything, one says, 'Let's imagine the worst. What would happen if we were to . . .?'

In such ways, emotional expression goes far enough to be identified, and is then countered with objective reality; hidden wishes are encouraged to color the discussion for a bit and then are contrasted with group purposes; imaginative fantasies are invited through brainstorming and are then screened for their practical gems; private purposes of individuals may dominate temporarily and are then translated into ideas about the unique contributions the person may make to the group's activity and program; gripes and complaints about lack of time, energy and skill are recast as operationally defined cautions to be observed, data to be collected, communication channels to be kept open. These dialectical confrontations keep the system maximally receptive to the greatest smorgasbord of individual initiatives and responses. The group is kept on an even keel, characterized by a nice balance among thought, emotion and action — no one of which is permitted to dominate for very long and thus discriminate against members who in that situation cannot operate authentically in the dominant mode. The group takes in stride streaks of pedantry, mob emotion, hard work and apathy, which reveal itself to itself. It is always open to any suggestion which catches the sense of (or is legitimated by) the overt and hidden agendas of the group.

The second equanimity-producing sort of action is stating the 'sense of meeting.' The group moves by expanding its recognized agreements; and it moves purposively by intention when the new agreements are put into words and consensually confirmed. Each new sense of meeting adds a bit of quasiobjective detail to the commonly assumed circumstances of the unfolding drama. It is the chief instrument for moving from interpersonal antagonism to purposive and therefore fullfilling cooperation.

The third action for equanimity mediates or monitors the tensions between the other two. It is the maintenance and insistence upon *distinctions* that are deemed essential to identity, mission and style. The quest for a pattern among the accumulating senses of meeting is centripetal; confrontations which demand new individual responses are, initially at least, centrifugal. When stressed, each member tends to mean whatever he wants to by the major terms of the group's discourse; and, through over familiarity and careless short-handism (or institutionalization) the group tends to become sloppy and to collapse its hard-won, once meaningful distinctions into the vernacular — as in confusing schooling with education, or scores on tests or examinations with understanding. Mediating between these two is the act of reinterpreting and reasserting, at some level of precision between vulgar collapse and useless pedantry, the key propositions of the group's rationale and identity. Moreover, to maintain definitions, norms and standards that are different from those generally prevailing in the larger overlapping systems is an active continuous fight against 'entropic degradation' or 'regression to the mean' in the field of ideas, purposes, self-concept and, ultimately, the mission of the enterprise.

We conclude that a productive system increases its own competence in consequence of its own operation. It learns to identify and use its own resources and make more of them available for use (inclusiveness); to organize itself more functionally, creatively and flexibly (adaptability); to encourage expression of individual concerns (vitality); and quite consciously to guide its own activity and, in the process, learn about 'life' (internalization). A system of this sort is educationally productive and the participants' experiences within it confirm, demonstrate and teach the value, meaning and significance of 'education.' A system deficient in these dimensions perverts and denies education, no matter how much or what tests 'show' or members say is going on in their heads.

We have discussed dialogue as the method of communication, comprehension as the nature of thinking and dialectic as the means for arriving at joint wisdom. We have referred several times to the educator as 'manager of dialectical processes' in policy-making, community action and classroom inquiries. The practical aim of this book is to clarify how he manages these processes. But there is a major question to be dealt with first: what about *his* dialect? What can be said about his 'inner habits, ideas and sentiments' about education? In what terms does he think of educational "growth" and of the ways education can facilitate the quests of the students toward self-realization and productive membership in society? It is to such conceptions that we now address ourselves.

Summary

Having considered comprehension-seeking (i.e. educative) inquiry from the standpoint of individual participants in dialogue, we turn next to the problems and dialectics of interactions among two or more participants. We distinguish internal private dialogue from external public dialogue and we hope that these two kinds of simultaneous activity will stimulate each other constructively. We suggest that the quality of dialectical inquiry will depend on five characteristics of the group engaged in dialogue: inclusiveness, meaning participation of the people whose inputs are needed for adequate comprehension; adaptability, meaning the system's ability to organize effort in whatever way will best facilitate the group's intentions; vitality, meaning engagement of participants in active internal dialogue; internalization, meaning development of an 'intuitive' grasp of target situations in such a way that one's suggestions are appropriate and realistic; and equanimity, meaning utilization of the system's centrifugal and centripetal tendencies as a dynamic to drive insight and commitment. I intend these systems criteria to guide all educative inquiry, whether by professionals, concerned citizens or students in classrooms.

Notes

1. H. A. Thelen, 'Educational Dynamics: Theory and Research,' *Journal of Social Issues*, vol. 6, no. 2 (1950).

2. G. A. Kelly, *The Psychology of Personal Constructs*, (W. W. Norton, New York, 1955).

3. C. Argyris and D. Schon, *Theory in Practice* (Jossey-Bass, San Francisco, 1974).

4. The concept of 'conflict' is basic in all efforts to conceptualize personal, group and social dynamics. For a systematic, if abstract, treatment, see Kurt Lewin, 'Frontiers in Group Dynamics: Concept, Method, and Reality in Social Science; Social Equilibria and Social Change,' *Human Relations*, vol. 1, no. 1 (1947), pp. 5-41.

5. B. Giuliano, 'Dialect,' *Colliers Encyclopedia*, vol. 6 (1958), p. 440.

6. John Dewey, *Democracy and Education* (Macmillan, New York, 1916).

5 The Educational Goal of Growth: The Three Faces of Adam

The scope, sophistication and structure of the theories of education that actually influence educational policy and practice depend on how one conceives the purposes of education. For some educators, the cultural archetype is theory enough. Everyone 'knows' what education is for, and the only practical problems are economic and managerial. In this view, education boils down to information-oriented acquisition of knowledge; and the method of education is mostly performance training. For others, myself included, education is conceived philosophically as a process of individual 'unfolding' and self-realization, through which, either directly or indirectly, a better (i.e. more educative) society will come into being.

Given these concerns, my most fundamental question is: what shall we assume about the nature of life not only 'in general' but in the classroom as well? We must identify its growth themes, its story lines, its recurrent dramatic conflicts that it processes into personal history. I shall adopt the word 'paradigms' as the label for these themes.[1] Three are most fundamental: *adaptation*, to be clarified in terms of evolution and the destiny of the species; *participation*, to be clarified through the relational and functional properties of societal interdependence; and *transcendence*, to be clarified in terms of cosmos and becoming.

The Paradigm of Adaptation

The classical view of evolution posits that life is a process of interaction between organism and environment. The organism has certain competences and the environment makes certain demands, offers some kinds of nurturance and confronts the organism with certain kinds of dangers. If the competence of an animal enables it to meet the demands, assimilate the nutrients and escape the dangers, then the animal will live. The competence of the animal depends on its genetic inheritance *plus* its 'acquired' or learned skills. Individual animals differ in this competence (or viability), and those with the greater competence have the better chance to reach adulthood and to propagate more animals, who will tend to have the favorable inheritance. Over time, so the logic goes, the species will be modified to resemble more closely its more competent (or better 'adapted') members. If the environment changes then different competences will be required and 'selected,' and the species must either adapt or lose out. Thus a species that spent most of the day hanging upside down in trees wouldn't stand much chance if trees were to disappear. (The predator and destroyer of the environment who has put hundreds of species on the endangered list is man; and in justice it may be that he is about to make the list himself.) The trick for any species is to develop specializations which capitalize on the particular beneficial abundances of the environment without at the same time losing the more general or flexible — if less 'efficient' — capability for life under a wide variety of changing environmental circumstances.

In *The Human Animal*,[2] Weston LaBarre reconstructs the sequence of adaptations through which man evolved. The story of evolution is one of the greatest adventure stories of all time. It tells of the gradual dominance of vision over smell as the instrument of knowing; the development of the grasping hand, tool-using and comprehension of self-object and means-ends relationships; the elaboration of consciousness through the development of symbolic recording, communication and experience-sharing; the acquisition of the habit of comparing situations and of imagining new ones; and finally, with man having to think about and learn much of his performance, the necessity for a long period of infancy and schooling.

Even in the earliest period there was social organization: the family, for reproduction and rearing; and the tribe or pack for defense and foraging. With the development of tools, means-ends thinking and directed consciousness, the human animal underwent a major reconstruction. There was now the possibility of choice; and of the corresponding internal goals of freedom and autonomy. Purposes could be formulated and effected through the exercise of rationality — and technology was born.

Technology started out as a new kind of competence which was adaptive for the environment at that time. As technology developed, it changed the environment. As the environment changed, the technological competence became maladaptive. The crucial turning point from adaptiveness to maladaptiveness of technology was when we realized where our technology was leading us: from a world of infinite resources to one of finite resources, and from a biosphere which could regenerate and restore itself after being wounded by man to a traumatized world in which man's depredations were irreversible.[3]

Meanwhile, the nature of social organization and human relationships underwent corresponding changes. The earliest animal association was the set of social arrangements required to protect and maintain the 'genetic pool' of the species. With the development of consciousness the association became invested with beliefs, myths, explanations and know-how; the distinctively human community was born. With the further development of reason, classification and consciously directed inquiry, division of labor emerged and, with it, society. With the development of technology to the point of overkill, society became completely dominant over community. As community languished, the individual lost the means of becoming a person. The end result is that participation has lost its source in, and utility for, human self-realization and has instead turned into psychologically empty acts of servicing the societal megamachine.

There is no question about the significance of the present trend. Life is increasingly maladaptive as the once benign and bountiful environment becomes depleted. The human adventure of the next decades must be a species-level Operation Bootstrap, through which we can develop new adaptive capabilities. The invention of new adaptive capabilities will probably be through the rediscovery, reinterpretation and, ultimately, redeployment of human capacities that have long been suppressed, derided and ignored. Some recent discoveries[4] that seem suggestive in this quest are: the neural 'firing' of the hypothalamus, the nature of dreaming and sleep, the alternative states of consciousness (studied through drugs and meditative regimes) and biofeedback control. We also see the reinstatement of the primitive pack in communes, the resurrection of emotions in sensitivity and encounter groups, the alleged strengthening of individual autonomy through open schools, the reaction against over-specialization seen in various forms of job enlargement and the atavistic return of tribal consciousness seen in movements of protest.

It seems to me that three primitive adaptive capacities are being resurrected in these diverse activities.

The first is that 'instinct for survival' which connotes our deep appreciation of, and personal identification with, the destiny of the human species. That part of the culture which gives expression and authority to these appreciations is religion. The sort of reorganization now required will give a central place to the concept of caring — its mystique, commitments and potentials for self-realization.

The second adaptive capacity is the role of the emotions in dealing with stress. LaBarre tells how the biologically engendered emotions of fight and flight reflexively activated claws, hooves, wings, immobilization and other special adaptive equipment in nonhuman beasts. He points out that we have the same reflexive emotional arousal in stress situations; that we lack the adaptive anatomical specializations through which other animals survive danger; and that we have developed consciousness and all its manifestations in knowledge, technology and so on as a compensation for our lack of the equipment of more primitive animals. We have *substituted* consciousness and its works for emotional capability; it is time now to *integrate* consciousness and its works with emotionality.[5]

The third adaptive capacity which we have systematically starved and ignored is for stable interpersonal relationships. I do not know whether we shall have to develop some modern equivalent of the traditional society's kinship system, or some new association in universal brotherhood, as Professor LaBarre advocates. What I do know is that in olden times an animal alienated from the pack had little chance to survive, and that this deep analog is incorporated within the 'wisdom of our bodies.' We need to rethink the meanings of interpersonal relationships, especially intimacy, and we need somehow to use these understanding to reverse the trend for technological benefits to be purchased at the cost of human relationships.

It is to the concept of association and of participation in associations that we now turn.

The Paradigm of Participation

The broad term for what it is that people participate in is society. Societies may be agrarian, high, religious, civic, national, racial, village, etc. When it comes to tribes, states and communities in general, cultural anthropologists discern the same set of properties; and knowledge of this list is extremely helpful to our understanding of participation in the educational enterprise at all levels.

All people have some way of gaining a living through the technology they have developed; they have some way to distribute goods and services (economics); they live or associate together in families, groups, kinship, networks, clubs, classes and congregations (social organization); they participate in arrangements for governing their activities (politics); they develop and share ideas and assumptions about the nature of the world, life and cosmos (philosophy); they seek with others to express and celebrate their faith in the unknowable design of which they feel a part (religion); they express their felt sense of the form in the world through language and art; they share and defend their moral understandings of what is right and desirable (values); and they help transmit their assumptions, understandings and patterns of thought (culture) to upcoming generations (education).[6]

These understandings are deeply internalized and they are sufficiently diffused among people that interdependent behaviors produced separately by individuals tend to maintain rather than destroy the society. This commonly understood corpus of manners, purposes, authoritative reasons, modes of thought and action constitutes the 'culture.'

The content of culture differs from society to society; and it also differs among groups such as ethnic and religious cadres that have distinguishable ways of life within society. Cultural variations are least with respect to operations on the physical world because the nature if not the physiography of the physical world is everywhere the same. Cultural variations are greatest with respect to practices and speculations that are not subject to objective test or to logical demonstration. The various components or aspects of culture are developed to different extents in each society and there are trade-offs within their patterns. Thus, in a society with little technology, religion or kinship will tend to be more prominent than in a high-technology society.

Action and learning groups form distinctive patterns which are different because their functions are different; and the subcultures of any two action groups tend to be fairly similar because of common understandings within the larger culture of what action groups 'are' and what they are for. Every association has a place within the larger culture, draws selectively on this larger culture in developing its own way of life, and tends to be especially interdependent with other associations that serve similar purposes. These networks of associational interdependency may be regarded as functional subsystems within the society; for each such network is responsible for maintaining some aspect of the society for the ultimate benefit of the society as a whole.

It is especially important for educators not only to recognize these connections but also to examine them: it is these connections that make the classroom educative, that is, that make it possible for learning in the classroom to be operative also in other parts of society both at the time of learning and in the future. This line of reasoning compels us to think of classrooms as adaptive microsocieties of 'whole' children not as isolated cultureless islands on which to do limited things to the abilities, information and other isolated fragments of persons.

But let us now turn from the description of society to its dynamics: the tensions and conflicts that 'drive' both the development of the person and the development of the culture. Two kinds of tension are directly implied in the description above. First, there will be inconsistencies *within* the operations of each subculture; and they will have to be ironed out, swept under the rug or denied. Second, incongruencies *between* the prescriptions and performances of different subcultures will have to be dealt with. Every culture has ways of coping with these problems — and these ways differ markedly between open dialectical societies and closed traditional ones. In addition, there is a kind of tension that appears in many guises and with different degrees of urgency in situations throughout life. In popular parlance, each person has to continually come to terms with two opposing 'needs': to 'do his thing' on the one hand, and to 'conform' to institutional expectations, on the other. It is often felt that to be a 'good member' of a group must be at the cost of self-expression and self-development.

Many persons have grappled with this issue and have helped to clarify its dimensions. Riesman saw its polarity in terms of inner-directed versus outer-directed. Bettelheim and Redl focus on controls from within and from without. In psychiatry, there is a tendency to associate 'doing your thing' with impulsiveness and childishness. In transactional anaylsis, the 'child' and 'parent' within us get into conflict which is then reconciled by the 'adult.' Freud invented the id and superego, whose conflict is mediated by, and develops, the ego. In education in the United States, the junior high school was invented to help the transition from the self-centered orientation of the child to the socially-responsible orientation of the adult. Many progressive educators have associated leadership with independence and followership with dependence, without seeming to realize that *inter*dependence is the mediative or adaptive condition.

Students of societies and organizations have tended to see the issue in terms of the sorts of associations that are conducive to development of identity, character and personhood versus those that engage only certain fragments of the person, such as special skills and competences. In the former, intimacy is possible, expressiveness is valued, the person *qua* person is precious, individuality is appreciated and hence fostered, and the individual is a unique irreplaceable event. Associations of this sort are families, kinship groups and friendships based on interpersonal attraction. The emphasis is on interpersonal interactions and relationships. The other type of association is oriented to getting jobs done. Each person is expected to 'contribute' in a self-disciplined way. Rationality is encouraged and emotionality suppressed. People with the same skills are interchangeable. Individuals 'represent' interests, know-how, expertise or power to other groups or levels of attainment. The goal is to solve problems, make something, formulate recommendations, decide on procedures, plan strategies and so on. In these two sorts of associations, the way of life is obviously very different.

The ancient Romans called these two kinds of association *communitas* and *societas* — community and society. More recently, Hsu distinguished participation of the person in the kinship system from coordination of his functional role in getting jobs done. Cooley distinguished primary groups — face-to-face, interactive, affective, familial — from secondary groups — functional, impersonal, performance-oriented. Tönnies used *Gemeinschaft* and *Gesellschaft* — the spirit of congeniality versus the impersonal spirit of functional necessity. Jennings distinguished psyche- and socio-groups — the voluntary, personal, anxiety-reducing affiliative group versus the compulsory, role-demanding, goal-oriented group. Mumford uses the rhetoric of the person as a human being versus as a cog in the megamachine. Organizational theorists get a lot of mileage out of the informal versus the formal structure. And, of course, our evolutionary sketch portrayed the difference historically: the community and then, with the introduction of technology, the society.

Thus a fundamental distinction is made between community and society as different forms of association or, more to the point for modern living, as communal and societal *aspects* of life in *all* associations. When the communal aspect is dominant, the important thing about the individual is what sort of person he is; who he relates to; what *interpersonal role* — child, lover, parent, friend — he occupies; what familia, ethnic or traditional way of life he represents; how permanent, affective and intimate are his relationships to others. When the societal aspect is dominant, the important things about the individual is what he can do; what he knows; how much power he has;

how his functions locate him with respect to the functions of others; what *functional roles* — farmer, dentist, official, welfare recipient, student — he occupies; what sort of brightness, skillfulness, resourcefulness or power he represents; how he enters into casual, formal and regulated relationships with others.

There are very few occasions when either the interpersonal or functional role is so dominant that the other is inoperative. Both are manifestations of the same personal internalized culture. Within this culture they may be completely congruent or in virtually total conflict. Thus the child whose interpersonal roles were formed in a middle-class literate family generally has very little difficulty in the functional role of student in a middle-class achievement-oriented school attended by people just like him. On the other hand, a child whose interpersonal roles were formed in a poor, powerless, disorganized and resentful community generally has great difficulty being a student in any ordinary school. Similarly, the teachers in the first situation lead a smooth, relatively unadventurous life compared to the teachers in the other school.

There is nearly universal consensus that functional roles and societal aspects of life too strongly dominate interpersonal roles and communal aspects of life. The cry is for humanization, self-realization, intimacy, emergence, personal security and so on. In a recent piece, Green proposed that the *sine qua non* for improving schools is restoration of some modern equivalent of *communitas*.[7]

We conclude from this examination of the societal component that education must be deeply and continually concerned with the question, 'What is the nature of participation in today's interdependent living?' In the classroom we must ask, 'How can the student be helped to recognize his options in every situation? How can he learn to choose wisely among them?' The pedagogical details must of course differ among children and situations; for options depend on opportunity, style and capability, personal goals and social responsibilities. To cope effectively with these questions, the classroom will have to continually recalibrate the balance between the modes of *communitas* and *societas*, between the confrontation and reinforcement of interpersonal and functional roles, and between periods of challenge to and integration of internalized subcultural assumptions.

The Paradigm of Transcendence

Suppose an observer followed another person around all day and wrote down 'everything he did.' The record would describe how the subject behaved in a long series of distinguishable incidents. In some episodes the subject would appear to act with practised familiarity, out of habit, calmly and adequately. Much of his activity would not even 'register' with him — consider how hard it is, when we are suddenly asked, to remember whether we locked the front door on the way to work. In the grip of habit one goes through the day making the expected responses, but with very little sense of any overall design or purpose beyond meeting the next cue on schedule. It is as if the person acts but is not changed in the process of acting; as if he experiences nothing and learns nothing.

Since we are considering incidents in which the organism is not itself changed, then the behaviors used to deal with stress do not enter awareness. Such behaviors are affective, reflexive, unmonitored, 'acting out' — as when the angry boss pounds his desk and yells, 'Damn it, I am *not* mad.' An upset boss banging his desk is equivalent to a startled bird taking wing, although a lot less graceful. Later on, the bird and boss settle down and the latter rights the wastebasket, apologizes and the routines again take over. It should be noted that 'acting out' is but one mode of emotionality or of affective expression. Other modes include the sort of discovery one makes in spontaneous or creative dancing and the sort of insight one obtains from awareness of how he feels in situations. In acting out, the emotionality is not integrated within a pattern of thought and action; in the other forms it is a component of the total pattern of intentionality.

Returning to the log of observations, one would note that there are some incidents during which the subject appears to learn something; that is, his experience seems to 'register' with him in such a way that a perception or habit is modified. A small increment of learning is gleaned from each incident and, if these learnings are self-consistent, they add up over time to a very large difference, as between a child and an adult. The instrument of learning is feedback. A person acts and then becomes aware of other persons' or nature's reactions to his act. Their reaction, if displeasing or incorrect, cause him to study his own behavior — and improve it. It is through consistently available feedback and correction, however gentle, that the child picks up language, manners, approved attitudes and the rest of the content of common culture. In this sort of natural 'shaping' or 'behavior modification,' the person is usually aware that he 'learned something'; and he would probably explain that this something was an improved way of doing things he was already trying to do. He would see the learning as a gain in efficiency, appropriateness or quality, but not as a new sort of capability.

This brings us to the third kind of experience that our subject may have at different times. The observer may miss some of these times because the experience is internal and may or may not be reflected or transacted in noticeable behavior. The experience is characterized by some patterning of three qualities: it is felt to be new or novel; it is felt to be on a 'higher plane'; and it is felt to be part of one's becoming. The label for such experience (or aspect of experience) is *transcendental*.

Transcendental experiences may be as dramatic as Joan of Arc's communications with God, as quiet and familiar as the appreciation of a sunset, as dramatic as a sudden insight. Transcendental experiences, as reconstruction, reformulation or reorganization of patterns into new, more powerful forms, is the essence of education as distinguished from training.

There have been many suggestions about what can enhance the transcendental component of experiences. Among the suggestions are: certain ways of believing in God, primordial guilt, primitive instincts, hallucinogenic drugs, receptive-meditative posture (with or without deep breathing), need deprivations (hunger, sleep, sociability), need satiation (communal orgies, saturnalia), need for harmony and closure and personal obsessions and delusions. While this is not the place to examine these possibilities in detail, it is worth noting that the variety of agents is so great that one may assume the thirst for transcendental experience to be equally pervasive and, with such a heterogeneous assortment of sources to consider, one should be on guard against those that only produce symptoms rather than the genuine experience (e.g. hallucinogenic drugs, orgies). In order to pursue these ruminations more effectively, let us examine two examples of transcendental experience, one extreme and the other memorable but common.

Perhaps the most striking feature of the extreme experience is its cutting loose from all moorings in conventionally understood realities. It is free from the constraints of the real world, with its hidebound ideas of cause and effect and its expected ways to do things; and second, it is free from the constraints of language, with its defined topics, time frame and syntactical forms. Such totally free experience would have to be completely subjective, inside the person, and it would also be prelingual — a precursor of meaning rather than a meaning in itself. In short, the experience would be deeply felt and sensed, but the individual experiencing it would not know what was happening to him. There would be a feeling, a spirit, a sense of going beyond the ordinary and mundane to some presumably higher plane. Here is an example:

> It is like being a ghost in an unfamiliar nonplace with no idea of how one got there or, for that matter, how one became a ghost. One has an apprehension of something immanent, as if the ghost were about to materialize. There is also the presentiment that one's experiencing is of a different and 'higher' order of sensibility; but since one has gone beyond one's file of benchmark facts and one's everyday tools of comprehension, one cannot prove a thing. One is left with the faith that the experience happened, that it contained some kind of message, and that if one could read this message it would beckon one toward a higher quality of significance in life.

This account, of course, is only one effort to describe something which by nature is indescribable. If the participant himself were to try to tell others about it, he would have to use content drawn from the culture as internalized in himself.[8] What content he would use would depend on his station and aspirations in life — his internalization of the culture, etc. Thus, one person's report might be

> I was neither dead nor alive and was standing at the door of heaven wondering if I could get in. God appeared — I didn't really see Him, but I knew He was there — and He gave me to understand that someday I might sit at His right hand. I was filled with ecstasy and wanted to know what I would have to do, but by that time He was gone.[9]

Generally speaking, the more the sense of supernatural in the encounter, the more likely the religious content of the culture would be drawn on. And, conversely, the more an individual was preoccupied with supernatural and cosmological ideas and faiths, the more likely he might be to have transcendental experiences through which the ideas would acquire new meanings and certainties.

More common but nevertheless memorable transcendental experiences are connoted (in some contexts) by words like empathy, recognition, appreciation, apprehension, dedication, identification, celebration and sacrifice. Consider this recollection by a high-school student.

It was an art class. We were all told to draw a picture. I didn't want to — I have no artistic talent and the teacher was always impatient with mediocre drawings because he thought they were caused by lack of trying. And everyone in the class could hear his comments. I had almost finished my picture. I could sense the teacher coming up behind me and looking over my shoulder. I stopped drawing. There was a long silence — I was in limbo. Then the teacher's hand reached down and he put his finger on a certain spot and, in a gentle voice, he said: 'I think it could use a little more black right here.' That moment was timeless; it was inside; there was no class. I'll remember the incident as long as I live.[10]

Transcendental experience has been valued for different reasons. A mad man, whose thought processes are not understandable to ordinary people, may be assumed to have ways of knowing, such as revelation, which transcend garden-variety inquiries. Such a person may be seen as a Child of God or as a true prophet. In any event, the emphasis is on the product of the experience: authoritative, wise or meaningful statements that can offer solace or guidance to weak, confused and self-centered human beings.

Transcendental experience may also be valued as consummatory — valuable in its own right — quite apart from whatever conclusions it may reach. In this sense, it adds a new dimension to life: the process of continually seeking meaning by experimenting with ways to reorganize knowledge in the hope of achieving greater resonance with intuition.[11] It is in this sense that what most people mean by the processes of 'integration of personality' must involve transcendental qualities. In so far as the sign of the process is partly in terms of knowledge, one might suppose that transcendental experience might be facilitated by certain beliefs or affirmations, expressed as formal propositions, whose content is to be ascertained by each individual in terms meaningful to himself.

The private subjective transcendent experience is unique to each person and therefore has most to do with possibilities of 'self-realization.'[12] As we have suggested earlier, this self-realization is the consequence of private reconstruction of meanings during participation with others in publicly oriented dialogue.

It is easy to see how these three paradigms fit together in comprehension of the multidimensionality of the person and of the way past, present and future are joined within him. The species-adaptive inheritance represents the past as vitally alive today; the participative aspects represent the present; and the transcendental aspects are the sentient stirrings of the future within us.

Classroom Life

These concepts of the processes of adaptation, participation and transcendence have their own implications for educational methods.

The fact that the child acts on and reacts adaptively to the environment is the starting point for education. It reminds us that educational agents are outside the child and that they operate by manipulating external things: events, materials, demands. Through changing the environment, the educator regulates the situational stress the student will feel; and, if the educator's calculations are correct, the child will then act spontaneously to reduce the stress and the way he proceeds will involve educative learning. Miscalculations are, however, quite frequent, for the student's strategy may be non-educative, as when he lowers his standards, lashes out destructively, cheats, becomes dependent or despondent. In these cases, the educator must help the child understand the nature of the adaptation he has attempted and start him thinking about a more constructive mode.

In broad terms, adaptive efficiency will depend on relations between the expectations of the classroom and the internalized culture of each child. There are four logically distinguishable possibilities. First, then, the child may perceive that when he enters the classroom he places himself in unaccustomed jeopardy. He feels that he has moved from a pleasant well-adapted existence in the Elysian fields to a desert island on which he will have to struggle mightily; that unless he can produce a complicated, possibly arbitrary or even senseless string of performances he will fail — with all the short-and long-range consequences which that would entail.

The second possibility is that he will perceive the classroom as a land of opportunity, a veritable paradise compared to the wasteland outside. In this case every demand from the teacher will be taken as an invitation to personal growth which until now has been prevented or inhibited by lack of support, stimulation or encouragement.

The third possibility is that the child will perceive himself as moving from one relatively congenial environment to another — like moving from San Francisco to Copenhagen. The adaptation in this case does not involve personal security because basic learned modes of survival are not threatened.

The fourth possibility is that the child moves from one terrible sub-sistence-level situation to another equally deprived and brutal situation. He will bring his survival techniques with him and, knowing no others, will use them. If his classmates are in the same boat, then their way of life will take over and the teacher's demands and expectations will be in severe conflict with the children's lifetimes of experience.[13]

Both at the level of microscopic activity and of macroscopic way-of-life, the teacher's job in this adaptive view is to work on the environment (verbal, material, interpersonal) in such a way that the perception of opportunities to be grasped can voluntarily rule as much as possible of the child's behavior. The societal-participative life constrains the adaptive life because the adaptive strategy used by one person may hinder or facilitate the strategies of others. Rules are needed and the most fundamental is that, 'Your right to swing your fist ends where my nose begins.' In short, social order is necessary along with some sort of authority capable of maintaining it in a way that protects or even optimizes the 'rights' (i.e. freedom to choose among adaptive alternatives) of all.[14]

The teacher is expected to be the instrument of this authority; and how he wields it and with what educational consequences depends on what he conceives to be its source, nature and responsibilities. He may help students understand and share in the exercise of this authority or he may hug it to himself and allow the children to learn about it only on occasions when he uses it to frustrate their expressions and coerce their actions. In principle, as least, the easiest authority to explain is the authority of reason in the service of shared commitments; and the most difficult to explain is the authority of personal private needs and drives which the teacher is not even aware of and is likely to deny. These two sorts of authority in the classroom conduce respectively to insight and conformity.

Activity in the societal life is governed by expectations that the child will get 'involved,' will make decisions and will carry them out; and that he will act alone or in cooperation with others. Although we usually cannot predict much about how the child will experience these functions, we can often infer something about what the experiences 'must have been like' as the partial cause of changed subsequent behavior.

In the third life, the transcendental, relations between activity and experience are the most nebulous and difficult to define. The educative processes are entirely within the privacy of one's head. The meditative life shows little outward sign. The teacher facilitates this quest neither by direct demands nor by 'structuring' problematic situations. (The quest is too fragile, subtle and voluntary for such crude interventions.) Instead, the teacher controls this life by controlling himself: by presenting himself as an exemplification of graciousness, humanity, intellectuality and decency. Such a model, when genuine, is believable because it resonates with humane intuitions. The teacher participates in the animal and societal components of classroom activity; but it is his reactions to his own and the children's overt participation that contributes to the transcendental cultural level. He senses in all activity, however imperfect, the universal striving for fulfillment; and he feels compassion for this striving, regardless of his awareness of its 'ulterior' motivation. He is armed with knowledge of the myths, parables and formal propositions that men have created to help them keep cool; and he is serene in the unflappable faith that thought — and action congruent with it — is still man's best hope.

Conceptions of man may enter education in at least four ways. First, they may be included in academic subject matter to be taught. Second, they may suggest 'objectives' for education: capabilities, understandings and attitudes whose development should enable the person to live more fully and effectively.[15] Third, they may characterize phenomena in the classroom whose understanding by the teacher will enable him to teach more insightfully, responsively and compassionately. Fourth, some of these phenomena may be signs of students' needs which the instructional method or curricular design attempts to ignore or suppress, thus driving the needs underground and generating the hidden curriculum. Another possibility is that, by reflecting on how these aspects or paradigms of man's nature react with each other, we may be able to define more precisely the characteristics of a classroom which is also an educational microsociety. But our thinking about processes as complex as instruction really has to start in some agreement about the values it is to serve, and so we next offer some reflections on this meaty topic.

Summary

We shift our concern from the processes to the content of effective social inquiry. Granted that improving education means coping with its phenomena, how shall we indentify and conceive the phenomena in such a way that we can deal with them? How shall we conceptualize the lives of students in which we interfere or coparticipate in the name of education?

It seems useful to think of life as a complex of three intertwined quests: for adaptation, participation and transcendence. The teacher's role in order to facilitate these quests is, respectively: manager of the environment (to which the student adapts); authority for maintaining expectations and safeguarding individual rights; and exemplary model of the humane and civilized way of life.

It is noted that ideas about these processes suggest goals for education, content to be taught, assumptions to inform teaching strategies and criteria for educative classrooms.

Notes

1. I am using 'paradigm' in the sense of T. S. Kuhn, *The Structure of Scientific Revolutions* (University of Chicago Press, Chicago, 1970).

2. Weston LaBarre, *The Human Animal* (University of Chicago Press, Chicago, 1954).

3. Herbert J. Muller, *The Children of Frankenstein: A Primer on Modern Technology and Human Values* (Indiana University Press, Bloomington, 1970). Other major pessimists on technology have been identified by Manfred Stanley in 'Technicism: A Study of Demonology as Social Theory' (Mimeo, 1970) as Jacques Ellul, Hannah Arendt, Lewis Mumford, Martin Heidegger, Herbert Marcuse, F. A. Hayek, Ludwig von Mises, Sheldon Wolin and Wylie Sypher. For a brilliant contemporary statement, see Robert L. Heilbroner, 'The Human Prospect,' *The New York Review of Books*, vol. 20, nos. 20 & 21 (1974), pp. 21-34.

4. *Scientific American* has collected and reissued its most interesting articles on *Altered States of Awareness* (W. H. Freeman, San Francisco, 1972).

5. This seems to be very much to the point of Carl G. Jung, *Psyche and Symbol* (Doubleday, New York, 1958).

6. A representative work from this group of cultural anthropologists is Melville J. Herskowitz, *Man and His Works: The Science of Cultural Anthropology*. (Knopf, New York, 1948).

7. Thomas F. Green, 'What Should Our Schools Become?' in N. J. Anastasiow (ed.) *Educational Psychology: A Contemporary View* (CRM Books, DelMar, California, 1973).

8. The notion of going back to the beginning and rethinking a better culture for ourselves is fairly common — the myth of voluntarily being reborn in a more advantageous condition. See, for instance, Theodore Roszak, *The Making of a Counterculture* (Doubleday, New York, 1969).

9. This mode of articulation appears to be in line with Herbert Marcuse, *On Liberation* (Beacon Press, Boston, 1969). In the sense that one might choose among internalized cultural subsets of content, the process is analogous to the description of roles selection in Erving Goffman, *Presentation of Self in Everyday Life*. (Doubleday, New York, 1961).

10. This incident comes from an unpublished study conducted in Swiss Catholic High Schools by Father Augustin Berset.

11. See Eugene T. Gendlin, *Experiencing and the Creation of Meaning*. (Free Press, New York, 1961).

12. See Carl R. Rogers, *Freedom to Learn. A View of What Education Might Become* (Charles E. Merrill, Columbus, Ohio, 1969). For Rogers, transcendent knowledge is phenomenological, and is generated by 'forces of growth from within.'

13. Jules Henry stands alone in his writings on cultural conflict within the classroom. See his *Culture against Man* (Random House, New York, 1963).

14. This can be seen as the problem of developing and maintaining social norms, both as internalized and as 'objective' constraints on personal freedom. A recent, scholarly and tightly reasoned conceptual scheme, to which my ideas are indebted, is that of Dennis Constance Sims, *Self-image and Social Change: Towards an Integrated Theory of Cybernated Behavior* (Stanford International Development Center, School of Education, Stanford University, 1971, Mimeograph).

15. Speaking substantively rather than paradigmatically, the three aspects can be viewed as levels of developmental maturation, and contact can be made with Kohlberg, Erickson, Piaget, Bruner, etc. I think that my formulation is closer, however, to the notion of 'levels' in Abraham H. Maslow, *Motivation and Personality* (Harper, New York, 1970); of 'layers' in Francis Hsu, 'Kinship Is the Key,' *The Center Magazine*, vol. 6, no. 6 (1973), pp. 4-14; and of eight hierarchial 'patterns' in Clare Graves, 'A Systems View of Values Problems,' *Systems Analysis and Cybernetics* (October 1969). For an elaboration of Graves in a larger context, see James F. T. Bugental, *The Human Possibility: An Essay toward a Psychological Response to the World Macro-problem*, Educational Policy Research Center Report 6747-16 (Stanford Research Institute, Menlo Park, California, 1971).

6   Monitoring Educative Activity: Trade-offs Among Values

Have you ever asked a curriculum-maker how he justifies some curriculum he has just 'developed' for a school? I have. Among the answers I have received are, 'Compared to the present curriculum in the school, this one is much more precise and clear; teachers will know what they are supposed to teach and they will be able to tell if they have taught it.' And, 'The students are regularly failing to pass college entrance tests. This course of study will get many more of them over those hurdles.' And, 'The subject matter of the old curriculum is hopelessly outmoded. The new course was developed with leading experts in its field.' And, 'We got some money to develop a program for the gifted; and this curriculum will really challenge higher-ability students.' And, 'Our parent group is pretty sophisticated. They want more "inquiry" in the classroom and, by heavens, they are going to get it.' And, 'The present curriculum was designed for middle-class students. Ours are lower-class and they must both develop more self-esteem and have their cultural horizons expanded.'

If you ask a teacher to justify his style of teaching, you get a range of answers which may include: 'After 15 years I know these kids. They like my course and so do the parents'; 'Why, what have you got against democracy in the classroom?'; 'It is important, especially in these times, for students to learn to accept responsibility for their behavior. That's why I make it a point to discuss all bad behavior with the class'; 'For me teaching is an exciting adventure. I love to continually try out new activities in class'; 'Students respect a teacher who has high standards and makes them work hard'; 'Look at the mess the world is in. My students are going to learn to come to grips with real issues, such as the racial prejudice of the leaders in our community.'

The question that such responses raise is to what extent and in what ways does firm knowledge of the lives of students enter into the determination of curriculum design and instructional policies? One sees the interests of policy-makers, subject-matter experts, parents and teachers in these replies; and certain capabilities and 'needs' are *attributed* to 'the' student. These attributions may be based on generalizations from sociological study of a large population of

'14-year-olds'; or on psychological insights on 'resistance to change' obtained from the teacher's experience with an adult sensitivity group; or on some rough and ready diagnosis of what minorities have to learn to be able to 'compete'; or on some provocative method of behavior modification that seems to work in homes for juvenile delinquents; and so on.

But do any of these reasons, principles or pressures give the teacher any *confidence* that what he is doing really is in the best educative interests of his own flesh and blood students that he faces everyday in class? Are their 'needs' really reflections of the teacher's own needs for security and approval? On days when class goes badly or a student becomes a 'problem,' is the teacher's conscience bothered? In all those decisions a teacher has to make every day about time allowance, standards, encouraging or punishing, activities to set up next, whether to express or suppress his personal feelings, etc., what considerations or concerns dictate the action? It is all very well to say that decisions ought to be based on assessments of costs and benefits, but in what terms are the trade-offs to be conceptualized? Even if one could begin to know the direct costs and benefits to his own students, what are the principles for arriving at a favorable balance?

In short, what 'guarantees' the rightness of the teacher's decisions and actions? What policies, what concerns, what criteria can legitimate the teacher's management of the educative dialectic in the myriads of changing situations that he must cope with? And by 'legitimate' I am raising issues about the educative welfare of his students. This is a hard question and it probably cannot be answered in any simple, flat, absolute way. Answers like, 'Well, they passed the tests,' and, 'They were intensely interested,' only invite questions in reply, such as, 'How do you know that the test measures anything educationally important?'; and, 'Are interests a safe guide to worthwhileness?,'

But perhaps we can get a start on the question by specifying our aspirations. I think that three are most salient.

(1) Teachers and managers cannot be all-wise and perfect. Let us be satisfied with the best they are capable of. This is not by any means a cynical answer: students are probably better educated by teachers who are actively and intelligently taking the risk of laying their best efforts on the line than by hypothetically perfect teachers who don't have to risk anything. The teacher's involvement, risk-taking and effort contribute to the guarantee.

(2) The teacher's dominant purpose in the classroom is not to indoctrinate, condition, mold or shape the student into a pre-conceived image of 'the' good student. Nor is it to enact as perfectly as possible 'the' role of teacher (kind, well-groomed, modulated voice, subject-matter expert, etc.). No, we shall assume that the dominant purpose is to facilitate each student's growth toward whatever self-realization and effectiveness he is ready for.

(3) The teacher's efforts are informed by adequate conceptions of the nature of the lives he is intervening in. It may sound corny to say it, but a good craftsman knows intimately, as if by instinct, the properties of the material he works with. And teachers are more than craftsmen.

If we accept these propositions, then we can begin to reflect on the concepts presented in the preceding chapters and we can ask how we draw from them propositions about the conditions that 'facilitate' educational development.

As we have seen, every person is to be regarded as a member of species, of society and cosmos. The aspects of his life viewed from the standpoints of these belongingnesses are, respectively, adaptive, participative and transcendental. These components are in continual dialectical interaction within the person as, in each situation, they stimulate, provoke and weave in and out of trade-offs and balances with each other.

In this chapter, we are concerned with the conditions in the situation that optimize the dialectical processes among these three components. The quality of interaction between adaptive and transcendental aspects depends on the state of *authenticity*; between participative and transcendental aspects, quality depends on *legitimacy*; and between participative and adaptive aspects, the criterion is *productivity*. I shall refer to these three qualities by the acronym, ALP.

The Criterion of Authenticity

Undergirding the quest of the species-adaptive life is the individual's intuition that he is part of the history and destiny of the human animal. Without locating morality in the biological characteristics of the species, one can at least feel that denial of our animal nature is dangerous. We must respect our need for nourishment, movement, novelty, love and an input of challenges to face up to. The human being, with his great gift of mind coupled to his affective virtuosity, channels intuition into awareness when situational expectations or demands violate his sense of his own capabilities — calling for more or less strength, endurance, cunning, fleetness, rationality, etc. than he has. The species-adaptive quest, then, attempts (among other things) to help the individual understand 'who he is' in terms of his capabilities, history and congeniality with various environments and demand-settings.

At the same time, the transcendental life, proceeding through inner organization, is an effort to define or create conceptually some higher meaning to justify our being alive and developing our potentials. This quest, too, is concerned with 'who am I?' not as given but as becoming. And again, in some situations one intuits that his prospects are violated, his view of the world worth working for falters, his faiths seem inconsequential or'merely' subjective. So the quest continues.

The two lives, seeking to accept and understand being and becoming, complement, constrain and stimulate each other. The concept of being is empty except as it apprehends becoming; and the concept of becoming is fatuous if there is no sign in being of tendencies to become. The two concepts grasp the tension between the two lives. For the individual has to risk his being in order to become. Being tends to consolidate itself by sensing and reinforcing its own pattern — its own equilibrium.

Taking the two quests together, their outward manifestation is that part of behavior which modifies and reconstructs situations (and comprehension of situations) in such a way that the inner questing (experience) can go forward. The quality of activity which facilitates the dual search for 'who am I?' is *authenticity*.[1] And this is the first criterion all educational activity must meet.

An activity is authentic for a person when he feels emotionally 'involved' and mentally stimulated; when he is aware of choices and enjoys the challenge of making decisions; when he feels he has something to bring to the activity and that its outcome will be important for him; when it has the quality of 'life' and is not compartmentalized or merely a game; when through the activity new relationships develop among his thoughts, attitudes and action tendencies; when his internalized culture (the pattern of informal, formal and technical elements) undergoes reconstruction.

An activity is not authentic for the person if he cannot imagine himself or anyone he identifies with spontaneously or voluntarily engaging in it; if he feels that his motives are irrelevant to the activity; and if he feels that his participation is mostly just to remove an extrinsic threat, demonstrate his good will or otherwise placate some real or imagined superior force.

In order to clarify the 'meaning' of our abstract ALP concepts, we may define them in terms of the operations by which their quality could be actually measured. Let us take another look at the study reported in Chapter 1. Out of our deliberations on these concepts, we came up with an instrument for measuring them; and we have since collected data from 49 classes in five contrasting high schools in the US Midwest. I should like to present not only the items of the measuring instrument but also the results.

The ALP instrument consists of 24 statements. Eight of the statements are keyed to authenticity, eight to legitimacy and eight to productivity. The statements are on separate slips, and the student or teacher is given a simple procedure for sorting and ranking the statements in order of how well they describe his classroom. The statement ranked first is the most descriptive or accurate; the statement ranked last is the least descriptive or most inaccurate. We asked the students to each describe a class they were in when they took the instrument. Here are the items for authenticity and the average rankings of classrooms.

(A8)   *It [the class] made me think some new thoughts of my own.* Rank: 2.

(A24) *I felt like contributing to the activity.* Rank: 3.

(A11) *I felt that during the activity I could be the sort of person I wanted to be.* Rank: 15.

(A23) *I felt that time passed quickly for me.* Rank 16.

(A2)   *I felt really challenged by things others said.* Rank: 17.

(A13) *I felt activity clarifies some previous personal experiences.* Rank: 20.

(A9)   *I felt like rapping with the teacher and other classmates after the meeting.* Rank: 21.

(A17) *I was excited by what was happening.* Rank: 23.

With regard to authenticity, the average ranks suggest that the students do have thoughts 'of their own' and that they do expect to contribute or participate in activities; these items fit the conventional understanding of the role of student. But what about the person? Self-freedom and self-satisfaction are relatively low, along with being absorbed in the activity (i.e. time passes quickly) and being stimulated by others. The classroom is perceived even less as a place to clarify private experiences; one does not talk candidly about class activities with others — either because the activities are not that interesting or because classmates are not that good friends. Finally, it is hard to interpret the 23rd place of the last authenticity item in any way except that classroom activities are just plain dull. (When we analyze our 49 classrooms separately, we find, of course, that some classrooms are *relatively* exciting, and so on. These may have something to tell us.)

The Criterion of Legitimacy

In the societal-participative life, beings are interdependent, and both their rights or freedoms and their duties or expectations are subject to authoritative agreements in all spheres — moral, political, economic, etc. These agreements are explained or rationalized by organized bodies of knowledge and are justified by consensus on the values they serve. The agreements may be expedient and rash or they may be compassionate and enlightened. Clearly, the former block transcendental life, whereas the latter encourage it.[2] Moreover, the converse also holds: when the transcendental life is submerged in adaptive necessities (e.g. to find food) the societal agreements will respond mostly to (economic) problems of distributing scarce resources. When the transcendental life is protected and encouraged (e.g. as in a genuine community) societal agreements and policies tend to reflect mutual aspirations (values) for a higher order or quality of life.

Individual and group behaviors, then, are regulated by authoritative cultural agreements which *legitimate* the behaviors. An act which is within the boundaries of freedom protected by agreement and understanding — usually elaborated in precedent and parable — is legitimate: it is admitted to, and assimilated within, public affairs and public dialogue. An illegitimate idea or behavior is outcast, alien and threatening, and will be treated accordingly.[3] A radical idea may be introduced into public dialogue provided one goes about it in a legitimate way.

In the classroom, the inquiry with respect to legitimacy asks what set of agreements, having what sort of authority, provide the justification for the activity and the rationale for interpretations of experience in the activity. What principles, morals, policies, laws and the like are illustrated, exemplified or embodied in the class's awareness of their activity? What organized body of thought, doctrine or expectations is understood to bear on it? Thus, an allegedly educative activity acquires a modicum of legitimacy when its ideational content is understood to illustrate general principles; when its method of investigation exemplifies an explicated mode; when its particular choices are seen as microexamples of the same choices made regularly in the society or the discipline; when its blundering trial and error is seen as a recapitulation of similar trial and error at early stages of the subject's development; and when its way of coordinating activity is noted consciously to exemplify a democratic (or other) political ideology. In short, an activity acquires legitimacy when it is examined from the standpoint of a defined, organized, coherent frame of reference, be it interpersonal, political, economic, educational, religious or other.[4]

Our legitimacy items and their rankings are as follows.

(L14) *Some of the things we found out will be useful in other situations*. Rank: 1.

(L12) *We understood the nature of our task and tried to see what it would require us to do*. Rank: 8.

(L7) *We concentrated our activity on the significant aspects of our task*. Rank: 10.

(L16) *The problems we had of working together occur regularly in other groups as well*. Rank: 11.

(L4) *As a group we had good reasons for what we did*. Rank: 12.

(L6) *Our meetings at times really exemplified good group process*. Rank: 13.

(L22) *The issues that troubled us in our group are also prevalent in the larger society*. Rank: 18.

(L21) *Our shared purpose was strong enough to help guide our behavior*. Rank: 22.

For our large sample, school work is legitimated or justified by the belief that things learned there will be useful later — certainly a common and popular belief. Then in ranks 8-13 — not strongly characteristic — we find that what one does is justified by the requirements of tasks; and that focus is on things that are 'significant.' The notion that group experience can generalize to other groups (i.e. the classroom as a laboratory for learning about other groups) is ranked next, and the sense that the group has good reasons for its activities is right in the middle — neither characteristic nor uncharacteristic. Also in the middle is the judgment that the group tries to meet the criteria of a 'good' group (presumably orderly, middle-class, etc.). On the rejected side are the notions that the classroom group has relevance to society in that it has the same issues (e.g. racial, brightness) as the larger society. Finally, we find that shared group purposes for the most part do not guide the group; they are not the reasons given for why people do what they do in the classroom. The overall impression is that classes exist to meet task requirements. They have little relationship to society and in the absence of shared purposes and of personal meaning (authenticity) they appear more as processing plants than as humane committees.

The Criterion of Productivity

'A square peg in a round hole' is unproductive. The peg is the adaptive affective-instinctual core of personality; the hole is the cultural-societal participative expectations of interpersonal and functional roles. Productivity is greatest when the adaptive-affective style adds flair and effectiveness to roles and when the demands of roles give the flair opportunity for growth in artistry. Or, as Getzels and Guba put it: when the *nomothetic* (role aspects) and *idiosyncratic* (personal aspects) are 'congruent,' then activity enhances both.

When the two are in conflict, the activity carries the extra burden of being the vehicle for resolving the conflict. Since societal functional demands are usually accorded higher legitimacy than are purely personal needs, conflict is usually 'resolved' by 'adjusting' the individual: suppressing or denying his needs; isolating his 'job' from his 'life,' etc. The energy used to maintain such 'adjustments' is unavailable for the purposes of the activity; and the activity is deprived, especially, of whatever component of creativity, judgment or wisdom the person might have contributed to it.

Productivity can be defined in several ways: the amount and quality of product or output (e.g. school-test achievement); the quality of the process (e.g. fairness, openness, standard of evidence) through which the product was produced or the conclusion reached; and the growth of capability to produce more effectively (as measured by either process or product).

It is our view that dialogue is the heart of the educative process; and that educative dialogue develops the classroom culture, including the role expectations and controls over the participative aspect of life; and that at the same time, development of this culture in an educative direction enhances the personal capability of students in the affective-instinctual personal domain. Productivity is the extend to which the development of personal capability by each student directly or indirectly enhances the development of personal capability by the others. Mutuality of personal growth is the hallmark of an educative classroom society; or, more accurately, it is the hallmark of concerted effort to move from the initial accidental collectivity toward a fully educative classroom community. This movement is multidimensional; it includes augmentation of individually supportive expectations, differentiation and recognition of special individual skills, contribution of individual resources to the attainment of mutually valued goals, aspirations for higher standards of performance, development of solidarity through interpersonal appreciations, adaptiveness of the informal structure. In this view, *what is educative is the intelligent striving with others to develop the educative culture of the classroom*. One may act like an educated man when that is the normal adaptation to an existing educative culture; but one *becomes* an educated man by participating in efforts to make his own culture more educative.

Of course, one does not set out to develop a good or educative society nor to improve a culture. These are byproducts or residues from purposive engagement in activities, studying one's experience of the activities and, in the process, generating readiness for further activities. The conscious aim is to achieve the purposes for which the activity is designed; but whether or not such achievement will be educative depends on what meaning the achievement has. It is the pooling of these meanings through dialogue that reconstructs the classroom culture and, along with it, the classroom way of life.

The items we used to assess productivity and the findings are as follows.

(P15)   *We ran into problems and solved them*. Rank: 4.
(P5)   *We knew how well we were progressing on our task*. Rank: 5.
(P10)   *One thing flowed from another*. Rank: 6.
(P3)   *We accomplished a great deal*. Rank: 7.
(P19)   *We all helped each other*. Rank: 9.
(P1)   *We decided what we wanted to do and we did it*. Rank: 14.
(P20)   *We each contributed our special skills to make the meeting*

productive. Rank: 19.
(P18)   *The diversity of our individual backgrounds aided the group*.
Rank: 24.

The first four items, ranks 4-7, show how prominent is the structure of tasks and assignments. Then it appears from the rank of 14 for (P1) that the group does not have much part in deciding on the tasks, and (P18), and (P20) reject productivity as utilization of individual resources and enhancement of individual competence through group dialogic activities. Thus (P18) asks to what extent individual differences are helpful; and the answer is that they get in the way; (P20) asks whether individuals contribute to the activity — that is, whether they are first-class citizens — and that rates rank 19. Finally, as to helping each other (P19) the range among the five schools is over ranks 5-19, and the mean value of nine for all five is strictly accidental.

Trade-offs among the Three Concerns

If you are concerned about authenticity — personal development, awareness, clarification of experience — then the picture that emerges from this study is disturbing. If you are concerned about legitimacy — the authority that justifies practices — you find that the authority is in the fact of the tasks themselves, not in the purpose the tasks should serve. And productivity boils down to each person doing the jobs in a parallel, possibly competitive, way rather than in the cooperative fashion required for the resources of individuals to be of any use or significance to anyone else. Is this good or bad? Should we be pleased or angry? Under these conditions can students learn what we think is really important?

To answer these questions we must clarify what we mean by them. All the description tells us is something about the average way of life in classrooms. That way of life, with its emphasis on problem structure and task demands and its disinterest in personal reactions, might strike a mathematics teacher as just right for carrying out his mathematical activities. On the other hand, a teacher of literature, gung-ho for individual personality integration or maturation, would be appalled at this way of life. If you see classroom learning as a process of inquiry, you will be struck by the very low rank accorded to group purposes (rank 22) and you might feel that 14 is too low for student decision-making. If you are sold on bussing as a way through equalization of opportunities to maintain democracy, then rank 24 (bottom, rejected) for (P18), the utilization of individual diversity, may make you weep.

Such thoughts imply that classrooms exist to carry out tasks, and/or to accomplish a small number of subject-related or political purposes. In this case we may expect the definitions and relative emphases of A, L and P to differ from one activity to the next. But classrooms have another aspect: they are relatively stable microcommunities; each develops its own ethos, dialect or subculture, which has different degrees of congruence with the lifestyles of different students. If the classroom is a good place to live, then students should perceive their actual and imagined ideal classes fairly similarly. Let us see what the discrepancies between actual and ideal suggest about the students' own concerns for authenticity, legitimacy and productivity.

The students perceive that classes are dull, and that they should be less so (by 14 ranks). They would like more opportunity to 'contribute our special skills to make the meeting productive' (up nine ranks). Part and parcel of the same longings are their wishes to move up: 'we accomplished a great deal' (from rank 7 to rank 1); 'we all helped each other' (from rank 9 to rank 2); and 'we decided what we wanted to do and then did it' (from rank 14 to rank 6).

It seems to me that the term which best captures the flavor of these wishes is the desire to be members of a *productive team*.

Turning to what they want less of, we find three items that are downgraded from quite to indifferently characteristic: 'we knew how well we were progressing in our task'; 'one thing flowed from another'; and 'we concentrated our activity on the significant [to whom?] aspects of the task.' Along somewhat different lines, we also find 'the problems we had of working together occur regularly in other groups as well' (downgraded from rank 11 to rank 23) and 'the issues that troubled us in our group are also prevalent in the larger society' (dropped from rank 18 to rank 24).

In sum, the students seem to want less dominance of the problem and task structure (which may really mean less imposition by the teacher of specific procedures); and they want fewer societal or social constraints on the class. Both themes fit very well with the preferred image of productive teamness.

There are a number of conclusions one might try to base on these findings. But for our purposes, I think the interesting point is cultural: that is, since the 'ideal' is part of the common culture of this age group of students in their various subcultures, the pattern of discrepancies describes the ways the schools fall short of what the students have been led to value. In fairness, I must also add that the teachers' perceptions of ideal and actual classes also show discrepancies of about the same magnitude; and to the extent that the gaps are the same for teachers as for students, the interesting question that arises is: *how come the classroom is the way it is when the participants do not want it that way?* By now you are probably way ahead of me: the processes required to develop a more appropriate and effective subculture are neither traditional nor technical; they are dialectical. And, as we pointed out in Chapter 2, these required processes are weak if not downright rejected not only in today's classrooms but also in the larger society. In short the big trade-off has been the sacrifice of educational effectiveness for the comforts of drifting without comprehensive understanding.

The ALP Dynamics: Diagnosis

The criteria of authenticity, legitimacy and productivity represent three active *concerns* whose interaction generates conflict, support, confrontation, closure, etc. In these terms, the 'best' situation is not one in which each quality is maximized independently of the others, but rather one in which the pattern of the three is optimum for that situation. A familiar middle-class pattern of events may help to clarify this matter.

Suppose that a number of people come together because they are 'concerned about our schools.' After the necessary ceremonial formalities, the members are asked for their views. They begin to express themselves and, after a few exchanges, different members begin to say things like, 'It is clear the problem is . . . Let's go to work on it.' Such comments act only as temporary distractions, and the members go on expressing feelings. But after a while, they begin to get restless and look to the leader to become more active. The catharsis has run its course, and it is now time to find a 'focus.' Many efforts are made to formulate the 'issue' or 'problem' and, after a while, someone comes up with a 'sense of the meeting' which seems satisfying, and is followed by suggestions of concrete actions, such as collecting information, interviewing school personnel, reading a book, visiting a school, drawing up a conspectus for a new school, etc. The meeting 'feels' finished when it is clear what the agenda for the next meeting will be.

This 'natural history,' which is repeated over and over in different groups (unless the leadership is too doctrinaire, insensitive or impatient), reveals shifting patterns among the three concerns. The first phase, of smoking out individual expressions, is dominated by the intuitive concern for authenticity: 'this is supposed to be our meeting and it is our problems we mean to work on.' It is only after this concern has been satisfied somewhat that efforts to find a 'focus' begin to gather momentum. Finding a focus is clearly the service of legitimacy: the focus will simultaneously establish the authority of group purposes and of significant issues in the larger society. Once this authority is sufficiently clear (by which I mean that each member feels the focus makes sense to him and also to the other members), the group then becomes concerned with its action strategy and with what activity to usher in next. At this point, the concern for productivity is dominant.

One can carry the scenario further: at the point where each individual must really carry out the action planned by the group, further anxieties about personal authenticity surface: 'Is this really me? Am I really sure I want to do all that work?' As these questions continue, they begin to verge into reexamination and elaboration of legitimacy: 'Is the problem really so serious that something must be done? How will other members of the group act if I let them down? Would it be immoral of me to forget the whole thing?' In other words, the normal authentic ambivalences at this point are brought under control through the authority under which the group is operating. Finally, having decided to work, questions of the form, 'What shall I do first?' and the like reflect the dominance of concern for productivity.

In addition to the sequential, possibly cyclical domination of the concerns, there are also interesting tensions. Some kinds of legitimizing authority are more authentic than others within a person's way of life. For example, either group consensus on purposes or demands of intellectual scholarship might serve to legitimize an activity. But the group may have a strong feel for the sanctity of group consensus and simply not have had any experience at all with 'demands of scholarship.' Activity legitimized by the intellectual criterion would be mighty unauthentic compared with activity legitimized by the more social authority. However much an educator might prefer personal needs, understanding and conscious inquiry to be the central component, respectively, of authenticity, legitimacy and productivity, the fact remains that, in most classrooms, he will have to settle for something less. And, instead of trying to 'train' or persuade the group somehow to adopt his criteria, he should be more concerned with understanding *their* criteria and then confronting the one with the other in such a way as to maintain dynamics through which growth will, seemingly, 'just naturally' occur.

In educative classrooms all learnings, even of the most basic skills, are ultimately in the service of the transcendental. Each person is to develop his potentials; and, as both cause and effect of such 'growth' the class develops more sophisticated agreements and a more enlightened social order. These developments — the optimization of authenticity and legitimacy — depend on each other. Productivity is conceptually the measure of the extent to which the interdependence is mutually facilitative. One sees that the teacher's task, calling for all his art and skill, is to conduct the class and supervise its activity in such a way as to move its way of life toward this integration of supportive personal relationships with civilized aspirations and the humane use of knowledge.

Teaching as Management of the Pattern of Values

Underlying practically all explanations of the development of persons, societies and groups is the concept of opposing forces which maintain dynamic stability of the organism; which, in the case of minor disruptions, restore its 'quasistationary equilibrium'; and, in the case of major confrontations, move the organism to a new kind or quality of provisional steady state — a new integration of biological life and psychological meanings. This proposition means that our paradigmatic aspects of life are by no means separate and independent of each other; that they weave in and out of support, conflict, reconciliation and reemergence of conflict; and that the dialectical processes among them 'drives' the development of unique personhood, character and learning of all sorts.

This is a great theory, but it is of little help to the teacher because he cannot split the child's classroom life into three parts, observe each, describe the conflict among them and then figure out how to reduce it, increase it or otherwise manipulate it according to some higher wisdom. (And for this we should all be thankful.) But he *can* tell when the conflict exists; because he can observe signs of tension, exploration and various well-known types of affective or emotional responses to the existence of inner turmoil. He intuitively senses the *drama* in the situation. What should he do? He realizes that the conflict or drama is necessary to growing up, that it is a sign of readiness for maturing development to take place. But it is the child's (or the group's) development that produced the drama, and it is theirs, not his, that is at stake. His aspiration then, is to do what he can to optimize the qualities in the situation that will be most helpful to the child's 'resolution' of the conflict in a growth-producing or educative manner. The deductions of this chapter suggest three major 'qualities in the situation' that are most likely to be salient: authenticity, legitimacy and productivity. The teacher, then, is 'concerned' about these qualities. He tries to pick up cues from the students' behavior as to which of these qualities needs to be augmented or soft-pedalled, and he acts accordingly. (I have labelled this sort of action 'management of the classroom dialectic'; in Chapter 9 we shall become action-oriented and show what is involved in such management. I believe it is this dialectical management which has most to do with 'educating' the child.)

But we must not allow ourselves to be carried away. This talk of 'qualities' and 'concerns' points more to style than to goals. The teacher still plans lessons, and tries quite purposively to set up learning activities. The child participates in these activities and, for the foreseeable future, takes tests. There is still a curriculum. It is as the child grapples with these realities that the conflicts and drama emerge. Thus the curriculum serves a dual purpose: it provides planned activities, challenges, problems and projects through which the child can learn to how to deal with the existential and conceptual world; but it plans these activities in such a way that the conflicts and drama necessary for educative growth are likely to arise. It is this aspect of curriculum that has tended to be overlooked. It is this aspect that the students in our study were, I think, sensing intuitively in their wish for productive teamness; and it is this aspect that critics have in mind when they call schooling inhumane and 'mindless.' Without this aspect, the child learns to know and to understand, but he cannot comprehend within his own dialect or world view the larger meanings and significances of experience.

Returning to the management of dialectic, we have suggested that, in different situations, different balances among the qualities of authenticity, legitimacy and productivity are probably most facilitative. Hence the teacher's course of action depends on what balance he is striving for. We shall see that the practical conditions that maximize one are at the expense of the alternative conditions that would maximize another. Neither a classroom nor a school nor any other organization can accomplish everything at the same time. Hence there is always a trade-off; and because one needs to understand the whole system in which the child lives and the trade-off occurs, I have said that the kind of thinking involved in reaching the appropriate trade-off (or favorable balance among benefits and costs) is comprehensive understanding.

Finally, and perhaps not a moment too soon, we can try to answer the question we started with in this chapter: what 'guarantees' that the teacher's acts, policies and decisions will be in the best interests of his student? 'Best interests' means educative growth or, if you like, 'unfolding.' The most fundamental variable under the teacher's control (with respect to which he must do his best) is the balance between the conditions for A, L and P. So the question is, what guarantees the teacher that he will strike the right balance? There is no one single proof, but there are a lot of contributing probabilities: the extent to which his theories of life adequately inform his intuitive grasp of classroom situations; his sensitivity and receptivity to the dramatic; his genuine personal concern for authenticity, legitimacy and productivity; his repertoire of behaviors, through which he can vary the conditions associated with these qualities. But perhaps most convincing are the results of his comprehension: the maturation of his students, as shown in their expanding capabilities for effective classroom life as well as for tackling increasingly sophisticated curricular challenges; the growth of the classroom community toward a more educative culture, ethos or dialect; and his own sense of being alive and looking forward eagerly to the adventures of the next day. But, as we said at the beginning, nobody's perfect, and so I would add one more probability — that his quest for comprehension is active and experimental: if what he does is not working, he assesses the situation and tries something else. For this is how people learn and develop, and the teacher might as well set the example — and make it seem like fun.

Summary

Having a general idea about the process quests of life, we now ask what to do about them. Which quests should be facilitated, which suppressed, under what conditions, and to what extent? These 'should' questions force us to think about values. I propose that the relationships among three major values tend to determine which quests will in fact be facilitated.

Relationships between the adaptive and transcendental quests determine and are controlled by authenticity; similarly, participative and transcendental quests relate to legitimacy; and the participative and adaptive quests relate to productivity.

The teacher monitors these values and decides what trade-off among them is appropriate in each situation. We show how different trade-offs best facilitate the various activities involved in the sequence of an action-oriented group. We suggest several classroom symptoms that can be used to tell if the authenticity-legitimacy-productivity (ALP) balance is appropriate.

Notes

1. In our framework, much of Maslow's thrust is in the domain we call 'authenticity.' His interest was in the study of 'good people and good organizations'; the interpersonal transactions which must develop throughout democracy; and the 'change of mind out of the temporal and into the eternal order.' These matters are discussed in the posthumous *Politics 3*, Robert Kantor (ed.), Research Memorandum EPRC 6747-12 (Stanford Research Institute, Menlo Park, California 94025, 1968.)

2. The concept of legitimacy as a kind of authority over behavior is treated in Max Weber, *Theory of Social and Economic Organization*, Talcott Parsons (ed.) (Free Press, Glencoe, 1947.)

3. The concept of legitimacy as linkage between individual and institutional *patterns* — cognitive justification, internalized values, situational norms — was more central to Talcott Parsons, *Essays in Sociological Theory* (Free Press, Glencoe, 1954).

4. David Easton, *A Systems Analysis of Political Life* (Wiley, New York, 1965) gives explicit consideration to ideology and its place in thinking about social systems.

7   Propositions for Educative Classrooms

In this chapter we shall attempt to portray the nature of the classroom group and to show what, within its nature, makes the group educable under what sorts of policies of teaching.[1] Because this is a fairly complex matter, I had better anticipate my strategy. I shall start with the by-now familiar assertion that classrooms are microsocieties which have the salient and distinctive tendencies of the 'larger society.' I shall then present some researches on classroom grouping and will show that they become highly interpretable if we assume that classroom groups are indeed miniature versions of larger societies. The grouping studies will help us recognize explicitly three basic activities and structures of classroom society that we have already identified as components of all societies: psyche-group activity, socio-group activity and task activity. We shall spell out for each some properties which seem most suggestive for education.

Having torn the classroom entity apart, it behooves us to show how it can be put together again, and this will lead us into the matter of how to teach. We have been assuming that, in almost all teaching, some practices violate at least some aspects of the nature of the classroom society. I shall suggest that the gamut of present violations tends to form a pattern, and that the basis of this pattern is the image of classroom activity as *labor*. I will then say a few kind words about *work* and, finally, try to show how the concept of work can be used to deal integratively and educatively with the psyche-, socio- and task facets of the classroom.

Society[2]

Born into an existential world in which they must find food, shelters and the other necessities of life, men have had to learn the properties of this world and how to 'participate' (Chapter 5) in its workings to get what they need. Here, then, is the reason for knowledge and know-how, collected over millenia, organized codified, symbolized and passed on from generation to generation — with revisions. In addition to pooling ideas, men have also learned to pool their individual efforts: faced with a difficult or even hostile environment, they tend to band together in the common cause of overcoming the enemy whether it be starvation, illness, acts of God or alien ideologies.

For concerted effort to be possible, men require language, expectations, authority and legitimization of common purposes; these are developed and enforced through agreements, both implicit and explicit. Society's major purpose is to produce the things its members need. But when the relationships between production and consumption (of food, art, ideas) can no longer be clearly seen, maintenance of society tends to become an end in itself; the 'good' society comes to fit a traditional image whose reason and justification may have long ago been forgotten. The society then becomes, in some respects, part of an existential world whose properties must be studied and interfered with in the same way as the rest of the environment.

Within the action context of tasks and the relationship context of organizations, the individual reserves for himself, autonomously, a small bit of psychological space. Here he cultivates his private wisdom, his secret apprehensions, his unspoken hopes; and these become known to him through his reactions to groups, to established knowledge and to demands for his activity. He selects other persons to assist him, and these preferences generate informal groupings oriented to the individual's mostly private concerns about himself.

All parts of this picture are *necessary*. To get jobs done you have to have organization; to have organization you have to have members; to have members, persons have to know who they are, what they value and what the *quid pro quo* is. On the other hand, the person cannot develop a 'self' except as he tries to participate with others in a variety of enterprises; in order to participate with others, there has to be organization; and for organization to exist there has to be some purpose.

Hence we see in society three major and necessary components, each with its own function, organization, body of knowledge and legitimizing authority: the task force, engaged in transactions with the environment; the socio-organization, engaged in maintaining a social order and organization; and the psyche-group, comprised of voluntary groupings or 'informal' associations through which each individual comes to terms with his private problems and anxieties.

In the classroom, the approximate equivalents of the three major components are: the students working on lessons (task force); the teacher giving instructions and enforcing his rules (organization and social order); children whispering to friends or playing with them outside of class (psyche-groups). Just how genuine these 'equivalents' really are remains to be seen.

What Grouping Studies Show about the Classroom Society

The classroom group, students and teacher, may be regarded as a microsociety. No doubt some features of the society or group will be affected by who the members of the group are — their interests, emotional defenses, values and capabilities[3] (to name a few). In other words, what the persons are like (what they bring into the group) affects how the group operates (management problems) and at least some of the outcomes of its efforts (achievement).

There have been many attempts to select students into classes which will have certain characteristics of process or outcome, greater manageability, greater achievement, greater ego support for individuals, greater security and less anxiety in the teacher. Homogeneous grouping by 'ability' is the most common form of grouping now in use. Insofar as 'ability' correlates with race, sex or moral character, grouping by ability is also a form of segregation of these other sorts. Insofar as ability correlates with prestige, ability grouping can satisfy what appears to be a condition that exists (according to Washburne[4]) in all societies: that there be an in-group and an out-group. This would also be in line with Bettelheim's suggestion[5] that the principle of social stratification, threatened by ending of racial discrimination, can be preserved by ability segregation. Apart from these dirty reasons, however, the notion that it would be advantageous to narrow the range of brightness, aptitude, speed, prior knowledge, etc. of the class is a popular and plausible idea. It is assumed that the teacher would have fewer 'individual differences' to contend with and would therefore teach more effectively.

At any rate, whatever the explanation (or excuse), the findings resulting from comparing achievement in homogeneous groups with achievement in heterogeneous groups are prefectly clear: the two organizations are superior to each other in about the same number of instances. Three carefully controlled, properly designed studies by Passow,[6] Drews and Borg[7] show the homogeneous groups to be superior on some scores (achievement, attitude, interest) and the heterogeneous groups on others. Moreover the patterns differed from one comparison to the next, and the patterns are mostly uninterpretable. Thus, a fourth-grade homogeneous class may show higher scores in spelling than did the heterogeneous class; but the same classes in the fifth grade may reverse their standings.

The failure of homogeneous ability grouping to generate clearly positive outcomes certainly means that the 'plausible' reasons for this form of grouping must now appear a little less plausible. Technically, what the findings suggest is that IQ plus achievement is a much less influential factor than some other factor that was not controlled and which *really* accounts for the differences. The popular hunch about narrowing the range of brightness to make the teacher more effective would make sense if verbal fluency, speed and extensive memory for an assortment of information — which is what group IQ tests tend to measure — has much to do with successful participation, but these are simply *not* the traits demanded in most classroom activities. The notion that academic ability indirectly *indexes* other things like self-directiveness, interest in school work and creativity is assumed when the course is changed to fit the bright or slower student. Unfortunately, most of these assumptions are wrong: there is no evidence to show that bright students like to work harder or are less dependent than slower students when confronted with equally difficult situations.

We do not have to look very far to see what factor *does* account for the differences in the grouping experiments. Ekstrom,[8] in her survey of all published accounts of ability grouping, points it out: the teacher. She suggests that a slower homogeneous class which has an emotionally warm and supportive teacher may achieve better than would the same students distributed throughout regular classes; and that a strongly work-oriented no-nonsense teacher may get good results with a homogeneous 'bright' class. She leaves open the extent to which teachers have any awareness of these qualities, and the extent to which they are due to teacher personality or teacher strategy and procedure.

Shane studied 32 ways of grouping students into elementary-school classes.[9] He concluded that the most important factor governing the success of any method of grouping is the extent to which the teacher believes in it and is committed to making it work. This seems to suggest that the teacher has a whim of iron; that he has very great power or potency. This is indeed the case, as shown, for example in the works of Withall, Flanders, Anderson, Hughes, Perkins[10] and now of

Kounin[11] — all of which show that one can predict the morale and achievement of a *class* simply from knowledge of the *teacher's* behavior. Or consider the Lewin, Lippitt and White studies which demonstrated how deliberate shifts in the role performance of the teacher led to vast differences in the behaviors of pupils. Finally, let us throw in the hopper one further generalization, from Bloom[12]: that the method of teaching seems to have little or no influence on learning of *information* that is, that when the same teacher teaches similar classes by different procedures (telling as against audiovisual, for example) there are not significant differences in the amount learned — even though there are differences from one teacher to the next. (However, procedures make more difference with respect to the learning of 'higher mental processes,' because demonstration of a rationale is required in such learning.)

These studies suggest that the teacher has great power, and that this power is exerted in relationships and through aspects of transactions that lie below consciousness. In short, teacher 'personality,' not method, materials or procedure, is the most important factor.

We are forced to see that the organizing principle of the classroom society is the personality of the teacher, and therefore the way to improve the classroom through grouping is to fit students to the teacher in such a way that the educative tendencies within his personality will be most reinforced. Short of intensive clinical study of teachers and students, educational theory at present would offer no suggestions as to how to effect such matching. However, we can make a beginning: we can give the teacher a classful of students he *can* teach. In such a class the teacher should most effectively achieve his goals — whatever they may be. The reasons for my reluctance to equate the teacher's goals with education will be apparent before long.

One study made such matchings to 13 teachers ranging across five academic subjects and four high school grades in eight suburban schools.[13] The matching was accomplished by having each teacher name students whom he considered were 'getting a lot out of his class' and students having the opposite experience. The two lists of nominees were extensively tested on a 405-item battery of classroom-related attitudes, preferences and associations, and items which empirically discriminated between the two lists were incorporated in a scoring key. Next the students from whom his next year's classes were to be chosen were tested on the same battery and scored by the special key. The top thirty students most like the ones earlier nominated as 'getting a lot out of class' were selected into the experimental, 'compatible' group for the teacher. The teacher was also given a control class, composed by the usual methods in his school.

There were many findings that emerged from the study but a quick summary may suffice for our purposes. The teachable students from one teacher had little in common with those for another, and for no teacher was IQ a desideratum for the 'teachable' students. Eleven of the 13 teachers gave higher marks to their teachable classes (and one gave the same marks). Nine of the 13 teachers preferred the students in the teachable class to work with or chat with; the students in eleven of the 13 teachable classes preferred each other more than did the students in the control classes. There were fewer observed problems in the teachable classes, and the teachers were observed to talk some- what more of the time, to express more affect and to be seen by the students as more interested in the class.

It is obvious that the teachers achieved their purposes better in the experimental classes. This is shown directly by the higher marks and indirectly by the greater liking for the students. It is also mentioned in testimony from five teachers who were followed most intensively — each got what he wanted: more vigorous, personally involving interactions with students; deeper penetration into the principles of algebra; faster coverage of the content; a pleasanter, friendlier, less work-oriented class that he could feel more adequate with; more counselling combined with teaching.

But this is not all of the picture. Eight of the *control* classes got higher gain scores on achievement tests given at the beginning and end of the year; and nine of the control classes liked the teacher better than did the corresponding experimental classes. This suggests two things: (a) for at least seven of the thirteen teachers, whatever the achievement test measures is less important to them than other objec- tives; and (b) judging by pupil liking for the teacher, some of these more important objectives may well have also been a bit exploitative psychologically. What we helped the teachers get appears in some instances to have been at the expense of the students' well-being. For example, certain teachers seemed to want mostly to be comfortable; others to have a quiet, orderly, punctual and respectful class; and others to get responses that would reassure them of their expertness, love or rapport with the kids. The pupils were selected to give them these things, but the children did not necessarily like it nor are these things necessarily educative.

The major job of the classroom society is to accommodate to the teacher's way of life. By picking students like those who have demonstrated *this* ability (IQ indeed!) one gets a classroom whose culture is more coherent, whose societal solidarity is greater and whose accomplishment of common (i.e. teacher's) purposes is greater.

But it is interesting that having a more manageable class does not, in itself, make the teacher more educative — only more effective. Presumably, to the extent that the teacher has wanted to try new things but has been held back by anxiety, he would be more likely to 'grow' with a teachable class. But to improve the quality (i.e. the objectives) of the teacher, he will have to get new insights and attitudes; he will have to be helped to be more conscious of his fantastic power, and to learn to use it consciously and wisely for educative purposes.

The teacher might well ask what power and authority, other than that exuding almost unconsciously from his personality and office, is available to guide the educative process. There are two answers to this question. One answer is that of the behavioral scientist: that the children are energy systems, and that they *have to cope* with problems of being a person, a member of the group and a producer of something. In other words, they too have quests. The problem for the teacher is to see how the encouragement of these legitimate quests of the student can also be the encouragement of educative experience. The second answer is that of the philosopher and epistemologist: knowledge has certain characteristics and, when 'learned' in certain ways, knowledge is useful, but learned in other ways it is useless. It is these scientific and epistemological insights, internalized within the teacher, that legitimate and justify his power and authority.

The Psyche-group[14]: The Interpersonal Network

Any device which raises the level of the student's awareness and articulation of personally important or authentic concerns also legitimates activities that lead to his meaningful acquisition and assimilation of meaningful knowledge. In the classroom, there is such a device which tends to operate spontaneously when appropriate to personal questing. This device is the psyche-group. The psyche-group is a mode of social organization; it forms voluntarily, is initiated by stress and is composed of people who choose and trust each other. It has no prespecified or assigned agenda, and its interactions have a quality of privacy, intimacy or confidentiality. Its structure can be described sociometrically as a pattern of interpersonal likes and dislikes.

In the classroom, students may be invited to form psyche-groups (self-selected) to talk over anything that has them emotionally aroused. They can reduce anxiety, try out their ideas on friends, be stimulated with more ideas, rehearse how they are going to report their ideas to the teacher and develop a greater sense of adequacy and confidence in their participation when the class next meets as a whole. The 'content' of such discussion might be called *self-knowledge*. You will find a lot of such stuff in novels: it is the medium of personal interaction. Self-knowledge has a special kind of validity: a statement feels exactly right or it does not; each individual is the authority in this matter, and conversations between friends usually keep going until the right words have been found or until the parties *decide* to let it go for now. All those parts of educative activity which require commitment or motivation from individuals could well be 'cleared' through open discussion in self-chosen small groups, for this is the sort of conversation by which one normally reduces his ambivalences preparatory to great undertakings.

We see psyche-operations in the back-stairs gossip when there is a new principal; in coffee breaks at meetings; in over-the-fence gossip sessions; in the endless telephone conversations of our children. We also see it in the eye-to-eye eyebrow raising of cronies at a business meeting, in the familiar 'deterioration' of a meeting into side conversations or in those rare moments of truth when a whole meeting is momentarily sharing a common emotion.

The teacher may sometimes overtly be a member of a psyche-group for some child; he is very likely to be a covert member with whom the child carries on active, imaginary conversations. The teacher's power is, as we have seen, largely exerted in the deeper unaware ways of the psyche-group, and much of this power probably comes from the student's *identification* with the teacher. The development of the class as a cohesive group during those first few weeks of the new school year is probably quite dependent on the development of identifications of students with the teacher and on their own awareness that they have this identification in common. The psyche-groups, meeting outside of school, or illicitly during class time, or under the guise of working committees, are the major mechanism of adjustment and adaptation for most students. Events in psyche-groups are to be understood in much the same way as events in therapeutic groups through the use of personality theory and psychotherapeutic models.[15]

The Socio-group: The Legislative Network

There is a whole realm of knowledge that has to be legislated, a domain of things that are true simply because people agree that they are true. This is the realm of manners and morals. It includes just about everything that is not true by logical deduction or by empirical test: what fork to use, what to do in order to be bad, how to address the teacher, what will happen to me if I do not keep my promises, how late I can be and still be excusable, what language I can use to cuss with, how openly I may display my autocratic leanings. What do we expect of each other by way of what sorts of participation, leadership and conformity? What do you have to do to 'belong'? What things can the individual freely decide by himself and what things must be discussed with others? When the group makes a decision, what recourse is open for the individual who cannot go along with the decision? What are acceptable ways to dissent, attack, express affection and run away from hard jobs? These questions can be discussed.[16]

The rules, boundaries and opportunities for interaction within the classroom social order are legislated by teacher fiat, by conscious group agreement and by subconscious sharing and concensus. Implicit and explicit rules and expectations 'define' the social situation, and the two most important aspects to be clear about are the nature of the authority which governs activity and the location of the boundary between that which is public — that is, a legitimate concern of the group — and that which is private — that is, its communication to others is at the discretion solely of the individuals. If the authority hierarchy is not clear, then classes and individuals have no way to legitimize their decisions because they do not know what criteria their decisions must satisfy. If the public-private boundary is unclear, individuals cannot tell what part of their experience (or, more precisely, of their reactions to their experiences) is relevant for the organization; hence they are at sea as to what ideas and feelings of their own can or should be expressed and thus 'tested' and learned from.

The imperative that sets the socio-group into operation is lack of predictability or lack of confidence. These are serious conditions, for without predictability I cannot behave intelligently, and without confidence I may not be able to behave at all. Under conditions of the 'rule of law' a person knows what to expect others to do in response to his behavior, and he therefore can use knowledge of probable consequences as an aid in making decisions about what to do. All groups 'legislate' the expectations needed for predictability; this is a major function of the initial shake-down period. The person who has the greatest power in the group, being most able to influence legislation and opinion, also can predict best the consequences of action. He is therefore the most 'free,' taking least actual risk when he sticks his neck out.

There is, of course, a *quid pro quo* involved. If I want maximum freedom, I must belong to the socio-group, for only those who belong can fully 'know' the rules. And I must not only follow the rules myself (including rules about how to change the rules) but also help enforce them on others. In other words, I must share in making the self-fulfilling hypotheses come true. And I will find myself tending to oppose other members who try to change their own roles, for such changes mean I no longer can predict their behavior and therefore my freedom is diminished just a little (even though theirs is increased until the others get them pegged again).

When a child is described as good or bad, it is quality of his membership which is ordinarily being evaluated, for good and bad behavior are socially defined. The good child 'helps' the organization, 'fits in,' abides by the organization's rules, supports its norms and influences the group to adopt 'better' norms. The bad child makes problems and difficulties for the organization: he violates the norms, lives at loggerheads with the organization, does not belong. The approved pattern of behavior is the member role. Differences in the quality and extent of membership (in the way the member role is actualized) are always found. Some members are more influential, or 'central'; they are accorded more prestige; they have more worth than others. The various aspects of membership can be rank-ordered; members can be arranged hierarchially, and the organization has a social structure.

The child who does not 'fit in' to the social order or organization has not been socialized; he is asocial within *that* organization. And he is punished, ostracized, made to feel bad. For the most part, the social order is maintained through habit, and the habits we need to 'fit in' may, as with the family, be instilled long before the child has the equipment to think about them. When the classroom social order is organized around values, language and thought patterns similar to those of our family, we will normally 'fit in' with the classroom organization. But when our socialization in the family is along quite different lines, we will, as members of the classroom group, be located at the bottom of the various membership hierarchies; and we will be 'out-group.' We will be deprived of what other members expect as a matter of 'right.' From our point of view, the 'in-group' members are 'privileged.'

The Task Group

In task activity we are concerned with the student as doer, problem-solver, creator, producer, investigator. These are functional roles carried on *vis-á-vis* the environment rather than *vis-á-vis* the self or other persons. The nonpersonal environment contains ideas of the then-and-there, not merely of the here-and-now; it contains objects, natural phenomena, records of past events, technologies, arts and artifacts; it embraces agriculture, manufacturing, transportation. It is the 'larger society' and all its works — the objective world for which the student is being readied. Much of this environment the student does not know at first hand; it is represented by words, by books, films, relics, myths, encyclopedias. This representation is continually altered, filled out and reorganized: this is the established knowledge which men have accumulated, the 'funded capital of human experience.' The environment thus has two manifestations: as 'real' things and events, and as knowledge-symbols. The common characteristic of these two things is their *externalization*: they exist 'outside' of personality and outside of membership. They have an inherent nature of their own quite apart from the student's needs or capabilities and, in dealing with the environment, the student must change his information, his ideas, his skills. He must accommodate himself in some way to this objective external world.

We have to experience the objective external world in order to influence it or be influenced by it: contact must be made. The medium of contact is activity. The activity may be primarily a transaction between the student and the objects and situations of the environment, or between the student and the organized sets of symbols which represent the environment. Performing a chemistry experiment is first-hand direct experience with the objects and situations of chemistry. Reading a book is direct first-hand experience with an organized set of symbols. When a student is doing an experiment, he is doing his business with the environment, and the extent to which the data of his senses — what he sees, smells, hears, feels — become translated into verbal symbols may be minimal. When a student is reading a chemistry textbook, he is doing his business with the world of verbal, symbolic representation presumably of the world of objects and situations. But the verbal world is an abstract world, devoid of sight, smell and touch but replete with assertions and conclusions. The presumption that activity in the verbal world has inevitable correspondence with activity in the existential world is certainly dubious. By itself, activity in the verbal world prepares one to carry on conversations and to answer word questions, such as those in most achievement tests of the present-day school. By itself, activity in the existential world is unique to each situation, and what an individual learns through each particular activity may not increase his power in coping with later activities. Both types of activity are necessary if knowledge is to make a difference in a person's life. The experienced existential world provides the sensory data to interpret and utilize; the experienced symbolic world provides the tools of thought for relating one experience to another and for coping with the widest range of situations in the future.

The activities of the student depend on the school 'subject' under whose auspices the activity is conducted. Some school subjects, such as physics, chemistry and biology, purport to help the student cope directly with the world of objects and situations; other subjects, such as mathematics and foreign languages, purport to help the student cope with the world of symbols; still other subjects, such as social studies and literature, seem for the most part quite unsure of where their interests lie. Considerations of this sort are at the heart of the true business of curriculum, but the curriculum field has become stagnant because for the most part it concerns itself only with one world, the world of organized symbols.

But let me now put our three classroom components back together again, using a contrast between *labor* and *work* to lead us to a conception of integrative teaching.

Labor

Controversies about education tend to 'involve' practically everybody, because the educational microsociety closely reflects the larger society and is much easier to fathom. The issue of individual versus society has been around a long time and takes different forms at different times and places: activity versus passivity, subject-centered versus child-centered curriculum, inner- versus other-direction, traditional versus emergent values — these are not equivalent issues but they provide vocabularies for discussing the same set of perceptions.

For our purposes, Hannah Arendt's brilliant exegesis of the distinction between work and labor[17] enables us to organize the ideas we need to see how the three components — psyche, socio and task — of the classroom society can be kept working together for educative purposes. And, as a sort of bonus, we find that Bion's work fits well with Arendt's, and Bion's *flight* and *dependency* emotionalities are close to Arendt's labor.[18]

Work, then, is effort that makes a difference. It changes the situation — solves a problem, produces some useful object, develops a new insight. Work is guided or directed by one's understanding of the demand-structure of the situation one is trying to cope with. (We put the load close to the wheelbarrow's wheel because that gives us the best leverage, not because that's the way Joe likes it or because that's the way we always do it). In other words, work is reality-seeking effort. Work is also 'molar' and 'significant' to the worker: it is no mean thing to 'make a difference' through one's efforts. (Recall the disgruntled shoe makers in the factory: when they made the whole shoe they were working, but when they shifted to assembly-line methods with each person just doing a small part of the work, they were laboring.) Work is also creative, involving reorganization of ideas and making of judgments: one is truly coping. During work one has a gamut of feelings, depending on how things are going; one feels involved; one senses the dramatic quality of existence. One participates in work as a 'whole' person. Work is the highest lot of man and is necessary for self-realization.

Labor is pretty much the opposite of the goodies just described. Labor may make a difference, but not in its own right and not to the laborer. To somebody else it's just dandy to have a ditch; to the ditch-digger, the ditch is just a grave with both ends knocked out or it's a trough out of which one's daily bread can be extracted. Laboring, unlike dancing and work, has no consummatory value. Labor is directed by someone else, for his reasons, and according to his procedures; and the basis of these reasons and procedures in insight or tradition may not even interest the laborer. Labor is uncreative, partly because the involvement of the laborer in the task is not great enough to generate much by way of discovery, and partly because it is not intended to be creative: it is the application of a formula or technique over and over; it is practice which may perfect the efficiency of a technique (like learning to run covariance analyses on the computer), but it does not improve the technique. Labor is easy to direct because the tasks are cut and dried. This is the genius of mass production. The laborer is not psychologically involved enough to ask any genuine questions about the task (only about the conditions of employment).

When the activity of the classroom is labor, the corresponding method of teaching is 'shaping' or conditioning or training in the narrow sense of training of specific skills.[19] The teacher sets up the activity and makes clear the procedures to be followed. He then gets the students started and tries to keep them delivering the required behaviors. He uses a combination of interventions: warning against 'wrong' behaviors, punishing wrong behaviors, encouraging right behaviors, rewarding right behaviors. These interventions occur as the students are laboring. The product of the labor is a test or exercise completed, and the student may be rewarded or punished additionally for the quality of the product. It is simply assumed that engagement in labor is educative and that the educator must therefore keep the students laboring.

Under these conditions — of laboring rather than working — interaction between students must be either suppressed, or simply tolerated as an unavoidable source of inefficiency.[20] Having set up a face-to-face group, the teacher has to contend with the *inevitable* psyche- and socio-processes of a face-to-face group. But his method and concept of teaching regards these processes as irrelevant rather than as a tremendously potent dynamic that can be capitalized on to drive learning. There is a curious bifurcation in the teacher's thinking. He says, 'Let me manage the class and then I will be able to teach them.' He has, in effect, two different theories, one having to do with 'management' and the other with 'teaching.' Trying to serve two masters at once calls for pretty fancy footwork, or it calls for assigning the masters unequal power, so that in the case of conflicting demands he knows which to obey. Generally speaking, the management master dominates the teaching master: you may know very well that if you will listen to the children they will, possibly, learn more; but the kids' talking may turn out to be so noisy that you tell them to be quiet. In the labor-oriented classroom, the verbal is emphasized to the virtual exclusion of the existential. For the verbal is neat, finite and tidy; and it requires neither purpose nor rationale. An 'assignment' is what you come up with by dividing the number of pages in the textbook by the number of school days in the year.[21]

In any classroom, three kinds of knowledge are utilized, whether one knows it or not: knowledge of self; knowledge of the society in which one participates (i.e. the classroom group); and knowledge pertaining to externalized events, processes and artifacts. Schools which are labor-oriented concentrate only on the third kind of knowledge, considering the other two irrelevant, distracting, soft or somebody else's business. But any theorist worth his salt must vigorously disagree with this stance. Since self and group processes largely determine the educative outcomes (not necessarily revealed by achievement tests) of the student's transactions with the external world, the teacher, at least, ought to know what is going on at the other two 'levels.' I think it is fair to say that when instructional activities are largely confined to practice exercises, lecturing and any other sort of prestructured activities, not only is there no justification for having students organized into classes, but indeed such classes may well foster seriously maladaptive understandings of social and organizational process.

Work

Work has many forms and guises. Assessment of situations, making decisions and carrying out action is the work prototype in business. Having a feeling to express and doing so through painting or music would be work in the world of creative art. In a society, sensing a discrepancy between expectation and behavior, diagnosing the cause and taking action, either to revise the expectation or enforce it, — would be work. Two individuals, both of whom are upset about the latest edict from on high, may help each other become aware of what they feel and think — this, too, is work. Work is reality-seeking, trying to understand, in one's own terms and with reference to his own perceptions and needs, what the world is like and how to operate in that world.

Given a class of children who are required to meet every day for forty minutes, there are certain things they can do easily and naturally and other things they cannot do so well. What they can do easily and naturally is *work*; what they can do only at a fearful and miseducative cost is *labor*. The method of teaching that makes most sense to a behavioral scientist is that method which keeps the child working, not laboring. The elements of this method are that the child purposively contributes skills and ideas to common goals by coordinating his contributions with those of others; the child helps maintain the group as a viable decision-making and communicative medium through which individual goals and contributions can be monitored, assimilated and legitimated by the larger classroom organization; the child finds support, anxiety-reduction and awareness of his own thoughts and feelings through interaction with selected other children in small groups. Activity is purposive and genuinely meaningful, which means that old ideas, attitudes and skills are inadequate so that one is under some stress. The stress is different for each person: one is annoyed at the unexpected difficulty of the task; another is reminded of certain painful experiences from the past and temporarily confuses them with the present activity; another child is extremely sensitive to feelings of being imposed on. Whatever principles the individual has to live with may be called into question. The student must be able to deal with unique personal stress in such a way that he can keep on functioning as a member and a doer. And this is the *raison d'être* of psyche-groups within the class.

When the method of learning is through work, spontaneously arising interpersonal and group processes are objects of interest and attention. For these processes (e.g. expressions of emotion, confused actions, acting out, conspiracy, intimacy-seeking) provide the evidence that work is going forward, is being resisted or perverted or is becoming snagged in frustration and pointlessness. During classroom activities, the situation is continually changing as the result of each bit of public overt behavior; and, as the situation changes, so also do the personal, group and task demands that govern the activity.[22] Since work (by definition) attempts to maintain contact with reality, work activity is continuously responsive to changed demands, and therefore the work curriculum is emergent, flexible, natural; and the human processes of the classroom are sacred.

Work-oriented teaching will make room for self-knowledge, socio-knowledge and externalized knowledge, and will organize the class in whatever way is appropriate to get the kind of knowledge needed at each moment. When individual reaction, awareness, commitment and anxiety-reduction are imperative, the class will be in small self-selected groups. When a wide range of 'bright ideas' is needed as a basis for creating interesting hypotheses, the whole society will be put under highly permissive leadership long enough to get out the ideas. When many individuals have many different ideas as to purposes to be adopted, the entire society will undertake an analysis of the different ideas, seeking for common threads or underlying themes that can be converted into an agenda. Once a variety of topics or questions has been set up for investigation, and each individual has committed himself to start on one or another question, the work will be done individually, with the students working on their existential and symbolic worlds, not on each other. Thus work-teaching continually attends to the patterning of organizational arrangements, varieties of knowledge, and self, group, and task purposes.

The prominence of psyche, socio, and task structures of the classroom continually shift relative to each other. The teacher picks up cues from the children in order to decide which mode of organization to facilitate next. After the class has seen a dramatic movie, the children are likely to express the feelings it aroused and the teacher, seeing this, may allow the class to divide into small self-selected psyche groups to give each individual the opportunity to articulate and 'get hold' of his feelings. After the class has been working in task or project groups for a while, the teacher may find it useful to invite them to meet together as a socio-group to legislate 'ground rules' for the activity. When a period of working is found to be unproductive, the class may attempt to analyze what went wrong and consciously to anticipate and circumvent similar difficulties in the future. When discussion begins to be repetitous and dull, the teacher may realize that it is time to plan another challenging work task so that the students will have some first-hand experience to come to terms with in a more meaningful discussion.

If we want students to work, we shall have to redefine social norms and we shall have to encourage supportive informal or psyche-operations. A major revision of social norms, has for example, to do with failure. In the labor view of education, the student fails because the teacher judges that he incorrectly remembers or applies information. In the work view of education, wrong answers simply show the student that he is on the wrong track; and they are therefore quite helpful. The only failure is failure to learn anything from wrong or unproductive attempts.

Integrative Teaching

A major aspect of teaching is the supervision of learning activities. We have suggested that to the behavioral scientist there are a number of 'givens' which seriously influence the child's experiences and therefore the presumed educativeness of learning activities. The psychologist tells the teacher to avoid antitherapeutic interventions, to be sensitive to anxiety states and confusions of individuals, to find ways to support the child's ego and to build on his strengths rather than his weaknesses, to operate the class as a psyche-group. The sociologist or group dynamicist tells the teacher that students will perform better if they participate in making the decisions that govern their performance, that problems of accepting 'membership' and leadership may produce hidden agendas, that group norms are all important and that the teacher's influence on norms is very great. (Knowing these principles and others, you, too, can have a 'good' group). And politicoeducational leaders tell the teacher that classrooms are now instruments for alleviating society's distress over problems of racial prejudice and opportunities for minorities and that, under these conditions, achievement — standardized, automated, regularized, and efficient — must be the highest-priority aim of education. Finally, our consciences tell us as teachers that the child is precious and that it is up to us to decide through our actions whether he will live a rich, challenging and vital life; a scared, thin life; or a permanently dependent alien life as a ward of the state.

The question of how to teach is, however, not as 'open' as the arguments among 'experts' would lead you to believe. Let us see how the ideas so far presented help us to close in on the matter of teaching method.[23]

First, in every classroom there is a psyche-group structure of interpersonal attractions and repulsions. These feelings will generate a good deal of behavior, and this behavior is gratifying because it serves the useful purpose of helping individuals discover and maintain their identity. The inevitable occurrence of these psyche-phenomena presents us with the problem of how to utilize or channel these interpersonal interactions into educationally relevant activity.

Second, however the classroom is composed, it is still an involuntary enterprise. That is, the students have to come, they have to be together some of the time and they have to accept the teacher. They have quite a lot to make the best of! The psyche-activity helps them to some extent, but if that were the only kind of activity, the group would divide into anarchic, power-driven subgroups or gangs. No, a further kind of activity is needed, and the most appropriate further activity is working on a task to accomplish some purpose all the members feel is important. This is the *raison d'être* for nonfriends coming together: to take some kind of action no one of them can quite manage by himself. But in order to coordinate their efforts on the task, they need a body of legislation — expectations and agreements about who will do what, through what sorts of behaviors and expressions a member may channel his contributions, etc.

Third, it is quite clear that the psyche-group and the socio-group processes and problems will be determined pretty much by the particular composition of the group, students plus teacher.

Fourth, the demands of the psyche-structure and of the socio-structure may be partly reinforcing and partly in conflict. Just as an individual is usually prey to some ambivalence, wanting to work and face reality and at the same time wanting to evade the pain and trouble, so the group has to come to terms with its two natures. In short, it must operate in such a way that each person retains his integrity as a person and can meet some of his private needs and yet at the same time the group must be a social order and working organization with a well-developed body of 'rules' that everyone can count on.

Fifth, given the probable tensions between psyche- and socio-operations, some higher authority is required to adjudicate the conflict — to decide (when occasion warrants) between tendencies to cooperate versus seek personal gratification, to dig in versus to flight, to be self-directing versus to be dependent, to operate in a formal way versus to proceed informally.

Sixth, the teacher clearly does have the power and authority necessary to adjudicate all such conflicts — without even giving reasons, without any recourse by the students, without required reality-testing. Practically the only control over all but the grossest overt behavior of the teacher is his own sense of responsibility and commitment to something over and above his own personal desires.

Seventh, because the teacher has this power and because he actually wields it every time he opens his mouth, any child who cannot identify with the teacher's way of life (his professional as well as his hidden commitments) is going to have a tough time. In any direct conflict with the teacher, the child cannot win. The most he can do is make the teacher anxious, and this reduces the teacher's competence not only to teach this child but to teach the class. Therefore children should be fitted to the teacher, since the teacher is not going to yield; and if this makes it too easy for the teacher to do bad or stupid things the teacher should be fired or retrained.

Eighth, the teacher's way of life and authority may exalt an amazing variety of purposes and values. Yet whatever the psychological pattern, by and large the way the teacher actually deals with the class and supervises its activities can be pretty well understood as exemplifying labor and work orientations.

Ninth, the work orientation (but not the labor orientation) provides criteria and processes by which to adjudicate all the disputes in the classroom. This follows from work being a transaction with external-ized realities which give the class feedback as to whether behavior is on target. Thus there is a higher unarguable authority than the personality or position of any person; and the 'enemy' is a set of condi-tions or problems to be solved, not another person's unfairness or caprice.

Tenth, to be able to set up activities as work rather than labor, the teacher has to know the discipline of his subject rather more thoroughly than is typically the case in schools today. He has to be able to understand the study of his subject as a 'dialectic of inquiry' rather than as the communication of a 'rhetoric of conclusions,' to borrow two of Schwab's felicitous phrases.

Eleventh, the teacher needs to understand consciously some model or strategy or sequence of steps or other guide which enables him to interpret what is going on in front of his nose; and thus to make changes in the activity in order to keep it viable. He will need help from the students, and, therefore, they must be taught to give this help; which means that they too have to understand the strategy.

Twelfth, this increased role of the students, requiring them to take initiative when work is pointless, to help formulate alternative plans, to take many more responsibilities for the work, for themselves and for the classroom society — all of this learning, even though not only ignored but scoffed at in high places, is truly important to the inhabi-tant of the modern world. In other words, the teacher and students can use their own experiences to exemplify, in some respects, other societies; and the classroom can (and should) be basically a continu-ing laboratory for the study of social and societal processes — and for the development of the skills required to participate in these processes.

It seems to me that these twelve points are hardly arguable. Of them, the eleventh is the one that should be spelled out next: a model of work-teaching.[24] This is a very big subject and Chapter 9 wll be devoted to it.

Summary

The behavior of the teacher is determined partly by such concepts as we have been developing so far and partly by demands of educative situations. The most central demand is that the teacher must deal with a group of students in such a way that each gains educational experience. We find that behavioral science offers helpful notions: that the classroom group can be viewed as a small society; that the 'fit' between its mix of personalities and the personality of the teacher has a lot to do with the effectiveness of the teacher. We find that the classroom society tends to operate in three different modes: psyche-group (self-chosen, intimate, authenticity-seeking); socio-group (involuntary, legislative, legitimacy-seeking); and task group (inter-est- or competence-based, transactional, productivity-oriented). We distinguish between work which is educative and labor which is not educative but is what the cultural archetype calls for. The processes of work satisfy Chapter 4's criteria for effective dialectical systems. Implications for managing the class in work are deduced and help to define further the conditions of educative teaching-learning situations.

Notes

1. Much of this chapter appeared as 'Group Interactional Factors in Learning,' in E. M. Bower and W. Hollister (eds.), *Behavioral Science Frontiers in Education* (Wiley, New York, 1967).

2. So far as I am concerned, you may insert in place of this section the whole of Weston La Barre's classic, *The Human Animal* (University of Chicago Press, Chicago, 1954).

3. Five years of experiments with emotionality in groups, including comparisons of groups with different compositions, are described in D. Stock and H. A. Thelen, *Emotional Dynamics and Group Culture* (New York University Press, New York, 1958).

4. And this is just about the *only* property characteristic of all societies, according to Sherwood Washburne (Seminar Discussion, 1954).

5. Bruno Bettelheim, 'Segregation: New Style,; *School Review*, vol. 66, no. 3 (1958), pp. 251-72.

6. Passow and his associates report an excellent study, including a survey of preceding studies, in M. L. Goldberg, J. Justman, A. N. Passow and G. Hage, *The Effects of Ability Grouping* (Teachers College Press, New York, 1962).

7. My information comes from reports by Elizabeth Drews (Michigan State) and Walter Borg (University of Utah). Both studies were sponsored by the Cooperative Research Branch of the then U.S. Office of Education.

8. Ruth B. Ekstrom, 'Experimental Studies of Homogeneous Grouping; A Critical Review,' *School Review*, vol. 69, No. 2 (1961), pp. 216-26.

9. H. G. Shane, 'Grouping in the Elementary School', *Phi Delta Kappan*, vol. 41, no. 7, (1960) pp. 313-19.

10. These researchers used observational instruments to categorize and pattern the teacher's behavior. The behavior of the students was remarkably predictable from that of the teacher! See a summary by D. Medley and H. Mitzel, 'Measuring Classroom Behavior by Systematic Observation,' in N. L. Gage (ed.), *Handbook of Research on Teaching* (Rand McNally, Chicago, 1963), Ch. 6.

11. Of greatest possible interest is Jacob Kounin's finding, that the rate of misbe-havior in the classroom depends more on the teacher's 'thrust' or straightforwardness

and confidence of movement than on his techniques for dealing with the misbehavior! (Work versus labor?)

12. Reported in conversation.

13. The preliminary analysis of what would be involved in a study of grouping was H. A. Thelen, 'Classroom Grouping of Students,' *School Review*, vol. 67, no. 1 (1959), pp. 60-70. The final report is H. A. Thelen, *Classroom Grouping for Teachability* (Wiley, New York, 1967). A summary of findings appeared as H. A. Thelen, 'Grouping for Teachability,' *Theory into Practice*, vol. 2, no. 2 (1963).

14. The terms 'psyche-group' and socio-group' were, so far as I know, coined by Helen Jennings, and were first presented in her article, 'Sociometric Differentiation of the Psychegroup and Sociogroup,' *Sociometry*, vol. 10 (1947), pp. 71-9.

15. I devised a model for student inquiry oriented to self-knowledge. 'Personal inquiry' is an educative variety of situational therapy. See H. A. Thelen, *Education and the Human Quest* (Harper and Row, New York, 1960), Ch. 6.

16. A potent kind of training in human relations (T-groups) centers around the study of what agreements the group must reach in order to survive, how the agreements can be reached, what roles different individuals present to the group, etc. The most authoritative work in this field is L. P. Bradford, J. R. Gibb and K. D. Benne (eds.), *T-Group Theory and Laboratory Method* (Wiley, New York, 1964).

17. Hannah Arendt, *The Human Condition* (University of Chicago Press, Chicago, 1958).

18. Work, according to Bion, is learned and is reality-oriented, whereas emotionality attempts to evade work. See W. R. Bion, *Experiences in Groups* (Basic Books, New York, 1961).

19. B. F. Skinner, 'The Science of Learning and the Art of Teaching,' *Harvard Educational Review*, vol. 24, no. 2 (1954), pp. 86-97.

20. In 'The Triumph of Achievement over Inquiry in Education,' *Elementary School Journal*, vol. 60, no. 4, (1960), pp. 136-51, I present the thesis that although teachers would like to have work done, they supervise it as if it were labor. Very sad.

21. John Ginther and I found that teachers who follow the programmer's instructions to the letter have a terrible time with the class, because there is no common content which justifies their meeting as a class. See H. A. Thelen and John Ginther, 'Experiences with Programmed Materials,' in Wilbur Schramm (ed.), *Four Case Studies of Programed Instruction* (Fund for Advancement of Education, New York, 1964).

22. Steering the group on the basis of feedback from its processes is both intellectually challenging and fun. Two case studies are H. A. Thelen, 'Training for Group Participation: The Laboratory Method', in *Dynamics of Groups at Work* (University of Chicago Press, Chicago, 1954), Ch. 5; and H. A. Thelen, 'Teacher Preparation for the Future', in *Improving Instruction in Professional Education* (Association for Student Teaching, Washington DC, 1958), pp. 83-117.

23. The development of a 'behavioral-science' rationale for education is my continuing interest. In *Dynamics of Groups at Work*[22] I discuss the group 'realities' and in *Education and the Human Quest*[15] I speculatively create four educational models that seem to me to fit the facts.

24. In 1963 I tightened up the model and presented it in 'Insights for Teaching from Interaction Theory', which appeared as a chapter in *The Nature of Teaching* (University of Wisconsin, Milwaukee, 1963), pp. 19-32.

8   The Role of the Teacher: Some Practical Considerations

By now the reader may correctly suppose that our goal is a model of teaching which facilitates educative activity. Such activity is felt by students to be 'meaningful' (or authentic) and by teachers to be 'educative' (or legitimate). Facilitation implies that the student is engaged in doing something on his own and the teacher intervenes to help him do it better — 'better' as judged by both parties. Because the teacher is useful to the student he is welcomed and trusted by the student.

To intervene in the world of the student, the teacher must understand that world as it is known by the student; and to intervene facilitatively, the teacher must have a clear idea of the sequence of activities through which the student's learning develops from the confrontation that initiates it to the confident insight that terminates it.[1]

Our question is: how does the facilitative teacher act? We shall start by considering teaching in the case of one teacher and one student. Then we shall consider the complications that ensue when the one student becomes a class. As stipulated in Chapter 7, we shall think of this class as having the properties of a small society; and we shall review some of the concepts applicable to this view. We shall close with an assortment of perplexities that are bound to arise wherever one accepts the group nature of the class.

Individualized Instruction: Teacher-student Accommodation

I suppose that the purest form of individualized instruction would be one highly responsive teacher dealing with one pupil. The teacher would continually try to 'adapt' his own performance to that of the pupil; and he would not only correct and judge, he would also support, empathize and personalize. While the teacher and pupil together might be viewed as a social system — a dyad — for most purposes the system properties would be much less salient than the processes of interaction between teacher and student and between student and materials and problems. There would be little point in distinguishing between the roles of the student as a learner and as dyad member. Indeed, the child would ideally be seen as a complete person, and the concept of 'role' would be superfluous. The teacher would deal with the learner, citizen and group member all at once, without any need to sort out these aspects of the person. The teacher would theorize about the state of rapport he had with the student, about the student's apparent motivations and competencies, and about productive strategies to follow in order to keep the student's attention concentrated on the matter to be learned. Over time, he would gradually find out these things about each individual and he would govern himself accordingly. And, by dealing with each student separately from the others, he could give his own full attention to that one child, and could do exactly what he thought best for that child without worrying about the possible effects of his behavior on other children.

This sort of individualized dyadic instruction is tutoring. The fact that children often tutor each other quite effectively suggests that intuitive or spontaneous responsiveness (the sort of thing children are capable of) is an important component of teaching; and that sophisticated insight, rational alternatives and explicit verbalized principles are correspondingly less important — which is another way of saying that the 'theory' of dyadic teaching can (whether desirably or not) be rather minimal.

The one-to-one situation is in fact so easy to modify that even twelve-year-old student tutors (for example) typically do quite well following the method of trial and error: if a technique, question, flash-card or exercise does not 'work' (in the sense of keeping the learner productively absorbed), then they simply try something else; if teaching still gets nowhere, then they give up teaching temporarily and take the role of friend, coconspirator, hobbyist or any other role through which they might 'reach' the tutee. The explicit rationale of teaching centers around activities and games through which the learner is exposed and invited to practise desirable performances; but the social system, personalities, culture, group standards, etc. can all be ignored as objects of conscious attention, even though the teachers respond to them.[2]

Group Instruction: Role Maintenance

Group instruction is another matter. The free and easy experimentation with materials and the almost automatic accommodations that two persons of good will can make to each other are much harder to come by and usually do not exist until after a great deal of group 'growth' has occurred. Persons are no longer free to change the subject at will, to indulge in free associations, to play ideas back to check understanding. Instead, they must worry about wasting time, being lucid to everybody, avoiding semiprivate jokes and personal remarks, not asking stupid questions, etc. And, to govern a society, the teacher needs to have clear policies and principles, not just a few interpersonal attitudes to act out toward one other person.

The target of the teacher's actions is the group. The teacher tends to respond to a child not as a complex individual but as a member of the class — more or less interchangeable with any other member. The child in the group is anonymous, not in the sense of being unknown or invisible so much as being a nonindividual, a duplicate of other children with respect to the aspects of classroom life regarded by the teacher as being most salient. These salient aspects, usually prominently related to group management, have been encoded, formalized and ritualized in the archetypical role of the student. The child's 'education' is an accumulated byproduct of his continual enactment of the role of the student over a period of years. The teacher then addresses himself to the dialectical processes of defining, delimiting, activating and reinforcing that role. The major behavior of the teacher is that of stating and reiterating general and activity-specific expectations. Instructions for each activity project short-range or procedural expectations. Moral criteria, citizenship standards and social policies tend to be longer-range, and through their consistency they give stability to the group. Values, philosophical orientations and commitments to general purposes are basic assumptions or themes with which the child is indoctrinated and through which his culture is 'transmitted' to him.

The child has to produce the role of student. When problems of obeisance to expectations held by the teacher and supported by other children and parents occupy much of the child's attention, he may feel that the group is a demander of conformity, a stultifying trap. When the expectations to be met are discussed and when decisions are felt to be responsive to suggestions of individuals, then the legislated boundaries, deadlines, product specifications, etc. may serve to define the situation in such a way that the child can cope with it meaningfully. When the role expectations include not only task structures but also agreements on a great many further procedural choices that each child, invested with the authority of common purposes, can settle for himself, then the student is made 'free.' In this case expectations are seen as coming from (being inherent in) the 'situation' rather than merely in the demanding personality of the teacher. And such impersonal expectations provide a secure platform from which each child can take off on his own. It might then be said that the role of group member stimulates and coordinates a large number of internalized roles: manager, artist, rebel, warrior, teacher, friend, baby, team player, etc.

Role Reinforcement: Monitoring Student Behavior

For the most part, the children and teacher lead visible or public lives in the classroom. Their public is their image of the classroom group; and their behavior is directed to this image as well, at times, as to other individuals. Thus, when a single child acts up, the teacher reacts to the fact that one of the rules is being violated; and making the child desist is also seized upon as an occasion to reinstate or reinforce the rule for all. The time for noticing a child, then, is when his conduct deviates from group standards, common expectations and public policies. That part of his behavior we call citizenship is defined operationally or behaviorally through legislated laws; and, for that reason, practically all antisocial acts can be spotted. Hence the classroom can be an effective setting for 'socializing' the child. On the other hand, processes of learning (as distinguished from demonstrable symptoms that learning has occurred) go on inside people and are not for the most part observable. Therefore, learning 'laws' cannot be formulated at the level of stipulated specific behaviors, and hence deviancy during learning cannot be spotted. In the group it is not possible to have the dyad's continual interaction which serves at each moment to check what is being learned — tantamount to assessing the ongoing learning process. The teacher has to substitute some criterion of overt participation for criteria of learning, which means that the most informative activity would be one in which children act out their new information and skills as they are acquired.[3]

Thus if Johnny is adding $2 + 2$, his teacher can ask his answer, correct or commend it, say something humane, and let it go at that. The answer, 4, tells the teacher both that Johnny is learning the required matter and that he is participating effectively with his workbook (on the possibly leaky assumption that successful participation in carefully set-up learning activities practically guarantees that the anticipated learnings will occur). But with 25 Johnnies, the teacher can at best only sample each child's answers; and even if he spent all his time at it, each child would be unsupervised 96 per cent of the time. To know when to intervene with a child, the teacher must rely heavily on data that can be rounded up simultaneously and easily from everyone.

In a group, the time-honored way that students follow to bring data into the teacher's notice is to stop paying attention or to bother some other child. Both these behaviors are easily spotted from the teacher's desk, and the amount and distribution of such behaviors is the basis for diagnosing how well the activity is going. It is presumed that one is not learning if he is inattentive, and that unauthorized conversation likewise is not conducive to learning. These presumptions approximate the truth when the task, materials and procedures are specified in detail and when individuals compete with each other so strongly that all forms of cooperation are regarded as cheating. The prototypical feedback in highly structured (quasi totalitarian) classrooms is the attention chart, whereby each person's lapses of attention are tallied.

In an unstructured classroom, by way of contrast, purposes, procedures, materials and required behaviors are not stipulated well enough that deviations from them can be ascertained (except with regard to standards about the expression of emotion, loyalty, respect for the leader and other management or housekeeping aspects). It is not possible to describe 'health'; therefore, it is not possible to specify 'disease' and hence it is not possible to know what symptoms (individual behaviors) to look for. Under these wide-open conditions, one cannot assert what ought to be true and then check to see how true it is (e.g. everyone ought to be paying attention to the teacher's blackboard work but, in fact, half the people are not). However, an assertive 'dialectical' approach can give way to a 'problematic' approach,[4] which addresses itself to the question: 'What is going on in the group that would account for my feeling the way I do at this point?' In short, it can be assumed that *all* behavior is relevant or symptomatic, and that the diagnostic task is to propose a theme, concern or value which, if held, would make the behaviors in the group seem consistent with each other. The process of diagnosis will clearly involve a movement from a subjective sense of impatience, apprehension, joy or other feeling to a statement in words of 'the cause or nature of a problem or situation'; and from a private 'sensitivity' of one person to a publicly designated circumstance or purpose, value or cause that makes sense out of the behavior of all the members. While all behaviors are assumed to be relevant, some are more diagnostically informative than others. The most informative are the ones to which the children themselves appear to be trying to direct the teacher's attention. Thus, Johnny surreptitiously crumpling a piece of paper and dropping it on the floor says something very different from Johnny ostentatiously and noisily tearing paper, and then, whilst steadily looking at the teacher, throwing it on the floor with an exaggerated pitching motion. Children do study the teacher, and they learn quite soon how to involve him in their problems.

Teacher Inquiry: Interpreting What's Going On

As the teacher observes tell-tale behavior, he attempts to make sense of it. He is helped by knowing how to think about situations. Thus it is useful, firstly, to recall our analysis of group behavior: energy may be put into a job to be done or a purpose to be realized (productive system); into developing and maintaining the group as an organization capable of eliciting required behaviors (sociomanagerial-legitimating system) and into protecting the privacy, diversity and autonomy of individuals (psyche-authenticity system). It is also useful, secondly, to 'know what to expect' in a variety of circumstances: to anticipate the appearance of boredom and to know its behavioral manifestations; to understand why decisions tend to come unstuck at the point of having to act on them; to recognize the sorts of stress under which most people 'just naturally' turn to a friend. And it is useful, thirdly, for the teacher to have calibrated himself; to know under what circumstances he can count on himself to go passive, to get angry, to feel warmth, etc. He may have discovered, for example, that he becomes annoyed when asked to hand down a decision which he is unsure about; or that he becomes impatient and punitive when the group seems to have lost its thrust; or that he tends to withdraw from discussions when children start picking on each other. Having found these probabilities about his own behavior then, whenever he becomes aware of his annoyance, he is predisposed to suspect that he is saying things he has no confidence in; recognition of his impulse to punish may suggest that purposes are unclear; the tendency to withdraw (once he is aware of it) may suggest interpersonal disharmony.

The calibrated and informed human nervous system is the indispensable diagnostic instrument for facilitating humane processes but, considering the dangers of mere projection psychologizing, *ex cathedra* evaluation and (if I may say so) downright arrogance by some 'observers,' we need some further methodological idea that will tell us when a diagnosis is dependable. That idea is an ideal of truth. What is truth in a diagnosis? How can it be recognized? The answer is simple in concept: the closest possible approximation to the truth of 'what is going on in the group' is a theoretical reconstruction such that it explains why everyone in the group feels and acts the way he does. This definition implies: (a) that there is some underlying condition (e.g. source of frustration, threat, eagerness) in the group, and that all the members are affected by this condition; (b) that they are all affected differently or 'individually' — it makes one angry, another nostalgic, another pleased, etc.; (c) that each person in the group has been calibrated in the sense described above, so that 'the sort of thing' to which each would react with fear, flight, intimacy-seeking, dependency, etc. is known. Under these conditions, a diagnosis is produced by finding out how each person reacted to, or felt about, the period to be diagnosed; and then imagining a condition X as the most likely single condition that would explain why each person reacted the way he did. Condition X, then, is the 'true' condition.

Diagnosis can arrive most closely at the truth when the group is sufficiently cohesive that individuals feel secure in expressing their own reactions; when each person has participated enough to emerge as a known individual in the minds of others; when diagnosis follows closely on the heels of the situation to be diagnosed; when diagnosis is made a normal part of operation; and finally, when the classroom group considers itself to be a laboratory in which to investigate its own problems or work, resistance, communication, etc.[5]

Diagnosis asks how far we have progressed toward our stated goals (closed situation) or what our apparent goals are as judged by what we are doing (open situation). Through diagnosis in the closed situation a discrepancy may be found between 'where we are' and 'where we ought to be,' and the teacher would attempt to see what caused the discrepancy and what action would remove it. Some form of correction, stimulation, restructuring, reward enhancement, etc. may be called for. Diagnosis in the open situation yields a theory about 'what the group is trying to do' and evaluation of this direction in the light of larger purposes or more appropriate responses would result in a definition of the 'trouble' or 'problem.' The interpretation of the diagnosis, the evaluation of the presumed direction and the suggestion of what ought to be done about it would best come about through group discussion. The method of teaching in the microsociety 'builds in' diagnosis and decision-making as part of its own steering mechanism.[6]

The Classroom 'System'

Our concept of the classroom group, as we have suggested again and again, is that it is a miniature but complete society.[7] All the political, sociological, economic, religious and other social concepts can be applied to the phenomena and structures of the classroom. In this view, the classroom is to be regarded as having all the characteristics of a society, not just the ones the teacher finds convenient to recognize; the teacher must understand that he did not create the society nor can he rub it out. It is a part of the larger society; it is swept by the same controversies, issues, anxieties and frustrations — even though the forms in which they are made manifest are only those available to children. The reason for the overlap is, of course, that the students and the teacher do in fact also live in the larger community, and they bring its cultures, which they have internalized, into the classroom with them. And because of this overlap, incongruent or high-impact classroom experience can invest 'outside' experiences with new meanings.

The (cultural) way of life of classroom and larger societies may be seen as produced and maintained by three component systems[8] (partially discussed in Chapter 7): the productive-distributive (task group), the managerial-legislative (socio-group) and the interpersonal-informal (psyche-group).

The productive-distributive system is oriented to making something and then distributing the earned rewards. In the larger society, what is produced can be exchanged for money and the money can be divided up and spent for whatever things money will buy. In the classroom, what is made can be exchanged for approval by the teacher, and this in turn can be translated into grades, privileges and a variety of psychic rewards. One important difference between the classroom and larger society is that in the latter the production goals are reached through coordinated and concerted effort whereas, in the classroom, the goal of 'behavioral change' of each student is not one toward which cooperation of the whole class can be effectively directed. Any collective goal simply does not function to give the group cohesion or authority; it is an inadequate *raison d'être* for a group — a point to which we shall return.

The managerial-legislative system is concerned with the maintenance of the classroom society as an organization as distinguished from maintenance of an internalized 'way of life' (culture) or a purposive goal-directed strategy (production). The distinction among these three concerns can be illustrated: the value of personal safety in the sense of prevention of accidental death is fairly well ingrained in our *culture*. The *productive* system turns out automobile seat belts. The *legislative-managerial* system attempts through laws, propaganda and persuasion to get people to use the belts. Or again: in the classroom group, the cultural theme, let us say, is verbal learning; the productive system defines a great many performances to be produced and the managerial-legislative system contains the machinery of roles and power through which decisions are made, conflicts adjudicated, communicability protected, rights upheld, recourse provided for individuals and agreements, both implicit and explicit, reached.

Finally, there is the interpersonal-informal system whose properties were extensively revealed in our consideration of the tutoring dyad.

We saw that the way these systems (and the values they facilitate) relate to each other determines the results, educational and otherwise, of group instruction[9]; and therefore the relationships among the systems must be continuously diagnosed and corrected as necessary through insightful intervention. One way in which the relationships can differ is in respect to which system dominates the microsociety. Suppose, for example, that the interpersonal-informal system is the 'leading' one and therefore that the productive-distributive and legislative-managerial systems must adapt to it. The dominant demands are for active celebration of friendships (and enemyships?). The required learning (productive) activities are those through which interpersonal preferences can be explored and revealed as, for example, when a self-selected small group of three friends decides what they would like most to do and how they wish to do it. The 'purest' example of the whole organization being dominated by the informal structure is probably the collection of 'bull sessions' going on in a college dormitory almost any evening. The dormitory residents produce and maintain the rules of conduct (parietal, managerial-legislative); the small groups select such topics as will enable them to get to know each other in ways that are personally important; and the conversation may or may not result in planning and executing activities (i.e. projects such as parties, expeditions, protests, etc.).

Domination by the managerial-legislative system is, I think, revealed in the common wail that, 'You have to be able to manage the class before you can teach it'; and in the insistence that children must 'respect' the teacher, sit quietly during transitions between activities, take turns (regardless of intensity of need or interest), be treated alike with no favoritism, etc. Many a classroom apparently exists primarily to be or to celebrate the virtues of quiet, order, punctuality and respect. In such classrooms, the learning activities (productive system) are selected to be unexciting, unfrustrating, easily supervised, fair and readily justified. In a sense, participation comes under the aegis of citizenship rather than learnership or inquiry. The emotionality that might, if encouraged, threaten classroom quiet and teacher tranquillity is further kept in low key by suppressing interpersonal spontaneous interaction. In short, the interpersonal network is spiked. This sort of classroom is most likely to be found wherever the teacher has given up the effort to teach — in many inner-city schools, for example. But ones does not have to go to the slums to see the managerial system dominant in the classroom; this feature is incorporated in the traditional view of teaching. Many adults take it for granted that the worst crime in the book is to cross the teacher, and the brutality with which the rules are maintained in the English public schools seems to be worn as a proud badge of class.

Why The Productive System Should Dominate

A great variety of considerations converge in the third notion that the productive system should be dominant in the classroom.

This is what teachers almost always claim is in fact the case — even when they are martinets or nondirectives; so it is time for them to fit their actions to their words. As Jennings pointed out, groups form spontaneously (naturally) to produce such things as everyone wants but which none can get as well by himself.[10] Thirdly, for people to know what is appropriate, relevant, helpful, etc. to do in a group they must have an idea of its purposes and tasks. Fourthly, a purpose that everyone can see is a public purpose; a public purpose has as a target some condition in the environment; and such a target is externalized, objective and impersonal. This means that it can be thought about explicitly, consciously and nondefensively; alternatives can be suggested and tested, and progress can be seen and demonstrated. (Consider the ineffectiveness of wiping out prejudice as compared with attacking discrimination.) Fifthly, the greatest individual reward is in having one's own contributions picked up and used by the group, and this of course is not possible if the group has no goal or aim it is trying to reach. Many individual products or actions such as looking up information, writing essays or stories, outlining, planning, taping, drawing, etc., acquire meaning and consequence when they are part of the goal-seeking sequence of actions in the group. Sixthly, until the group can articulate clear goals or purposes it must engage in exploring its own attitudes and feelings, and its discourse remains semi private and parochial. But once its purposes are conceived in public language then warranted knowledge can, for the first time, be applied and learned. Learning or knowledge-using behaviors, like other behaviors in the group, are legitimized and examinable only when the group has and acts on related purposes. (Looking at the children's arithmetic skills, for example, would appear to be of doubtful legitimacy when the group's major purpose is to get out of the arithmetic class.)

Seventhly, and quite apart from the above more or less 'educational' reasons for making the productive system dominant, there is the demand in modern society for avoiding all forms of socioeconomic grouping, such as homogeneous-ability grouping tends to be. We must figure out some way to deal with a heterogeneous class, in fact, to *capitalize* on heterogeneity. The principle is clear: if everything is specified at the level of exact procedures, diversity is a nuisance; but if all that is specified is a broad purpose, then a broad range of different behaviors may all contribute. A shared commitment to common purposes makes diversity tolerable, and the clearer and stronger the commitment the more diversity can be tolerated and made a source of strength.

Classroom Action Research

The major diagnostic question in the microsociety is: what are the explicit and hidden purposes of the group and how effectively is each being achieved? When processes do not seem effective, one must consider whether the problem lies in the area of work, group management or personal feelings. The kinds of actions to consider would respectively be: clarification, examination or demonstration of task procedures and products; discussion of what the class expects from the teacher and from each other; and development of semiprivate dyadic conversation between selected individuals, possibly including the teacher.

It is clear that diagnosis and trouble-shooting provide the steering mechanisms of the microsociety; that they should be built into pedagogic method; and that a complete rationale for teaching would be a member of the family of systems theories.

In all such formulations, examination of participant behaviors and their perceived consequences provides some of the data needed for deciding on next behaviors. In the classroom as a microsociety, each person is expected to make his own contribution to group processes and understandings; therefore the students should be involved in the processes of diagnosis and trouble-shooting. All members need to participate in these functions at such times as their own thoughts, feelings or actions reflect the effectiveness of present experience. The basic sequence, whose details are monitored by action research, is planning, action, feedback, planning, action, feedback and so on. The perennial concern of the group is what restructuring is needed to keep the classroom society functioning effectively to meet the process criteria. The range of choices is by no means infinite, and the major ones, in my opinion, have to do with social organization and with kind of knowledge. Thus the teacher may decide at any time to have the students work alone, in self-selected small groups, in official committees, or as a total class. The teacher may also direct the discussion to the 'official' subject matter in the book or to the personal opinions of each student, without regard for their warrant or validity. Generally speaking, when the class has lost thrust, and its purpose is no longer compelling, one tends to allow the informal structure to take over, meaning that friendship groups and exchange of opinion are invited to provide a psychological bootstrap operation through which group purposes can be recovered. When purposes are clear and compelling, bureaucratic organization, rational action and systematic data collection are germane.

Every teacher must engage in diagnosis and trouble-shooting as his basic method for steering the group — for accommodating the lesson to the group and the group to the lesson. During much of this time, his action-research simply confirms that the activity is unrolling as hoped. But at some times, action-research, shared in some respects with the class, is targeted toward decisions about instructional strategy. Such critical times are: When the group does not know what to do, and pace, thrust and confidence have bogged down in inconclusiveness; when choices must be made among alternative courses of action; when the group is consciously concerned with self-training and wishes to experiment with agreements, roles, procedures and expectations that might improve its own operation; when the group has finished some phase or task and now needs to get a 'fix' on appropriate next goals; when the teacher adds to professional insight by trying to decide under what circumstances the present activity seems actually or potentially most appropriate and the children for whom it seems most helpful or contraindicated.

Some Implications of Viewing the Class as a Group

In my opinion, the most severe and widespread difficulty that teachers and researchers encounter with conceptions of group instruction is their failure to see a group. The group can only be seen in the mind's eye: a group is a theoretical construct. Nevertheless it must be talked about as if it were real and, if one defines what is real as what makes a difference, then the group is most certainly real — and the properties of groups that distinguish them from mere collectivities are also real. In this section I want to examine further some of these group characteristics that are most germane to educative teaching.

One of the most interesting questions for the classroom as well as for the larger society is: whose culture will dominate? One usually imagines that it will be a middle-class culture — a tribute both to the teacher's power and provincialism. But in a school which is both poor and black, many teachers are only partly successful in establishing their culture. Through force it is possible to get outward conformance to middle-class behavior; but the achievement motive is likely to remain unaffected. What is needed, of course, is an emergent culture developed dialectically (Chapter 4) through dialogue about alternatives suggested by all concerned.

All classrooms develop their own culture in the form of a set of expectations which become sufficiently well habituated that people can see how to relate to and communicate with each other. But it is a mistake to assume that any culture that may emerge is necessarily educative. Classroom cultures can indeed be organized around the intentions of achievement and inquiry; but they can also be dominated by the quest for comfort, for reassurance of the teacher and for toilet training (behavioral conformity to absolute standards of order, respect for authority, quiet and punctuality).[11]

Changes of cultural aspects such as language, attitudes toward social roles, nature of accepted authority, use of myths and degree of rigor in thinking are changes in the way of life of the group. Cultural conflict, whether manifest or hidden, is an important object for diagnosis, both as feedback to guide decisions and as evidence of group growth. Clearly, decisions about activities should bias the group toward the way of life of educated men. If such shifts do not occur, one may, I think, assume that the microsociety was treated as a collectivity, and that educational aspirations were compressed into mere cognitive and verbal outcomes. But to think about a group rather than just a collection, one has to assume that a group can and does have *purposes* and that the purposes may not necessarily be known to the members. This is another way of saying that the 'actual' purposes of a group are arrived at by interpretation of behavior: what purpose, if held by all the members, would account for the pattern of their behaviors? The notion that there may be hidden or unacknowledged or even denied purposes has its parallel in theories of individual behavior.

What one shall mean by a 'group purpose' presents severe conceptual problems. The notion that a group purpose is any goal or even demand stated by the teacher is, of course, ridiculous — unless the statement sums up the 'sense of meeting' which has developed over some time. The usual statement of purpose by the teacher is an *expectation* that he says he holds for the performance of the class; and it is also a warning to the class that he is about to make his expectation come true. But a 'real' group purpose is something that is being sought voluntarily by the children together; they are all contributing to the seeking. My own opinion is that group purposes are *qualities* (or models) *of experience that the group has tasted and wants more of.* Thus a group which enjoyed a movie may put forward considerable effort to get another movie; more generally, it wants to repeat the kinds of activities the members enjoyed. Group purposes are most clearly revealed by the consistency with which they respond to some expressions rather than others — by selective choice and apparent priorities and commitments. A highly directive teacher who gives the group no choices is unlikely to know much about its purposes.

Hidden purposes frequently refer to the present rather than the future; they are directed to maintaining some condition of balance, morale, power, etc. in the group. Prominent examples of hidden purposes are Bion's 'basic assumption cultures.'[12] Thus it may be 'as if' the group is putting its energy into evading coming to grips with real problems; and it may be seen as 'flighting' or running away through joking, sleeping, withdrawing, 'academic' lecturing, etc.; or as 'fighting,' meaning attacking the leader, the definition of the problems, scapegoats, themselves, etc.; or as dependency, which refers to hunting for a stronger person or leader, past legislation or report of somebody else's practice to 'pull them through' without having to really study the situation themselves; or 'pairing' which means pulling closer together in the interpersonal network for the sake of reducing stresses and anxieties felt by individuals. Opposed to these hidden agendas is the purpose of 'working,' which means not merely doing tasks but trying to cope realistically with the complete situation, of which the task is but a part.

A good deal of confusion attends the concept of 'group learning.' What does it mean to say 'the group learned the multiplication table through the sevens' or the 'group learned to operate democratically'? And, of course, if one decides that the 'group' learned something, can one also assume that all — or even any — of the members did too?

There are two ways by which the group could gain greater effectiveness; one requires learning, the other does not. Suppose, for example, that the class is now reaching better decisions on the basis of more alternatives weighed more realistically. In terms of learning, one would explain that each person (or most) in the group must have become more creative and rigorous in his thinking, that each person has acquired new, similar skills. The 'nonlearning' explanation is that no individual has changed but that somehow the group more efficiently activates that member who can help it most at any moment. The only 'learning' has been of how to coordinate more effectively the different resources of individuals: they somehow activate the original thinkers when new ideas are required, the cynics and pessimists when reality-testing is required and the most judicious person when probabilities are to be estimated. It is not, of course, impossible to tell which process of 'growth' has occurred: if the individual learned anything he should behave differently in a further and different situation; if he only improved his timing, then the nature of his contributions in further situations should be substantially unchanged.

One is reluctant to accept the notion that the group can 'grow' without individuals becoming more productive. It is here that the conception of the three systems comes into its own. Assuming no significant 'learning' in the productive-distributive system, what about the managerial-legislative and the interpersonal-informal? Clearly, the growth of the group through better knowledge and coordination of individual resources is a change in the managerial-legislative system, possibly supported by changes in the interpersonal system as well. In short, group growth may come from increased skills of membership and of personal self-confidence rather than from 'achievement' as usually tested in school subjects.

What we have been illustrating is that the roles of producer, member and 'individual' can be distinguished; and that all of them play a part in coping with a situation. Achievement testing has been primarily concerned with the skills believed to be necessary for 'production,' and secondarily with such attributes of 'the member role' as can be rationalized — proper attitudes, interests, responsibility, etc. Aficionados of 'mental health' are usually made acutely uncomfortable by such tests. As for 'personality,' that has not been considered among educational objectives; it is something to fall back on, with the help of a clinician, in order to prove that school failure is at least as much the fault of the child as of the school; and anyway, to assess personality would be an invasion of privacy.

In customary achievement terms, we see that the part of the 'educational product' that is evaluated is confined to the 'low-level' (verbal, rational) abilities within the producer role; and that the rest of the whole child — which, I may say, has at least as much to do with coping successfully with the world — is either ignored or left to the teacher's 'subjective' judgement. I hold the position that the member role and the individual are at least as educationally relevant as the producer or typical 'learner' role, and that only the concept of the microsociety is broad enough to comprehend all three in their relationships to each other and the environment. As pedagogical principles are extended to the notion of the classroom as an educative community, diagnosis and feedback will be seen as the navigational or steering systems, and the 'process' point of view — that teaching is judicious intervention in a complex social system — will begin to pay off. The evidence that a person is becoming educated will be that he is developing his own somewhat unique style of coping increasingly successfully with more and more complex, challenging and socially significant situations. And our 'evaluation' will consist of describing the situations he can cope with, rather than measuring fragmentary producer skills that 'everybody should have,' even though they represent only a small and uncertain part of the complete armamentarium with which individuals cope with the world.

Summary

We try to visualize the 'facilitative' teacher in action. We note that one-to-one teaching (e.g. tutoring) is relatively simple because the student's behavior shows immediately how effective is the teacher's behavior. In group instruction, however, the feedback that the teacher needs to maintain a high level of facilitativeness is much harder to come by. Student behavior relative to classroom 'management' is visible and easily monitored. But the internal processes of learning going on simultaneously inside of 20 to 30 students cannot be observed, let alone monitored, by the teacher. He can, however, keep track of the state of the classroom's small society as the milieu for individual learning. He can experimentally control the organization to selectively facilitate psyche, socio, or task processes; and this control also selects purposes and values.

Diagnosing the state of the group is basically a dialogic undertaking in which everyone participates, because everyone is responsible for the state of the group and for any repair work that will be needed.

Finally, we considered some of the questions a facilitation-oriented teacher has to contend with: group culture as dialectically emergent; group purposes as essential for interpreting behavior; 'group learning' as a sign either of collective individual learning or of better coordination of role resources; the nature of evaluation and the range of student outcomes it must encompass.

Notes

1. Much of what follows is excerpted from H. A. Thelen, 'The Evaluation of Group Instruction,' in *Educational Evaluation: New Roles, New Means*, Sixty-eighth Yearbook of the National Society for the Study of Education (University of Chicago Press, Chicago, 1969), pp. 115-55.

2. For an exposition of the dyad as a social system, see J. W. Thibault and H. H. Kelley, *The Social Psychology of Groups* (Wiley, New York, 1959).

3. J. W. Getzels and H. A. Thelen, 'The Classroom Group as a Unique Social System,' in *The Dynamics of Instructional Groups*, Fifty-ninth Yearbook of the National Society for the Study of Education Part I (University of Chicago Press, Chicago, 1959), pp. 53-82.

4. These terms, plus 'logistical' and 'operational,' are used by Professor Richard P. McKeon to characterize major methods of inquiry.

5. Supportive concepts are found in: Henry H. Murray, *Explorations in Personality* (Oxford University Press, New York, 1939); OSS Assessment Staff, *Assessment of Men* (Rinehart and Company, New York, 1948); and N. Polansky *et al.*, 'Problems of

Interpersonal Relationships in Research on Groups,' *Human Relations*, vol. 2 (1949), pp. 281-91.

6. See 'Implications for Practitioners,' in D. Stock and H. A. Thelen, *Emotional Dynamics and Group Culture* (New York University Press for National Training Laboratories, Washington DC, New York, 1958), pp. 225-38. See also my *Education and the Human Quest* (Harper and Row, New York, 1960); 'Insights for Teaching from Interaction Theory,' in *The Nature of Teaching* (University of Wisconsin, Milwaukee, 1939); and 'Group Interactional Factors in Learning,' in E. M. Bower and W. Hollister (eds.), *Behavioral Science Frontiers in Education* (Wiley, New York, 1967).

7. For more on the group as a microsociety, see D. Katz and R. Kahn, *The Social Psychology of Organizations* (Wiley, New York, 1966).

8. Talcott Parsons, 'Some Ingredients of a General Theory of Formal Organization,' in A. Halpin (ed.), *Administrative Theory in Education* (Midwest Administration Center, University of Chicago, 1958), pp. 40-72.

9. This is as good a place as any to cite a work that underlies much of this chapter: H. A. Thelen, *Dynamics of Groups at Work* (University of Chicago Press, Chicago, 1954).

10. Helen H. Jennings, *Leadership and Isolation* (Longmans, New York, 1950).

11. See also D. S. Whitaker and M. A. Lieberman, *Psychotherapy through the Group Process*, (Atherton Press, New York, 1964).

12. Bion, *Experiences in Groups* (Basic Books, New York, 1961); *Assessment of Men*[5]; and Elliott Jacques, 'Interpretative Group Discussion as a Method of Facilitating Social Change,' *Human Relations*, vol. 1, no. 4 (1948), pp. 533-49.

9 Teaching: Development of the Enquiring Community

The teacher has to do a lot of thinking on his feet. He has to know what educative activity looks like and what distinguishes it from non-educative activity. He has to understand and accept as part of the facts of life a wide range of motives and hidden agendas that are buried in classroom behaviors. He has to have some sense of what sorts of reactions, under what circumstances, can be expected in response to a great repertoire of possible interventions by the teacher. Wisdom of these sorts develops gradually over time. It is nourished by experiences in and out of class. It provides a frame of reference for decisions; it conveys the teacher's personal theories of education; it enables the teacher to locate himself within the educational enterprise.

In this chapter we shall present the 'wisdom' — in the form of basic propositions — that we think is most helpful to making the decisions required in teaching. We hope to give some idea of the nature of choices and the criteria educative choices should meet. Following this orientation we shall suggest a scheme for classifying activities and functions that constitute educative sequences. Finally, we shall offer in more detail a rationale for each of nine activities that are fundamental to educative inquiry by a class.

Propositions about the Nature of the Teacher's Choices

Our first proposition is that the teacher's mission is to educate children — as distinguished from baby-sitting, entertaining or 'shaping' them. This means that the basis of continuity among activities must be in the students' experiences: in how one experience generates the need for the next; in how meanings develop, commitments grow, worldviews expand and develop internal organization; and in how experiences today can help the student to live more fully and effectively tomorrow.

The teacher must assume that students are engaged in some sort of quest; and that this quest is to be facilitated by the teacher. If the teacher does not believe in and respect this quest — adaptive, participative and transcendental — then he cannot very well facilitate it, and it dives underground into the hidden curriculum. On the other hand, if the teacher believes in this quest, he supports and encourages it — and he becomes a partner in it. He uses his power, authority, wisdom and ingenuity to make sure that whatever opportunity the student is 'ready' for is in fact available and enticing.

Our second proposition stipulates that we shall regard the class, school or any other interactive entity as a 'state-determined' system. This tells us two things: that the total activity, both within and between persons, exists in a pattern or state that changes more or less continually as a result of its own operation; and that the state it changes to will be determined by the unassimilated tensions developed anywhere in the system. This holistic view implies that there is an organizing principle which regulates the manifold activities of the group and is maintained by these same activities. Such a principle must concentrate on part-whole relationships.[1]

Each behavior of a member alters the state of the whole group, which in turn changes demands on, and opportunities for, the behaviors of others. Even the case of two persons interacting directly with each other is to be viewed holistically — first, because the rest of the group sees these persons as testing or confirming behavioral boundaries and standards; and second, because through their interactions group-relevant thoughts, attitudes and roles of the two persons may be changed. It follows that, in order to appreciate and react educatively to much behavior that is most significant for the educational enterprise, teachers need to be 'group-centered.'[2] Further on, I shall spell out several teaching policies that I think distinguish and define the group-centered teacher.

It should be noted that the power of this second proposition depends on our ability to describe or characterize with precision the 'state of the group.' There have been efforts by scientists to discover and identify group variables such as 'syntality'[3] that seem to catch some sense of the group's 'groupness.' But even if one had several such variables for groupness the problem would remain of how they go together to determine the overall state of the group — what even more central variable would still be needed in order to organize the ones we have? This is, of course, the chief, largely unacknowledged problem of social and educational science: it is great at dissecting wholes into parts but very bad at recreating wholes from parts. (It can make artificial wholes, such as factors by virtue of the combining principles of mathematics and the large capacity of computers. But what name to give such factors — that is, how they correspond to the world of phenomena — continues to present serious difficulties.)

There are times when the state of the group corresponds well to one or more of Bion's 'basic assumption emotionalities' (Chapter 7).[4] That is, the group's action can be understood on the assumption that it has a hidden purpose; and that the purpose is to be dependent, to fight or flee, to seek intimacy, to work or some combination of these. Each individual reacts in his own way to this central mood, which he assumes is desired by everyone else. Suggestions counter to the mood are not heard nor taken up; and there may even be resistance to becoming aware of the mood the group is in. As the emotionality state continues, anxieties develop, restlessness sets in, and a period of transition — ultimately to establish a new mood — begins.

The basis of holism in the teaching model we are developing is *function* — the function which the group's activity seems to serve within a sequence of purposive activities. The state of the group may be characterized as whole-hearted functioning as planned; and each person's behavior will be taken as germane and productive. Or the state of the group may be somewhat less than whole-hearted, in which case the deviate behaviors may be tentative efforts to change the state of the group's functioning. The group may, alternatively, be in a state of transition between two more stable states. In this case, the nature of the new or future activity may be fully anticipated so that the group is impatient to get to it; or its shape may be so unclear that in order to recover effectiveness an unexpected diagnostic or trouble-shooting activity has to be introduced. All such variations in the state of the group are confidently ascertainable only to the extent that there is, at each stage of the inquiry, a clear holistic image of the productive state of class functioning to be sought.

In an actively inquiring class, activities are planned to achieve goals. Hence the function of each activity is *intentional* on the part of the class and teacher. When activities are productive, intentions channel behavior into effective functioning. When the discrepancy between intention and function becomes uncomfortable, diagnosis and reassessment of both may be called for.

Our third proposition is that the teacher educates children through his sensitive awareness and reinforcement of such tendencies in the class as he thinks have potential educative value. Conversely, he tries to avoid imposing plans whose activities violate the class's natural tendencies at the time. Clearly this proposition implies voluntary cooperation between teacher and class — voluntary in that the class's performance is animated by existing readinesses ('natural tendencies'); and cooperative because the teacher and class have similar interests in having experiences that are meaningful.

Thus, during some periods the class works effectively and the teacher's role may be limited to responding to individuals who, for whatever reason, want to talk with him. But when the class activity begins to lose its educational value, the teacher may decide to intervene. He diagnoses that in its present circumstances the class may be 'ready' for any of several new activities. Of these, some — such as to blow off emotionally (catharsis) — can be facilitated with very little effort. Others — such as to analyze 'what is going on' — may be so strongly resisted as not to be worth with the effort. Moreover, some activities, such as comparing notes with a colleague, may be significantly educative, whereas others, such as answering workbook questions, may, at the time in question, contribute only to 'discipline.'

The activity that is easy to facilitate is one that the class is already tentatively edging into. In this case, depending on its presumed educational value in the sequence, the teacher may support and encourage — 'catalyze' — the movement.

Our fourth proposition is an interpretation of the basic dynamic of the way of life that educates. Following Dewey, we may refer to it as *reorganization and reconstruction of experience*.[5] It is to be contrasted with the other two major alternatives, namely *acting out* and *conditioned socialization*. The relationships among these paradigms are akin to those, respectively, among ego, id and superego.

The acting-out (id) strategy discharges a person's stress without his having to understand or cope with reality. The person's fears or anxieties about failure, inadequacy, punishment, security, etc. are aroused and discharged through emotional expressions of dependence, intimacy, aggression, flight, etc. The motive is to get rid of unpleasant stress and return eventually to one's normal level of activity. When a class is in the acting-out mode, the different emotional behaviors of individuals cover a wide range. The class looks chaotic and the teacher's usual reaction is to try to suppress all the behavior rather than to channel its underlying tensions creatively.

The conditioned-socialization (superego) strategy is selective punishment or reward of overt behavior by the teacher, parent or other surrogate for 'society.' Socially desirable behaviors in the stress situation are 'reinforced,' thus increasing the probability that they will become habitual in similar situations. Undesirable behaviors are 'extinguished' by associating them with punishment or by ignoring them and thus depriving them of consequence. Criteria for what is accounted desirable or undesirable must be known to the teacher, who attributes them to 'society.'

Conditioned socialization dominates the conventional teacher's reactions to children; and its purpose seems to be to 'shape' each child to occupy the place in society that is expected of him by virtue of race, social class, intelligence and the status of his group in that area. Since much of socialization — language, manners, social relations, street sense — is learned through conditioning, one cannot argue in general against this mode of learning. But one can attempt to distinguish between situations where conditioning is the only choice and those in which more educative possibilities exist.[6]

Reconstruction and reorganization (ego functioning) is the educative strategy for learning to cope with stress in both present and future situations. The strategy calls for confrontation by interesting and fairly tough problematic elements, for being aware of what one does and what happens as a result, for correcting expectations and predictions on the basis of experience and for gradually developing more comprehensive and trustworthy principles for action (such as teaching) in the real world.[7] Clearly the individual has to be supported if he is to plunge into situations he does not yet know how to manage; and he has to be able to muster the needed resources of people, knowledge and time. These requirements make even individual inquiry a social process.

In the reorganization mode, the student is an *inquirer* continually examining his experiences and consciously seeking conclusions from it. The class is a *community*, oriented to the encouragement of individual inquiries. The class as a whole attempts to keep in mind common purposes that may be achieved by contributions from each person's semiautonomous inquiry. Thus our fourth proposition characterizes the educative classroom both as an inquiring community and as a community of inquirers.[8]

Since the decisions made by the teacher are to develop and maintain this community, it would be very helpful if all activities could be classified within a limited number of families or types, and if natural tendencies could be identified and counted on to move the class from one type to another in an educative sequence. In that case, when a change in activity is required the teacher would try (with such help from the class as he needs) to become aware of the increasing frequency of impulses to leave the present activity; would posit what tendencies, revealed in the impulsive distractions, could be encouraged to bring about the transition to the new, more educative activity; and would then decide which conditions, within his legitimate control, must be modified in order for the transition to occur spontaneously or voluntarily. These considerations generate our paradigmatic model of educative activity.

The essential proposition, number five, which best distinguishes our model from the others is that there is an intimate relationship between social organization and the ways in which the class can generate, manipulate, confirm and organize knowledge.[9] This proposition is so central to teaching that it provides the model's two basic terms: *knowledge* and *social organization*. Both terms are also fundamental in their own right.

Knowledge is fundamental because the basic act of inquiry is conscious examination of experience; and the content of consciousness is knowledge. It is essential to distinguish between two kinds of knowledge. *Personal Knowledge* comprises the opinions, guesses, policies, beliefs, hopes and moral attitudes — the personal culture — that people operate with as they cope with the world. Personal knowledge evolves from the experiences of individuals in their own idiosyncratic if not unique lives. Such knowledge may or may not be trustworthy or dependable as a basis for action but, when appropriately used, that does not matter.

As distinguished from personal knowledge, *established knowledge* is taken to be objective, the best approximation to the truth that has developed so far. The warrant or truth-value of established knowledge depends on how it was arrived at. In science, the warrant is validity — the demonstration that findings actually correspond with phenomena in the way that they are claimed to. In society, the warrant is consensus — that competent people generally agree on the soundness of the policy, law, role or institutional arrangement at issue. In religion and, possibly, humane studies in general, the warrant is revelation — creative insight that organizes universal concerns. (One sees that validity is the criterion of knowledge that is most useful for adaptation, concensus for participation and revelation for transcendence. Since all three of these processes are essential to growing up whole, education should traffic in all three kinds of knowledge. Presumably this would be accomplished through having the child take a variety of school subjects, each of which is accorded dominion over those experiences that are illuminated and investigated by means of its discipline.)

At any given time, the content of dialogue subscribes to personal knowledge and/or one or more of the three types of established knowledge. Since the teacher normally leads and monitors class discussions, he can easily bring about a shift from one type of knowledge to another. He simply invites contributions of the new sort that are appropriate to the logic of the inquiry and the maintenance of the inquiring community. If he has correctly diagnosed the class's readiness; it is able to come up with the invited contributions and move ahead.[10]

Social organization — the second fundamental term in our model — tends to set limits on and expectations for the quality of thought, feeling and action. In Chapter 7 we suggested that a person can make personal discoveries much better within a psyche-group than within the formal assembly. Purposive production is facilitated by team organization and culture; legislation by the formal assembly; introspection by working alone. Whatever activity is required to advance inquiry will be more effective when pursued in the appropriate (supportive and facilitative) organization. Moreover, it should be noted that the teacher is usually free — no matter how repressive the school is in other ways — to set up whatever social organization within the class he thinks will be useful.

Overview of the Teaching Model

The model distinguishes two kinds of knowledge (in the rows of Figure 9.1) and three kinds of social organization (in the columns). The figure thus has six cells and each cell comprises a kind or family of activities. By this I mean that, although the activities in a cell may differ in such dimensions as complexity, roles, content and depth, they serve the same basic functions in larger sequences. Thus the function of all the activities in cell 1 (individual, personal knowledge) is to arrest attention, arouse feeling, stimulate thinking and get the child 'involved' in or motivated for further activity. The function of cell 2 (psyche-group, personal knowledge) is for aroused students to use friends to help clarify their own thoughts and feelings and to prepare to contribute them to the class. A further function is to get group-building communication started. The function of cell 3 (formal assembly, personal knowledge) is to identify and define shared purposes that provide a *raison d'être* for the class as an inquiring community, and to plan directions for group-encouraged individual investigations that will contribute to the attainment of group purposes. In cell 4 (individual, established knowledge) the function is investigation of specific problems that are meaningful and appealing to individuals but are in the framework of group-anticipated ways to achieve their goals. In cell 5 (team, established knowledge) the function is facilitation, through productive team work, of investigations by several members who have chosen problems compatible in content or method. In cell 6 (formal assembly, established knowledge) the major function is for the class, reconstituted as a community, to engage in 'consummatory activity,' which draws on the expertise and findings of individuals and which attains the group's purposes (cell 3) or redefines them. A further function is for the class to get closure on its experiences of investigation and on the principles, policies and findings it has generated during the unit.

Figure 9.1: *The Teaching Model. Activities in the Inquiring Community*

Social organiz-ation / Know-ledge	Individual alone	Small group, psyche-group or team	Formal assembly (whole class)
Personal knowledge	Cell 1 Confrontation, involvement	Cell 2 Clarification of own thoughts and feelings	Cell 3 Commitment to shared purposes, plan investigations
Established knowledge	Cell 4 Individual investigations	Cell 5 Team work, team consultation	Cell 6 Consummatory activity, reflexive dialogue

The sequence of activities and functions during an inquiry by the class has both a logic and a psychologic. The logic is given pretty much by by the methods (or discipline) of chemistry, history or whatever school subject governs the activity. The psychologic is given by the nature of the human animal and, more particularly, of human experience. Its cardinal principal is that any activity tends to run its course and to develop readiness (if not imperatives) for some future different activity. Morever, certain of the transitions occur sufficiently regularly under typical classroom conditions that I tend to think of these transitions as 'natural tendencies.' Since the crux of decision-making by the teacher is in trying to decide which of several potential transitions to facilitate, I shall present the major transitions and their natural tendencies in more detail later.

But to give an illustration rather than compound a mystery, one transition which has the force of a natural tendency is for individuals who are stressfully aroused by some happening to seek a friend to whom they can blow off feelings, explore, organize and legitimate their hitherto threatening and tentative ideas. Thus after the class has seen a dramatic movie, the children tend to exclaim about it to one or more colleagues and, until they have done so, they are not likely to be very attentive to a lecture by the teacher.

Activities that are carried on voluntarily are both meaningful and dramatic to the participants. Such activities begin 'naturally' in tension, work through or reformulate the problematic situation and come to an end in new tensions that call for new activities. To the extent that each activity just 'naturally' gives way to its sequel, the sequence of activities through the six cells should tend to be reproduced quite regularly in accordance with the psychology of experiencing; and the sequence of functions inherent in these activities should constitute or at least be consonant with the logic of inquiry.

It is these relationships of activities to functions, to preceding and following activities and to group-supported inquiry sequences that make our paradigm useful. If the teacher can locate the cell in which his class's activity seems to fit, then the model suggests a number of possibilities about what may be appropriately facilitated. If the class is at the beginning or middle of an activity, then perhaps the teacher should try to assist the class to carry on; if the class is toward the end, then the next cell may suggest the most likely activity to facilitate. Under some conditions of ending, such as that the group has become frustrated, some other cell's function may seem more appropriate, such as a return to cell 2. If the activity of the class does not fit any of the cells, then its social organization may be inappropriate to its purposes. (Consider, for example, the prevalent misuses of subgroups!).

The regularities of the model are probabilities, not certainties. Variations are expected due to school subjects, age, social class and culture. But I suspect that the variations may be primarily in the way that time is distributed over the various activities. It could be that as the school year rolls on there is less need for psyche-group activities, partly because they are going on outside of class. Moreover, the personal-knowledge activities of the first three cells may properly be given a great deal of time at the beginning of a new unit of subject matter; but once the unit is well launched the transitions from cell 6 may go more to cell 4 than to cell 1. Inquiry is a 'wheels-within-wheels' enterprise and in the course of taking action many minor confrontations arise and have to be dealt with — possibly by reenacting the activities of the first three cells in a half hour or less. Clearly the cell to move into is the one that will best forward the particular inquiry of a particular class under its own particular circumstances at a particular time.

Finally, it does not follow that all of the persons will achieve closure through the class activities of cell 6. Their investigations may have opened up new ideas to pursue further or to try to express in art or in stories. Under these conditions, it would be sensible to disband the class for a few days so individuals may pursue their private interests a bit further. I will develop this suggestion in more detail later on.

The Major Functional Activities

Initial Confrontation and Involvement (Cell 1)

An educative unit begins when the student's attention is arrested, his feelings aroused and his ideas stimulated at both conscious and subliminal levels. Hence the first act of the teacher is to set up a situational confrontation that is likely to have these effects. What the teacher needs in order to engineer such a confrontation is some understanding of the nature of natural tendencies to get involved, and of the circumstances in which these tendencies are activated.

Four kinds of involvement tendencies that can be catalyzed by a teacher may be considered.

Triggering. There are some topics that people are so interested in that they start right up if you give them the chance. All the teacher has to do is give a cue that pulls the trigger and legitimates the discussion which is bursting to begin. Triggering capitalizes on the already-present instabilities in the organization of personal culture. It catalyzes action in the whirlpools of inconsistency, conflict and ambiguity. Thus for some age or subcultural groups, words like 'toilet,' 'sex,' 'God' and 'Watergate' trigger 'excessive' emotional reactions, which would be all out of proportion to their stimulus-value for persons whose way of life is more mature or integrated.

It is possible, of course, that sex, toilet and Watergate are topics pretty far removed from the subject matter of a course and that the teacher would prefer to occupy the student with some topic that can lead into issues more useful for his curricular goals. On the whole, triggering is not generally suitable for our purposes.

Speculation. The invitation to speculate almost always works under appropriate conditions. Speculation is the process of filling in ignorance with tentative ideas. Guessing games, detective stories, puzzles and practically all decisions about what to do next involve speculation. Under nonthreatening, reward-available conditions, most people enjoy speculating. Speculation involves searching the memory banks of the personal culture for useful content, and it generally involves some creative reworking of that content.

Confrontation invites speculation when the chemistry teacher performs a demonstration in front of the class without saying a word and asks the students to tell him what they observed, what his hypotheses were and what is proved. Another example is giving the class an old document and asking them to 'reconstruct the community out of which this document came.'

Dramatic Overload — Overwhelming. This is a less gentle confrontation, because the person has less control over his participation: the person is simply overwhelmed (but not to the point of disorganization, frustration or anxiety) by a rich variety of stimulating impressions, ideas or affects. As these accumulate, he develops the 'need' to organize the input, find central points, seek closure, 'get hold of himself.' He needs to sort out his cognitive smorgasbord, to abstract the essential things and discard the trivial: in short, to assimilate the 'new experience' within his already-organized personal culture.

This sort of confrontation was involved when a chemistry class visited a large down-town department store. Their instructions were to go through the whole store and find new products or new techniques for fabricating old products. This question organized and processed a vast amount of scanning and perceptual input. When they got back, the teacher asked, 'What was the *one* most interesting thing you saw? What was the *one* most important thing that happened to you on the trip?'

The demand to decide on the *one* most important, interesting, repulsive, desirable, . . ., etc. aspect of a complex experience requires the student to compare his ideas with each other, and arrange them hierarchically. During this process he discovers what dimensions of the experience were most 'meaningful' to him.

Violation of Expectations. This can be quite brutal: the person is shocked by the discovery that his intuitive sense of the world is, in some respects, untrustworthy. He can no longer take his adequacy for granted. He loses confidence that his predictions are accurate and therefore his sense that he can control the world is diminished. He has a strong 'need' to restore or recover security, and to do this he must revise his views. Discrepancies sensed between events and expectations (especially those that undergird faith) may be shattering. On the other hand, a wide range of jokes, all of which work through the sense of shock, are usually experienced as pleasurable.

Legitimate use of violation of expectations is exemplified in some recent studies of cognitive processes in small children. They are asked to predict what will happen in an experiment. Matters are rigged so that the opposite result occurs. The child's intuitions are outraged. He begins to ask all sorts of questions and the questions may be so shrewd that impressionable observers have been known to conclude that, given the right conditions, 'any kid can be taught anything, no matter how sophisticated.'

Teachers sometimes inadvertently violate expectations in ways that create problems which they do not care to deal with. Suppose a teacher goes off to a summer workshop and then, next fall, without any explanation to anyone, begins to teach altogether differently than his usual wont. His conduct violates the role expectations held for him by students and colleagues. He is no longer predictable; no one knows what to 'count' on. This troubles them. If a teacher or student wants to change his personal style or role in an organization, he has to be prepared to respect and cope with the tensions that will develop in others around him.

During confrontation, students are best left alone for a bit while they speculate, sort out and explain things to themselves. Some children can work alone, facing the uncertainties of the confrontation, for a long time; others come to the end of their resources or become prey to anxieties rather quickly. But, whichever is the case, after a short while most children welcome the opportunity to talk with friends. They need to think out loud with a sympathetic person so that they can become more aware of what they think and feel. During this conversation, the child may move consciously to connect present to past experience, express his feelings, consider further possibilities or formulate his discomfort into the projection of a problem to be solved or external circumstances to be changed through action.

Clarification of Thoughts and Feelings (Cell 2)

The teacher's second step is to organize the class into small self-chosen psyche-groups whose instructions are to go on speculating, sorting out ideas and otherwise reacting to the confronting situation and to each others' reactions to it. The psyche-group has supportive expectations for spontaneity, creativity, personal opinions, affective expressiveness, etc. Its most essential function is to legitimate and encourage the person's quest to get hold of what he 'really' thinks. It may restore his self-confidence by enabling him to find out that others do not regard his thoughts as crazy or incompetent. He may rehearse his opinions and prepare his 'official' version of his experience of the confronting events. Students stimulate each other to create new hypotheses. And, of course, they also engage in rewarding interactions and emotional adventures with others they have chosen. Reworking by students of parts of their personal culture through intimate interaction tends to produce high-affect discoveries.

Dialogue with friends is especially helpful for assessing the scope and significance of the confronting situation. Is it a trivial matter or a big problem? Does it somehow catch the essence of the world or only of a few accidental particulars? The aroused person often starts with extreme or exaggerated statements; his friends help him to focus his concern, narrow it down, pinpoint its relevance and find words to represent it more accurately.

Development of Shared Purposes (Cell 3)

When time is called on small-group activity, students are often intensely curious about what happened in groups other than their own. They wish to prolong the psyche-group gratifications — as shown in their resistance to reconvening the total class. An important item on the agenda of the reconvened class will be to rebuild the class into a viable, inquiry-oriented community.

Rebuilding a sense of community involves the development of commitment to a purpose or concern that all members have and that they cannot achieve by themselves. It means finding a concern that resonates with the student's intentionality and that legitimizes cooperative group effort. To facilitate the emergence of such concerns is the teacher's next task.

There are certain natural tendencies that can properly be channeled to accomplish these functions. Psyche-groups understand that they are to come up with ideas to present to the class, and they anticipate class discussion of their ideas. The personal emotional involvements in the psyche-groups may have been high enough to produce anxiety and a need for legitimation by comparing experiences with other psyche-groups. Moreover, in the newly reconvened collectivity, persons have a strong interest in restoring groupness through identification of common purposes which enable members to know what sort of contribution will, at each moment, be accepted and rewarded, in justifying their making demands on each other (in the name of the group) and in opening up prospects of adventurous action.

The teacher should encourage and capitalize on these tendencies. He calls the class together and lists on the board volunteered testimony from the psyche-groups. He asks (in effect), 'What are the different meanings our confronting situation had for you? What did you come up with?' At this 'brainstorming' stage, variety, including humorous or fantastic suggestions, is more essential than defensibility or plausibility.

Listing contributions on the blackboard serves a number of purposes: (a) it acknowledges the receipt of each idea, assuring the child that he was actually heard; (b) it visibly follows through on the promise implied by the teacher that he will want to know what they find out; (c) it displays the ideas in such a way that they can be easily referred to, compared and organized; (d) it gives tangible signs of progress, of getting somewhere as the list grows longer; (e) it depersonalizes ideas so that the person suggesting each one does not have to defend it — the ideas are now the property of the group and it is up to the group to decide what to do with them; (f) it contributes to the control, pacing and rate of reward of the discussion — writing down the idea clears the deck for receipt of new ideas; (g) and, finally, listing accumulates the group's ideational capital — a form of wealth which carries with it a mounting expectation of further interesting investments.

The list-making is sustained at first by a continuation of psyche-group rewards, but these recede as the class's formal operation becomes reestablished. Expectation of and support for spontaneity and 'brainstorming' is displaced by expectation of orderliness, teacher domination, systematic procedure, cooperation and achievement. The students find themselves back in the role of class members; they are responsible not only for contributing ideas but also for maintaining the social order of the formal assembly. Under these developing conditions the listing of ideas gradually becomes a bore.

When ideas start to come slowly or repetitiously, it is time to guide the class into examination of its own pooled and listed testimony. The agenda for the required dialogue is, in essence, as follows. (a) How do we perceive the situation and what degree of confidence do we have in each part of our description? (b) What about the situation is important, meaningful or valuable to us personally? (c) How can we express our intuitive feelings in the language of a shared significant concern? Note that 'situation' may be taken to refer to the initial confronting situation but that in reality it includes also the present state of the class.

The common concern may be couched in the language of feeling, policy, problems or even complaint. *It cannot be in terms of specific procedures (detailed plans) to be undertaken.* It must be sufficiently far from action that different individuals can project their own different 'meanings' on to it. The expressions will be something of an ink-blot and the subsequent activity of the group will be to ascertain both the public and the private meanings of the inkblot which they all agree is there. Thus the common concern has the nature of an action-anticipating 'sense of meeting.'

How does the teacher proceed from the blackboard list to statements of common concern? Several strategies may be offered. A very common procedure is to classify the ideas, putting together ones that have a common topic. By this means, a list of 25 items may be reduced to three or four — usually with a few left over for 'miscellaneous.' The three or four will, of course, be at a higher level of abstraction than the 25. One can, for example, examine the speculations about a community and then say, 'Well, now let's see . . . this item seems to have to do with earning a living, this has to do with buying and selling and this with what determines wages . . . these seem to reflect an economic interest. Do you see other items that also are sensitive to the economic condition of the community?' Similarly, attention could be called to notions relating to social structure, politics, education and so on. In social studies, scrutiny of the heterogeneous list may produce an inventory of the domains of knowledge normally used to understand communities and societies.

A much more dynamic procedure is to focus on contradictions within the collected testimony. Conflict would be sensed and pointed out. Students would be encouraged to take sides, thus splitting the group and creating apprehension: if the group is ever to pull together — that is, take action again — it will have to resolve this argument. In action-expecting groups, this apprehension is a natural and potent force. I shall never forget an instance in a teacher-training program. We started the course by taking the prospective teachers to visit several classrooms (overwhelming confrontation). Then we asked them what they had seen that was interesting or important. Most of the observed classes did not strike fire, but the kindergarten touched them off. The youngsters had been invited to skip before the whole group and each had had his turn. After a few minutes of discussion, our candidate-teachers were at each others' throats. Half of them took the position that the activity was cruel. They claimed that the children who could not skip were being shown up for dumbies — a mean and nasty thing to do to them. The other half took the position that it was fun for all. Each child was in fact rewarded and encouraged by the group for whatever skill he had; how else does anyone ever learn a skill? Having accepted both views as reasonable, we finally stepped into the maelstrom with the question, 'What information would we need to settle this argument?' It took the group two weeks to answer this demand — not only to learn what is involved in the sort of evaluative judgments that they had been making but, during this process, to find out something about group conflict and group-building procedures.

I have found — a third strategy — that the question which most often leads to a useful formulation of a class's deeper concern is, 'We have all listened and responded to interesting testimony from all of us. *Are we all saying different things or are we really all saying the same thing but in our own individual ways*?' The success of this gambit depends on the members' collective readiness to reunite as a group. In order to succeed they must find some commitment they can share. In terms of identity, the shared concern connotes that, 'We are the sort of people who worry about . . .,' and, 'We know who we are, at least in this situation together.' This knowledge legitimizes giving to, and getting from, each other; it legitimizes the group's existence. And, by the time commitment has developed, members ar ready — if not downright impatient — to get into action.

We note that any statement of common or shared concern encompasses only the communal, consensual or agreed sense of the discussion. Many things that were said and that were meaningful to the individuals who said them are not represented in the consensus but, because attention was given to them, they are tucked away in the memory of the group. They provide contextual and resource ideas within the group's developing culture.

In summary, our scenario for the development of group commitment is about as follows. The teacher pegs the 'climate' of group discussion at the level of intimacy characteristic of casual friends. He invites and encourages expression of the widest range of perceptual and value alternatives. As the listing proceeds, there comes a time when it is sensed that enough alternatives have been received; that further activity of the same sort will produce boredom, fruitless argument (in an effort to dispel the boredom) or inappropriate invasion of privacy (looking for excitement). It is felt that the barely reformed class is beginning to fall apart. The teacher reacts by guiding the group's examination and interpretation of its ideas; and interest revives. The class seeks to find words to symbolize its shared concern (or togetherness). The search continues until each student feels that the expression represents (or at least respects) his ideas and values. At this point the group has a sense of closure, achieved partly by shifting unresolved elements from the previous debate into the realm of anticipated action and promising to deal with them there. The successful legislation of the shared purposes gratifies the class, but it also generates uneasiness as to 'just what we are letting ourselves in for.' The agreements reached so far signify to the members more cohesion than they really feel; and this discrepancy adds to the uneasiness.

Because of its uneasiness, at the next meeting the group may express lack of confidence in its earlier decision; and it may want to spend time reviewing or rehashing it. After pointing out that such 'second thoughts' are quite usual, the teacher should suggest getting on with the planning. If successful, the planning will prove that the decision was adequate and meaningful; if unsuccesful, there will be time enough to reexamine the decision and the processes through which it was reached; and the further input from the attempted planning will be helpful.

Since the above comments center on group process, let us recall that there is also a subject to be taught. The teacher must bring to the discussion a deep understanding of the domain of knowledge, an awareness of the kinds of questions that will be fruitful to formulate and precise knowledge of the kinds of information that is available in books, libraries, museums, laboratories and even the course of study. Even as questions are being fielded and formulated, the teacher imagines what would be involved in investigating them. He selectively encourages and reinforces — usually with some explanation — certain questions that provide a superior entry to the subject domain. The teacher must himself understand the categories and issues that are the instruments of understanding in his field, so that he can recognise the students' testimony, however naive and blundering, as primitive but valid grapplings with key concepts in his field.

A Note on Personal Reflections of Students

I have been discussing the dialogue (cell 3) primarily as a process through which the formal class organization is regenerated and legitimated by finding a *raison d'être*. During this process each student has devoted part of his energy and consciousness to giving testimony, examining it with other people and reaching conclusions. We now wish to consider some other private but equally important things that the student may be doing at the same time.

He is likely to be perceiving and forming opinions about himself in comparison to others in the class. He may conclude, for example, that he is at the top for influence, at the bottom for thinking up bright ideas and in the middle for affection-giving. Being at the top means being central to the actual (possibly hidden) purposes of the group, in which case contributing to the group is consonant with realizing personal goals. On the other hand, if the individual defines himself along dimensions different from those valued by his peers, then he would seem to be responding to an 'imaginal audience' or reference group which is more potent for him than the actual class.

During dialogue, the student may be actively experimenting with his own role — trying out various ways to influence or provoke the group. Such experimentation, when undertaken voluntarily and accompanied by feedback of perceptions of others, substantially assists one's growing up. Such experimentation will be appreciated and encouraged if it is sensed as developing resources for the group.[11] But unexpected or inexplicable experimentation violates expectations and reduces predictability and security in the group's social order.

During dialogue, the individual may continue to gain knowledge of himself as a person — as distinguished from himself as participating member. He may note the kinds of behaviors or expressions that make *him* feel defensive or angry and the kinds that enable him to come into his own. He is likely to be especially attentive to how *other members* seem to define truth, justice, fairness and other sacred values, for these definitions rationalize the coercive or liberating group norms and they help define the boundaries within which a person, as a member of a group, must live.

During discussion each person may be deciding on his level of aspiration: how hard he will try and to what he will aspire. His observations of the quality of others' commitments, their emotional investment, the richness of their ideation and the rigor of their arguments all help the person decide on the quality and quantity of his own further efforts. In this connection it is worth noting that when group concerns are arrived at ritualistically, hypocritically or superficially, they are not likely to encourage serious efforts by individuals. Other things being equal, the best issue for the group to work on (from an educational point of view) is the one that engenders the highest aspirations.

Formulation of Problems for Investigation (Cell 3)

The process that built the group and generated its authority was the long search for common commitments. The common concern is expressed in generalities large enough to accomodate all the different individual interests and thus make agreement possible. To investigate such 'concerns' is to find out what the words mean in a variety of significant circumstances.

Thus, for example, a common concern, so deep that it is well-nigh universal in the western world, centers on 'freedom.' But how can one investigate the properties of such a broad omnibus idea? The class has to break down the concept. It notes that any intelligible statement about freedom must specify *whose* freedom — women, teachers, civic workers, children — you are talking about; and with respect to what activity — political, religious, educational, etc.; and in what community and culture — date, region, place. Given the community setting, we may list the distinguishable groups as rows in a table and the major areas of activity as columns. With respect to each cell, the same questions are asked: how may we characterize the state of freedom of this group (row) with respect to this activity (column)? How did this state of affairs come into being? What forces in society maintained it, and how did it change during the period we are investigating?

With anywhere up to 50 cells, all of which are equally useful to throw light on the nature of freedom, it seems reasonable to invite each student to select the cell that most interests him.

Students, like the rest of us, do not plan activities solely on the inherent interest of their subject matter. Students also want to know what they will have to do to carry out the investigation. What sort of artifacts, relics, apparatus, literature, interviews, surveys and media will they be dealing with? The state of freedom has been expressed, explained, prayed over and fought for through songs, stories, religious and civic celebrations, protests, etc. These have their own fascinations and may legitimately affect the selection of the problem.

Students, like the rest of us, want to know whom they can join forces with; they need to see what cells other persons are choosing. Often a team forms first and then parcels out a series of adjoining cells to its members.

The end product of planning is a list of specific projects which are such that their investigation is expected to produce dependable or trustworthy findings about problems through which a concern is ramified, which have been rehearsed sufficiently that the group is confident their investigations will be successful and which encompass enough different qualities or modes of anticipated experience that every individual can find at least one project to which he can gladly commit himself.

Individual Investigation (Cell 4)

Planning is complete when each student has his own problem. Now his task is to find his way from the given question (and its elaboration of meanings through context) to the 'conclusion' or 'findings.' The pathway through these steps found by a student reflects his strategy of inquiry. He may use trial and error, ask someone, make and test deductions, work backward, forward or sideways through the material. In one way or another, the student has to search for patterns in given or discovered data; and he has to interpret the patterns. The student must work in his own way — in ways meaningful to him; yet, at the same time, his work must go forward within a framework of expectations and anticipations imputed to the class and teacher as an imaginal audience whose interest in individual inquiries is both legitimate and supportive. He has received a great deal of instruction and considerable clarification of terms in the context of discussion up to this point. The context includes the things that have been said, responded to and acknowledged or allowed to pass by the teacher. These ideas and feelings are 'on the record'; they are part of the group's lore and public history; they may be referred to and worked over; they are cues and leads for further development.

The student also knows that certain individuals in the class feel very strongly about different subissues; that certain experiences he has already had have been judged relevant and that the class expects him to draw on them; and that the teacher thinks certain aspects are more important than others. Thus the student's task is multidimensional. As he plans his investigation to cope with his perception and appreciation of the shared concern, he will also be influenced by consideration of his role, position and aspirations for himself within the microsociety.

In working on projects and problems, individuals display quite different styles. They have different manners, modes and flair for investigation, as they do for life. Some prefer to work assertively and didactically, others diagnostically and inferentially. Personal style includes considerations such as the amount and distribution of searching within the sequence, the extent to which one thought must be completed or tied down before one can consider another, the extent of analysis into discrete subproblems and the amount, timing and use of reflection.

Just as students differ in their styles of solving problems, so they differ in deciding when to stop. (After all, there are very few problems — outside of logic — which have clear, unequivocal, immediately recognizable, all-or-none solutions.) Some students are ready to stop as soon as they have a first finding to report. Some stop when they are too frustrated and cannot develop sufficient confidence in next steps. Some can be distracted by a new thought or discovery. (One of the interesting problems for teachers is to encourage serendipity and at the same time get jobs done.) Some stop because the rate of reward is not enough to sustain effort. Some stop because they sense that nobody really cares what they find out. Some stop because they feel that what they are doing is trivial, or because a plan of attack seems aimless. Some stop because they do not know how to get, or interpret, the feedback they need to make sensible decisions.

Many of these obstacles are genuine confrontations, and the student needs to talk them over with other people. Conversation with teammates may help him get a new purchase, a new appraisal of his relationships to the problem, of what there is in it that is meaningful or impenetrable. He can get gas in his tank and get started all over again.

Team Work (Cell 5)

Inquiry alternates between discovery and dialogue, between working alone (cell 4) and working as part of a team (cell 5). If each individual's problem for investigation is unique, then the function of his team is mainly consultative. To the extent that a cluster of investigations are planned together, a concerted team effort makes sense — with each person taking greatest responsibility for his component.

The fullest potentials of team work are realized in action projects carried out jointly; each individual is strongly encouraged and assisted to learn to make the best contribution he can.[12] In developing the principle of least group size,[13] I suggested that the team should be the smallest group that can be selected to contain the resources of interest, technical know-how and skills of cooperation required to cope with the problematic situation. Each team ideally would consist of at least two persons who feel deeply committed to the problem, for they would reinforce and maintain societal expectations, and also two who will have original or interesting ideas and can engage the others in dialectical dialogue. In addition, each person would have at least one highly congenial friend for emotional and cultural support.

During production, the dominant subculture should be the technical-productive, and the most influential authority for decisions by the teams should be the requirements of the task. Nevertheless, much of the tension that drives production is between institutional criteria, demands or constraints on the one hand and interpersonally encouraged individual creativity on the other. Productive action respects and capitalizes on both and, in the process, mollifies and modifies both.

Integration of the various demands within productive activity is not easy, even for mature adults. It is hard to be citizen, producer and friend all at once, but it is not hard to grace these roles one at a time. It follows that production teams would, at times, give away to psyche-groups in which friends would help each other deal with their frustrations. And, at other times, the whole class would be reconvened to report progress and to assess the progress of the teamwork with respect to the overall societal purposes under whose aegis the teams were formed. Thus societal expectations may be continually revised to fit what production teams find to be feasible; also, anticipations for utilizing and assimilating products gradually take shape, getting the classroom community ready for the time when products are available.

Whether the individual tackles his project alone or as part of a team, he is likely to need certain kinds of help from his peers. Let us see what sorts of help may be involved. As problem-solving draws to an end, the investigator looks back over what he has done, felt and written; and he anticipates possible consequences to be realized in communicating his findings or experiences to others. It may be hard for him to select, screen and mull over what to communicate. Some of his experiences — his emotional reactions, for example — may be private and should remain so; other aspects are more speculative and tentative, and they cry out for reaction. He may need headings and subheadings, a pattern or theme, proper rhetoric or syntax. He may need to check that loose ends have been followed up and brought to terms; and that surplus meanings have been squarely faced and properly acknowledged. Very often an investigator needs help to organize his report and hit on the level of formality and rigor appropriate to the nature and purpose of the investigation.

He may need somebody who can make a disinterested appraisal of what the class is interested in, how they would perceive the various issues he has been tussling with, and what other students are coming up with that may be connected to his own work. If he is lucky, he may find someone to read his report and to sense what is left out and what might be followed up better; someone to recognize more objectively lapses of integrity and ineptnesses that mar communication of the 'real finding' and of what the experimenter thought was important. The most helpful person would not be the good friend to whom the student reveals everything. This friend will be too empathetic, too sympathetic and too interested in sharing the student's private experience. On the other hand, he does not need an expert who looks on with a fishy eye and does not even try to understand him well enough to see what is important to communicate. A small peer group that can help would, I think, be a committee rather than a friendship group. The primary loyalty of the committee should not be to the experimenter but to the class and, ultimately, to civilized aspirations in general. Its loyalty, in short, should be to the values of the discourse that the report will hopefully exemplify and promote.

Consummatory Activity (Cell 6)

Following the productive activity of teams and individuals, it is necessary to 'get the class back together again,' reinstate the sense of common concern and find some way in which the various findings can, in concert, 'throw light' on the common concern — and possibly uncover some new issue or concern to work on next. My favorite strategy for profiting from the projects is to present the whole class with another confrontation that would demand a 'consummatory' activity. Let me explain. We note that each student has been dealing with ideas, developing power with them, learning things that are unique. Presumably he is now more adequate in some special way: he has gained some special increment of strength, skill, information or confidence that he did not have before. Since all the investigations were in some way relevant to a common concern, we may regard each person as a potential resource-person with respect to some instance or aspect of the concern. What we need, then, is some further activity to which the class full of resource-people can contribute their resources; and in which they need each other's contribution in order to contribute their own — an interactive, interdependent project of some kind.

What might such an activity be? Here are two possibilities for a history class whose investigations have been into the life of, let us say, a colonial city. First, the class could confect a newspaper from the period. Each student would write an editorial, news item or advertisement which capitalized on his own inquiry. But just getting out the newspaper is not the point. Let us further stipulate that the whole class is to serve as board of editors. They must decide whether each article is authentic; they would have to question, in the light of their own knowledge, the historical facts and the article's plausibility to the way of life of the time. The consummatory activity, then, is the dialogue that would ensue, and it would be strictly in accordance with the discipline of history: 'the cross-examination of testimony by doubt' and also the 'reconstruction of the life of another time and place.'

The second activity would involve role-playing. Let the class enact a civil suit before a court of the time. Advocates, victims, witnesses, jurors and experts will be needed. Let each person take a role for which his investigations have given him special preparation. The class would work up the whole play, enacting, questioning and critiquing authenticity, and reenacting. This would be continued until the class felt, from its gradually pulled-together sense of the period, that the play was as 'right' as they could make it. Points of detail could, of course, send the investigators back for more research.

In general, I would characterize such a consummatory activity as follows:

(1) It is dramatic — open-ended and problematic; and the *dramatis personae* are characters with whom the students, by virtue of their own investigations, can identify personally.
(2) The setting of the drama would be one about which the students had, among them, gathered adequately detailed and comprehensive information. The dilemma of the drama would be congruent with the issues generated from the common concern.
(3) The play would be small in scope — probably one act. It would be divested of nonsalient detail; it would be a demonstration of the structure and possible resolutions of the dilemma.
(4) The discussion and critiquing should make the final enactment a prototype: a model, thoroughly understood from all angles, whose internal pattern would be internalized and give the student

a sense of form that would be useful in future situations which embody the same dilemma. That is, the experience would contribute to *character*, not merely to information, skills or other fragmented outcomes.

(5) The consummatory activity would be integrative in the sense that all three subcultures would operate either simultaneously or in rapid alternation. Thus the students would engage in means-ends thinking (productive subculture); they would define and respect the verities (institutional, societal, traditional subculture); they would have to take some personal risks and support the risk-taking of others (interperson subculture). It is precisely because of this fluid overlapping of subcultures that the activity would be integrative and would lead to reorganization of relationships within the total personal culture of the child.

Reflective and Reflexive Dialogue (Cell 6)

During relatively fast-paced activities of the sort we have been describing, individuals suppress the expression, if not the awareness, of much internal rumination. Some of their internal disequilibria may be brought to terms through conversations with friends outside of class. Others may be dealt with in dreams. The most educative means, however, is engagement in meditative introspection or reflection, and that is the next activity to be described.

The educative requirement of reflexive discussion is that the personal experience of the child during inquiry is to become internalized as a prototype for further experiences in similar situations. That is, it must go beyond itself, its own particulars, to make future living more informed, effective and fulfilling. As new stresses and problems are encountered, the educated person 'uses' his past *examined* experience. He has the sense that he has been here before; and he draws on his already-internalized understandings to help him mobilize his thinking, accept and interpret his emotion and more quickly arrive at policies and procedures for higher-quality (more enlightened and compassionate) action. In short, what is called for is *post hoc* revision or reorganization of past experience in such a way that it provides a more satisfactory basis for future experience.

The dialogue may begin with recollections of the group's experiences. Its agreed starting concern (cell 3) would seem to be a good point of departure. The questions to be asked are, 'How have our experiences illuminated and restructured our concern? In what respects have we clarified it or obscured it? Where are we now?' Some of the closure needed by individuals can be assisted by a joint effort to define the concept of 'concern' and to analyze or trace how it organized their own activities as a class. Other definitions of concern (and related concepts of purpose, worry, goal, etc.) should be explored — literary examples, political pleas, religious usages, past exemplifications, even the dictionary. It would be useful for the class to look at its own unit sequence of activities from the standpoint of each of these frames of reference.

The relationship of knowledge to the concern's content should be discussed. How did the findings from the various investigations change the 'meaning' of the concern? How did information gained by the class assist in 'breaking down' the concern into manageable bits? Since a concern is about the world — its existential situation — what sorts of information are needed for an adequate description? What categories of knowledge are required to inform a concern rather than leaving it at the level of sentiment or strictly subjective discomfort? How do individual concerns become socialized or generalized into actionable social issues?

To get the necessary knowledge, individuals had to undertake investigations, and the nature of their investigations determined the kind and dependability of their findings. What are the different ways in which members of the class carried on their inquiries? For example, one student will have worked through trial and error; another, primarily through syllogisms; another, by stating the conclusion first and working backward; another by analyzing the elements and seeing how they combine. Under what circumstances would each identifiable 'method of inquiry' be most suitable?[14] Why is knowledge so much more useful and meaningful when one knows how it was obtained? Why must all action to relieve the concern include a component of investigation to 'get the facts'?

Reflective dialogue builds on testimony of the students as to findings, methods of approach to problems, difficulties encountered and implications for the larger concerns and issues that generated the problems to begin with. In this dialogue, the teacher is concerned with both substance and method. The substance in this case is not the feelings and attitudes of students or the generalized orienting assumptions which these feelings and attitudes sample, but rather the correspondence of ideas with reality. It is here that questions of predictability and validity are introduced. The concern for methodology by the teacher is not so much with the sort of motivation that leads to a particular predisposition but rather with the formal discipline of knowledge in the subject field. The teacher tries to show how the paths of inquiry discovered by the students illustrate basic modes of inquiry that are explicitly understood and judiciously used as appropriate in more competent investigation.

The reflective discussion attempts to connect substantive findings to human action; relate truth status of ideas to the activities through which the ideas were gained; give one power to cope more adequately with further situations; distinguish between acting with the discipline *of* a chemist or historian rather than forever talking *about* chemistry or history. It attempts to reveal relationships between knowledge and disciplined action — relationships that make knowledge an instrument to be shaped and used by men.[15]

Individual Adaptive Assimilation

During the consummatory activity and reflective discussion, the teacher has been trying not only to get cognitive and emotional closure for the activities just completed, but also to use the testimony for entry into new vistas of problems, methods and commitments. The students have been encouraged to see what they 'need' to do in order to consolidate their own skills and understandings and to explore for themselves, as individuals, some new and appealing directions.

Different students have different concerns and readinesses. One student needs to practise with certain procedures or methods of problem-solving; another may wish to go back to the original confronting situation and examine it in the light of his subsequent knowledge; a third may wish to tackle further problematic situations in order to extend the range of conceptual or methodological generalization to new situations; another may wish to expand the context of his established knowledge by reading more about what other persons have demonstrated or believed.

Until now the strategy has been to have a division of labor coordinated by common purpose; now it seems important to set the individual free and to help him see what he has to do in order to make his whole experience up to this point meaningful, useful and transferable. Anticipation of further activity will invite him to discover and make more or less explicit his commitments and personal goals. In guessing what activity would be profitable to pursue next, he will become aware (i.e. construct a theory) of his goals, and to some extent, of who he 'is' as a person. The individual must voluntarily, in his own way, mull over alternatives and see how they 'feel' to him. While consultation by the teacher and other students may be helpful, the student must ultimately decide and be responsible for the consequences of activities he plans and carries out.

Thus, the class is dissolved as a formally cooperating investigatory agency in order to free the individual to carry on his own, necessarily unique, assimilative activities. But the class is not dissolved as a social milieu nor as a microsociety with norms and standards. Moreover, the class knows intuitively that the independent investigations can make a powerful indirect contribution to its way of life. They sense that the group will be better able to pursue its investigations and realize more challenging purposes as each individual develops strength and competence; and therefore the individual has some responsibility to the group to use his time wisely. In this way, the classroom group, like any community, has a considerable stake in freeing each individual to go off at times on his own.

When the classroom retains this sense of community, the 'societal' outcome of independent activity is readiness for participation in a new unit of inquiry as more fully functioning, more adequate, more self-assured persons within the classroom microsociety.

Policies of the Group-centered Teacher

No formal statement can capture the spirit of supportiveness, adventure and enthusiasm that animates the good teacher. Perhaps 'humaneness' — meaning enlightenment and compassion — comes close. In the context of the classroom as an inquiring community, it seems to me that the following policies of teaching would distinguish the humane or group-centered teacher.[16]

First, it should be assumed that each statement made by anybody becomes the property of the group. That is, statements are taken on their own merit; they are depersonalized items of content for the group to work with and dispose of in any responsible way it chooses. Stating an idea is tantamount to giving it to the class, and the class must make what it can of the gift. It cannot discuss ideas very sensibly if the discussion is also by implication a discussion of personalities, so that a choice (should it become necessary) among ideas is also a choice among persons. Depersonalizing ideas by writing them on the blackboard invites others to take them as their own, elaborate on them, turn them over in their minds without feeling that they are cheating or stealing from the contributor. The reward for the originator is not in the continual deference of the group to his idea but rather in the fact that the idea was sufficiently important for others to take it seriously. Under these conditions, children learn that the more valuable — shrewd or appropriate — the contribution, the greater the reward.

A second policy is that emotional behaviors of individuals should at least be considered as possibly expressing the need or feeling of the group as a whole. If one person makes a nasty, sarcastic comment, the teacher may guess that quite a few others feel like doing the same; perhaps the only difference is that these others have a higher threshhold of tolerance. If a period of bickering or fighting is prolonged, the teacher may assume that that is what the group wants. (The reasoning is simple: if they don't want it, why don't they stop it?) My own impression is that this proposition does not always fit the situation but nevertheless it is a good policy to wonder whether emotional expressions speak for or give emotional gratification to (and are therefore encouraged and supported by) other members. When a person's emotional expressions do not serve the group or violate its standards, other people sooner or later let him know, possibly outside of class meetings.

A third useful policy is based on the assumption that there are no problem children, but there are problems of the group. When Johnny acts like a son-of-a-gun and makes everybody mad they say they hate him. But Johnny is not the problem. The problem is that the group lets (sometimes even encouraging him) Johnny's behavior upset it. Thus, the policy is that, when the group is upset by an individual, the thing to investigate is not the troublesome individual but rather the vulnerability or inability of the group to cope with his behavior.

Another policy is that when the group is hunting for issues and purposes, the most useful approach to a new idea is not to ask if it is relevant, but to ask what it is relevant to: 'What issues does the contribution remind us of or mobilize in us?' The class automatically examines the idea, regardless of its source, for some germinal association, provocation or insight which can be turned to account. The reason for this policy is clear. If all contributions can be accepted as relevant to the issue that is finally formulated then everybody has a place in the subsequent activity; the issue or concern belongs to everyone because everyone's concerns or sensitivities are represented in it. If the members feel that the issue really belongs only to John and Mary and that the others have only been persuaded to go along, then the decision makes Mary and John central and all others peripheral in the group.

The next policy is the house rule that a problem is defined as what everybody feels to be a problem. This distinguishes problems from puzzles. A problem is invested with concern that people want to do something about. It is a concrete instance of some more universal issue, and the point of 'problem-solving' is to get better insight into the issue and our relationships to it. A puzzle is created by rational necessity; but without the action motivation, it is not a problem.

Another policy has to do with group decision, voting and concensus. When it comes to defining the issues for investigation, there has to be agreement that the sense of meeting has been caught. Everyone must feel that his private concerns, however poorly or inadequately they may have been articulated, can be worked on either directly or as a byproduct of the planned activity. Therefore the consensus required of the group is quite constricted: *it is only on the nature of the activity and its broad goal-direction*. It is not necessary that all people value the activity for the same reasons. It is important that they agree the activity is worth doing; and, since they all feel this way, they can trust each other to the extent of risking their own personal involvement. Given this understanding, it is useful from time to time to ask, 'How many of us feel we are on the right track?' Each individual is invited to judge in his own terms; and he is assumed to be a competent witness to his own feeling and sense of the situation. Polling is to test commitment, not truth nor even wisdom. It is not a substitute for rational examination of alternatives. It is not used to rule out an unexamined course of action just because people's first impressions are against it. It is used to ascertain how ready people are to move, and to find out if further discussion and analysis is called for before the group is ready to agree on goals.

When has a decision been reached? When people are confident enough to imagine themselves in action their language shifts from the subjunctive mood to the indicative, and from passive to active voice. They stop saying, 'If one were to do such and such,' and start saying, 'I am going to do thus and so.' When a person begins to rehearse his future action he has, to all intents and purposes, reached the decision to undertake that action. When students have to be restrained from getting out of their chairs in order to get a project underway, there seems little point in insisting on a vote. Voting, then, is a peculiar sort of ritual whose point is to demonstrate to everybody that a decision has already been reached.

Another policy is that all seriously intended contributions are to be responded to. This policy is insurance against the possibility of inadvertently discriminating against individuals. At this point (of hunting for common concerns) ignoring a voluntarily submitted idea is an act of discrimination against the person. It makes him a second-class citizen. It is much more cruel to ignore him than to tell him his idea is wrong, because the latter responds to the person and the former does not. The leader may have to stack up incoming contributions, like planes holding over an airport, and then land them one by one with appropriate recognition of each.

A final policy has to do with 'spokesmanship.' I suggested that spontaneous emotional expression by one person may speak to the needs of the group. But now I should like to note that consciously formulated, rehearsed, verbal statements quite often do not. When a person says, 'I sense that we all want to do thus and so,' I think the appropriate response is, 'Let's ask the others.' When it comes to making wants known, each person must speak for himself; this is his responsibility as a member of society. If the climate of the group is too threatening for this to be possible, then the climate of the group must be improved. But to acknowledge a self-appointed spokesman and thus let the group think that some one person can speak for them is dangerous: it relieves the others of actively thinking things through; it establishes a false premise; and it confers leadership without commensurate responsibility. And in the subsequent action, the others, having been 'uninvolved' in planning, may be pretty much at sea.

Benediction

Inquiry — even genuine inquiry — is not enough. One must also consider the spirit that animates the inquiring community. Students may compete, not for grades, but in assisting each other, in furthering the excitement and beauty of their experiences, in helping each other (and through this, themselves) to grow and develop. Let the child, in all the years of his growing up, live compassionately and with enlightenment; and let the quest for these qualities be accorded the priority to which human dignity is entitled.

Summary

Our teaching model attempts to pull together all the ideas, categories, principles, admonishments and exhortations so far presented. Since it is in action that ideas have real-world consequences, the model is one of teacher action: what would a teacher (who has internalized the inquiry so far) do in class? How does this activity facilitate the continuity of educative experiences of students?

The model suggests that the teacher acts to monitor the kind of knowledge that is the content of dialogue (from spontaneous personal opinions to text-book facts). He monitors the organization of the class (psyche-group, socio-group, task group, individual effort). He adapts his monitoring to the purposes of the class — and helps the class diagnose its purposes. He assumes that at any time the group has tendencies of different strengths — to work, to run away, to fight, to seek closeness, to be dependent — and that his job is to reinforce whatever tendencies have the greatest educational potential.

The basic unit of the model is activity. Six kinds of activity are identified, and the class is seen to move back and forth among them. The activities are selected to alternate experiences of personal 'discovery' with those of dialectical 'dialogue': the discovery generates input for dialogue and the dialogue structures opportunities for discovery.

Our model begins in confrontation and ends in consummatory activity of the class. Then several 'reflexive' functions are suggested: looking back over the experiences of the entire unit to see what can be learned in order to make the next unit more effective; dissolving the class and its expectations for a while so that each individual will be free to follow up on intriguing leads or questions that opened up for him during the inquiry.

Notes

1. H. A. Thelen and J. W. Getzels, 'The Social Sciences: Conceptual Framework for Education,' *School Review*, vol. 65, no. 3 (1957), pp. 339-55. Teachers must deal with the classroom as a society rather than simply as a collection of individual learners. This article provides a starting point for approaching the classroom as a 'system.'

2. H. A. Thelen and R. W. Tyler, 'Implications for Improving Instruction in High School,' in *Learning and Instruction*, Forty-ninth Yearbook of the National Society for the Study of Education, Part I (NSSE, Chicago, 1950), pp. 304-35: an early exposition of group-centered teaching.

3. R. B. Cattell, 'Concepts and Methods in the Measurement of Group Syntality,' in A. P. Hare, E. F. Borgatta and R. F. Bales (eds.), *Small Groups* (Alfred A. Knopf, New York, 1955).

4. W. R. Bion, *Experiences in Groups* (Basic Books, New York, 1961).

5. H. A. Thelen, 'Case Study of a Basic Skills Training Group,' in *Report of the*

Second Summer Laboratory Session (National Training Laboratory, Washington DC, 1949), pp. 70-7. This paper reports on an early human-relations training group (T-group) guided more by Dewey's ideas of inquiry than by therapeutic doctrines. See also John Dewey, *Democracy in Education* (Macmillan, New York, 1916); *The Child and the Curriculum* (University of Chicago Press, 1902); and *Experience and Education* (Macmillan, New York, 1939).

6. H. A. Thelen, 'The Triumph of Achievement over Inquiry,' *Elementary School Journal*, vol. 60, no. 4 (1960), pp. 136-51.

7. H. A. Thelen, 'Insights for Teaching from Interaction Theory,' in *The Nature of Teaching* (University of Wisconsin, Milwaukee, 1963), pp. 19-32.

8. H. A. Thelen, *Education and the Human Quest* (Harper and Row, New York, 1960). This book presents four models for educative sequences in schools and attempts to identify connections between behavioral sciences and pedagogy.

9. H. A. Thelen *et al.*, *Classroom Grouping for Teachability* (Wiley, New York, 1967).

10. H. A. Thelen, 'The Experimental Method in Classroom Leadership,' *Elementary School Journal*, vol. 53, no. 2 (1952), pp. 76-85.

11. Ibid.

12. H. A. Thelen, 'Social Environment and Problem-solving,' *Progressive Education*, vol. 27, no. 5 (1950), pp. 152-5.

13. H. A. Thelen, 'Group Dynamics in Instruction: Principle of Least Group Size,' *School Review*, vol. 57, no. 3 (1949), pp. 139-48.

14. H. A. Thelen, 'Reading for Inquiry,' in Helen Robinson (ed.), *Controversial Issues in Reading and Promising Solutions*, Supplementary Education Monograph 91 (University of Chicago Press, Chicago, 1961), pp. 35-53.

15. H. A. Thelen, 'Some Classroom Quiddities for People-oriented Teachers,' *Journal of Applied Behavioral Science*, vol. 1, no. 3 (1965), pp. 270-85.

16. H. A. Thelen, *Dynamics of Groups at Work* (University of Chicago Press, Chicago, 1954; Phoenix Edition, 1963), pp. 285-9. This book attempts to develop a group-centered rationale for six technologies: citizen action, classroom learning, faculty self-training, management, laboratory training and large meetings.

10 Curriculum Design: Context for Instruction

Chapter 9 has presented a detailed rationale for teaching viewed as an educationally facilitative intervention in the small society of the classroom. The analysis was at the level of the microsociety — the moment-by-moment happenings that the teacher participates in and the activity-to-activity transitions that the teacher invites in response to signs of the class's readiness and its individuals' needs. Our starting point for thinking about instruction was the notion that the class exists as a lively bunch of real children; and the teacher, within the boundaries and limitations of his position, is responsible for helping the class to channel its normal needs for activity and interaction into educationally constructive activities. The experienced teacher has a large repertoire of past experiences to draw on, and his decisions usually involve diagnosis of the *kind* of experience the class needs, review of many potentially facilitative activities of this sort that he has participated in in the past and consideration of possible strategies for leading the class, tentatively, into the new activity, and for either going ahead or revising his diagnosis on the basis of the children's reactions.

Among the limitations of the teacher's position is likely to be the fact that he has a school subject to teach. Activities are not merely to be 'educative,' but are required to help educate the child 'in' a 'subject' which is usually thought of as a distinctive field and/or 'discipline' of knowledge. Each subject is distinguished and justified (or legitimated) by the special contribution it is alleged or supposed to make to the child's overall armamentarium of skills, sensitivities, appreciations and useful or elegant information. Thus each subject makes its own demands on the class and teacher; and the pattern of these demands and expectations is the immediate context for teaching.

It is the function of curriculum-makers to design the subject's demands and expectations for different ages and kinds of students. The demands and expectations associated with or attributed to each subject are specified separately; and, according to the cultural archetype, the extent to which a child meets these expectations is counted as his achievement.

It is possible to imagine — and, in fact, most of us have experienced — subject courses whose demands and expectations for achievement were felt to constitute a heavy and senseless burden, so that what we learned was how to deal with the burden of senselessness. But we have also (I hope) experienced subject courses whose demands and expectations felt like invitations to adventure, to growing up, to delight in what we could learn to do. So it is not the fact that we have subjects, nor that they make demands, that makes some courses not very educative; it is rather the particular or peculiar appropriateness of the demands and expectations to the learner's style of life that makes the difference. Each subject curriculum not only emphasizes certain achievement objectives at the expense of others, but also conveys to the learner a set of intentions with respect to the quality and meanings of his learning experiences. As a context for instruction, each curriculum design has its own achievement-shaping ethos and functions like a containing subculture.

In this chapter we want to show how several different curricular designs can be generated in one subject; how each design directly and indirectly specifies a set of demands and expectations for students to meet; and how the presumed educativeness of such expectation-meeting by students can be forecast. Finally, we shall reflect on this analysis, together with that of chapter 9, to see what sort of educative scenario emerges for our subject — which happens to be art.

Behavioral Bases for Art

Art is a distinctive kind or component of human activity. To find out about art, you would hunt places where art is going on and you would seek to learn why, how and under what conditions. Then, as an art teacher, you would simulate or reproduce in the classroom these art-generating conditions.

But it isn't really that simple, because the art activity you would find and recognize as art is the art of artists, and that kind of activity is the side show (for a few students) rather than the main tent. The art that is justified in general or public education is the art of living, of aspiring after the humane, of developing more aesthetic, informed and interesting responses to a wide range of commonly occurring 'life' situations. These are situations to which everyone, somehow, responds. Our job is to recognize children's responses as 'primitive,' 'naive' art — or even merely precursors of art potentials — and to do what we can to improve their outer (cultural) form and inner (personal) meaning or value.

What, then, are some common activities that are not, *per se*, recognized as art but which can develop into or give rise to art activity; and where, within an instructional sequence, might each activity be placed? Our scenario in Chapter 9 began with confrontation and ended with consummation; it had a beginning, middle and end. Keeping the model scenario in mind, we may ask where each activity would fit and what function it would serve in an overall sequence of art-education activities. For the purposes of rough classification, five functions seem adequate: starting, orienting, assimilating, symbolizing and completing. Here is our list:

Starting

Starting involves the involuntary arousal of emotion in ambiguous, demanding or inviting situations; a sense of being confronted; displacement of equilibrium; loss of equanimity; behavior may realistically cope or evade the initiating stimuli.

A student might be frightened by the mottled gray areas in a Rorschach test and make up a scary story.

Walking down a cluttered, ugly, unfamiliar alley, a person may look around apprehensively and wonder what the world will be like after he is dead.

It is considered therapeutic (controlled mild stimulation) to have hospital walls painted in two or more pastel colors.

School architects can design gymnasiums and corridors that are riot- and accident-prone, or riot- and accident-free.

Composers, choreographers and dramatists program sensitive and skilful performers to build up and release tension in the audience.

Driving along the 17 Mile Drive in Monterey is also an experience of 'programmed' tension build-up and release. The driver moves through the environment rather than having the environment ever-changing before him.

A teenager finds school and family life bland, impenetrable and unresponsive to his emotions. He drops out or takes to drugs.

Urban redevelopment tends to homogenize the class structure of the community, thus producing a more self-consistent and predictable pattern of life. When it becomes too self-consistent and predictable, morale and morals deteriorate.

Orienting

Orienting involves seeking organization of details by prominent features such as landmarks and purposes; formulating alternatives; locating one's 'place'; putting self in the picture; 'to take one's proper bearings mentally.'

Someone lost in a strange city climbs a hill so as to be able to look out over the whole city and see the parts and wholes that make it up.

It is natural to look for landmarks that can organize environing details: Mount Rainier viewed from Seattle, the covered markets of Milan and Istanbul, the Vieux Carré, the Seine or Thames or Potomac flowing through a large city.

Walls, highways, drainage ditches, hills, shores and open fields are seen as 'natural boundaries' that make neighborhoods and neighborhood identity possible.

A student draws a map.

He takes a ten-question, true-false newspaper test on 'the perfect marriage.'

As a visitor, he drinks in the details of his host's place.

Assimilating

Assimilating involves accepting or rejecting elements of present experience into already-developed structures of ideas, expectations and/or moods; and reorganizing mental structures to accommodate new insights.

A well-told shaggy-dog story leaves the listener absolutely refusing to accept that there *really is* no punch line or point.

A person who is really sure that the world is an evil place can accept the kindness of another only by seeing it as selfishness.

Symbolizing

Symbolizing involves putting experience into words, processing experience for memory storage or relationship-seeking; connecting instances to universals; the language of art as cultural symbols (media, methods, materials) through which the culture is communicated and expressed.

George M. Cohan, who wrote the great World War I song, *Over There*, is quoted as saying that he would rather write the nation's songs than be president.

Finlandia and *Polonaise* helped hold nations together.

Nonexistent cultures can be made vivid in utopian writings and science fiction.

Parades, mobilizations, church services, festivals and graduations are successful as rituals if they remind us of the long sweep of human destiny.

Reinterpretation of behavioral meanings of truth, justice, equality and mercy is a never-ending process.

The balconies of New Orleans, the Ringstrasse of Vienna, the covered bazaar of Istanbul somehow catch the flavor of their peoples' ways of life.

Completing

Completing involves task completion; design closure, release of attention, disentanglement of emotion, solution, restoration of equilibrium, fulfilment, satisfaction of goal criteria, readiness for new adventure; sense of episodes, phases units, rebirth and drama.

Confronted with an unintelligible pattern of lines, the viewer suddenly sees a staircase.

Confronted with a sequence of brackets ([] [] [] [] []), the observer tends to perceive a series of completed squares rather than of I-beams or separate brackets.

Women's fashions use all sorts of optical illusions created from stripes and patterns in order to encourage us to complete the 'picture' most pleasantly.

A sign of musical illiteracy on the Seashore Test is to complete a Mozartian phrase with a hunk of *Stars and Stripes Forever*.

A jagged, broken line may be called 'peeweetee' and a flowing, curved line 'oolonga,' but not the opposite (which may suggest that opera is possible after all).

An infallible way to bring a late-sleeping, famous pianist downstairs is to hit an augmented-seventh chord; he just has to come down and resolve it by hitting the tonic.

Man is an organizing and pattern-seeking creature. Patterns and changes of patterns detected in his environment build up and release his emotion (starting); when he is snowed by details, he seeks a vantage point from which to organize the scene and locate himself within it (orienting); to the extent that he has past ideas and expectations organized into an intuitively satisfying pattern, he has the puzzle of what to do with possibly dissident (or congruent) elements from new experiences (assimilating). Not only do individuals exhibit these types of behaviors in their own ways; in addition, there are cultural or intuitive communalities among responses. Large numbers of people complete the same designs in the same ways, giving rise to the notion that some patterns are inherently more stable than others (completing); and artistic patterns and products give access symbolically to a whole culture, with its traditions, artifacts, and activities. (But be careful! The fact that these incidents occur does not necessarily justify elevating the behaviors to the level of major functions and then compounding the felony by acting as if they form a developmental sequence. But it *is* suggestive, isn't it? And what would you do?)

I suggest that *art education should concern itself with the contributions of art experience and experienced art to the refinement of the adaptive processes of starting, orientation, assimilation, symbolization and completion; and that the place to start is with those processes that exist or can readily be released in the present (art-classroom) experience of the students.*

Propositions for Art Education

(1) That need-meeting of all sorts takes place through making structures and patterns, and that the behavior involved may tentatively be classified as orienting, starting, assimilating, completing and symbolizing. Problem-solving, social action and artistic production are alike in utilizing these behaviors in order to seek patterns, respectively, in solutions, policies and art objects.

(2) That there is an affective component of life which signifies 'involvement' in structure-seeking. The artistic quest is expressive during the seeking, and its products are evocative. The performing artist programs tension build-up and release in his audience — just as the 'artistic' teacher does in his class.

(3) Artistic structures are intuitively satisfying, and this is the major criterion they must meet. Other structures, like problem-solving and action-strategy, also involve intuition, but much less prominently. It is assumed in art that people have intuitions, that they are entitled to them and that their manifestation through art is worthwhile.

(4) Patterns and structure cohere as forms which can be worked out in an infinite number of ways, but which have properties of their own: flexibility, complexity, penetrability, etc. The study of the properties of forms belongs to art and should become habitual.

(5) Artistic structures arouse emotion and feeling; they invite (if not

demand) affect from the beholder. A picture presents a man with a job: he has to complete it, resonate with it, resolve it, add something, find harmony or strength or authority in it. It is evocative because he cannot leave it alone; and it needs him for its own realization.

(6) As distinguished from artistic structures in general, great art is universally evocative. Any artistic structure will be evocative for a few people, like the artist and his model; but great art is more universally appreciated. It responds to a variety of needs because the beholder can complete it in a variety of ways. This universality stems from mastery of materials and techniques, which is, in turn, a mastery of artistic language as the symbol-system for cultural communication. Great art is universal because evocation is as broad and deep and meditative as the culture allows, transcending private idioms and family-restricted meanings.

As art teachers, we must assume that there is an aesthetic aspect of all the activities of men. Art is the endeavor in which this aspect is most explicit, demonstrable and manipulable. Basically, *art activity is a refinement of, and response to, a whole host of structure-seeking behaviors of men; and art education should facilitate these natural, valuable and inevitable processes*.

Varieties of Art Education

How shall we look at art education in relation to these propositions? To find out about art education as practised, I went through the *Report of the Commission on Art Education*, edited by Jerome Hausman in 1965.[2] I was curious to know what varieties of art education there are and whether they fit together into some sort of pattern. In fishing for patterns, I went back to the tried and true proposition that behavior is a function of personality and environment, $B = f(P)(E)$. This famous dictum of Kurt Lewin is similar to John Dewey's formula that experience is a function of internal conditions (meaning the 'subjective' inside state of affairs) and of objective conditions (meaning basically the things men can agree on, which means primarily the environment).

In art education, one apparently can put emphasis on each of the three terms: the *behavior* the child produces, the factors in his *personality*, and the demands made by, or imputed to, the *environment*.

Following this lead, I found two submodels within each emphasis, making six patterns of art education. Table 10.1 compares these models and provides the notes for the following discussion.

Variation 1. Emphasis on Behavior Shaping

This comes in respect to two kinds of learning: techniques and appreciations. The learnings are achieved through the same process used by Skinner to teach pigeons to play ping-pong.

In *technique-shaping*, the behavior of the student is to manipulate materials. The salient part of the environment is the corn flakes, crayons, bits of string and other high-potential trash furnished by the teacher from his handy-dandy bin. The goal of manipulation is to develop correct techniques, and the correct technique is whatever the teacher says is the correct technique. The authority for this goal, then, is the teacher. The process by which the child is to go from naive exploratory manipulation to correct techniques is correction by the teacher. This does not require the teacher to be nasty — although the temptation often is there — but the teacher does have correctional responsibility and he sees its exercise as part of his role.

In *appreciation-shaping*, the behavior of the student is talking. The salient part of the environment is great works and artifacts placed there by the teacher. The goal is correct obeisances; that is, displaying sincere attitudes of respect or contempt (as appropriate) for the objects and 'schools' of art. The process of change is supervision by the teacher: 'John, that's not the Hopi way.' The teacher clarifies for the student how he is expected to talk about objects and ideas dear to the teacher.

Shaping appeals to certain motives of students. Students who thrive on shaping may be trying to identify with the teacher. They do not know what there is about him that appeals, so they take over all his mannerisms, prejudices, etc. This is easy to do because the teacher is a very clear person; there is nothing fuzzy or ambiguous about him. Students can psych him out in a minute and then play him on their line. Then there are those who are dependent, who need a lot of reward and approval. There are even students whose families have taught them that learning art means the ability to display techniques and verbal content, so shaping seems just right to them.

Variation 2. Emphasis on Personality. Releasing

This model concentrates on releasing something from the personality, unblocking the personality, tapping a keg — like a good obstetrical

Table 10.1: Varieties of Art Education — from $B = f(P)(E)$

	(B) Variation 1: Shaping		(P) Variation 2: Releasing		(E) Variation 3: Transacting	
	Technique	Appreciation	Self-esteem (Inward)	Competence (Outward)	Communicate	Act
Behaviour (B)	Manipulate	Talk	Act out	Act out	Create object	Change environment
Environment (E)	Art Material	Artifacts	Permissive climate	Permissive climate	Student's life situation	Ugly part of environment
Goal evaluation dimensions	Correct technique	Correct obeisances	Self-esteem and confidence	Maturity and competence	Product's communicability	Humaneness of environment
Authority	Teacher	Teacher	Shared goodwill of teacher and student	Student's own aspirations	Reactions of others	Group-generated common purpose
Congruent motives of Students	Identification (introjection) Reward, approval Become 'educated' Social-class expectations Needs for dependency, predictability		Maintain own self-image Explore, mess around Relate to teacher as person	Discover own goals, values Seek competence Gain autonomy Relate to teacher as artist, critic	Communicate Receive acclaim Further career Identify with 'artist'	Improve world Learn social strategy Gain autonomy through group belongingness

delivery, in which the chief expertise of the doctor resides in knowing when to get out of the way. This is a major role of the teacher who attempts to release personality through art. There seem to be two routes that can be followed. The first model aims to build *self-esteem and confidence*; the second shoots for *competence* in art. The difference is that confidence-building is turned inward — who am I? — whereas art competence is turned outward — what is the world like? In both models, the initial behaviors are the same: acting out. The child is to do what makes sense to him, follow his impulses. The environmental circumstance that fosters acting out is a permissive climate; this is a consequence not of materials, but of the teacher's attitude. Both routes start with the same behaviors in the same setting, but the teacher responds quite differently.

To build confidence, the teacher reinforces the child's own sense of worth; to build competence in art, the teacher reinforces whatever behavior seems unusually mature, creative or competent. (I can illustrate this difference very readily. When I was working with student teachers, I visited an art class and the teacher said, 'Since you are interested in art education, why don't you do a little art yourself?' I said, 'Well, that is an interesting idea and, as a matter of fact, I have a picture in my mind that I would like to do.' I fell to, got paint all over myself, and produced a genuine daub. The teacher, who had seen me sweat, cruised over. She said, 'Dr Thelen, you know this is very reminiscent of early Picasso.' Shucks, I never had to do another thing. I walked out of there two feet taller and have never since dared to touch paper with anything smaller than a typewriter. Obviously the teacher adapted the experience to contribute to my self-esteem, not to help me gain artistic competence. She might have said, 'Tell me about it, what you are trying to capture here. Have you thought about such and such?' She might have accepted the daub as something meaningful to me because I had invested a lot of myself in it, and then helped me learn how to make it less dauby.)

The authority for the goal of self-esteem is the student and teacher united in a sort of conspiracy of good will. The authority for the development of competence is the student's own aspiration. The student controls himself, driving toward sights which are continually and realistically revised upward. The dynamic through which change occurs in the case of confidence-building tends to be uncritical acceptance by the teacher who does not want to be bothered by the art as art; he just wants to sympathize with the child's trying and give him an E for effort. The process that fosters more mature performance and competence is feedback which the teacher helps the child get so that he may reflect on what he was trying to do and how well it worked; diagnosis of ways to 'sharpen' the product; and probably a lot of speculation and wonder about what would happen if . . . This calls for dialogue between teacher and pupil and for the teacher to try to understand the effort and product in the child's own terms.

The motives congenial to confidence-building are to support a self-image of creativity, worth or independence. Personality releasing also appeals to the child who likes to mess around, exploring without let or hindrance — as is in fact highly appropriate at early stages of development in any field. The student may try to relate to the teacher interpersonally, but not in his role as critic, artist or expert. On the side of competence-building, the personal theme for the student is self-discovery plus achievement. He wants to discover what his goals are, what is important to him; and he seeks personal strength, power and autonomy.

Variation 3. Emphasis on Environment. Transacting

In the third variation, we concern ourselves with E, the environmental factor. Within this emphasis, two submodels can be seen: *communication* and (following Marantz) *action on the visual environment*.[3] In the communication submodel, behavior creates a product rather than merely practising a technique, talking about art or acting out. The environment is the student's own life situation in and out of class; he is confined neither to the studio nor to objects or models that somebody else provides. His art activity may take off from any part or occasion of his life. His product emerges from his own seeking or inquiry, but the goal is to improve its communicativeness. Unlike the person-releasing variation in which the product is to show something about the student, in this case the product is to be art and is to communicate with others. It goes beyond (or not as far as?) the self-revelation of the private and idiomatic. It belongs in the domain of public discussion of art.

The authority for development of communicativeness is the reward value of reactions from the teacher, students and public. Change is brought about by feedback from others. To improve communicability, there must be someone to communicate to, and some way to get their response.

In the action submodel, the behavior is to change the environment. The product is not a conventional art product, but it is art just the same: a patch of flowers in a waste triangle at a highway intersection;

a new children's playground growing out of a graveyard for beer c.. and discarded ambitions; an orderly and efficient garden. The part of the environment to work on is that which turns one on, and do not waste the class's time making academic designs for some change that you do not have the power to produce — or for some change that is merely convenient. The thing to work on is whatever everyone feels is truly ugly. The goal is to produce a more intuitively satisfying pattern, what Marantz calls a more 'humane' environment. This strikes me as a good word for surroundings that have qualities of stability, depth and evocativeness such that the passerby enters a little of himself in interaction with it.

The authority for the action product is, interestingly enough, a sense of common purpose generated by the class and teacher together: what shall we aspire to? How excellent shall our work be? How big a job shall we tackle? What criteria shall we try to meet? These decisions must evolve from the class and teacher together, because they are the ones who must take action and therefore must know what the criteria are; and the way they are going to get the criteria sufficiently internalized to serve as guides to action is through developing the criteria through a considerable expenditure of their energy. The development of the sense of common purpose is crucial. Without it, the whole activity degenerates into competition and policing; but with it, the perpetual question is: what can each individual uniquely contribute to the whole and how can he facilitate the contributions of others? Strategy for dealing with environmental ugliness can be generalized to apply to such things as getting rid of rats, finding play space for children, lighting the streets, etc. The model throws light on how certain methods of 'group operation' increase the creativity and autonomy of individuals.

Students motives congruent with art action are to improve the world and, as Marantz says, to develop the habit and expectation of being responsible. Those readers who are old neighborhood buffs will recall that a fabulous array of motives may activate neighborhood improvement and citizen action. Consider, for example, the variety of motives, hopes and targets of those who join mobilizations these days.

Here, then, are the patterns I can tease out of the writings — with a little prejudice of my own thrown in for good measure. I think these models cover most of the flavours of art teaching as it goes on today.

Comparative Evaluation of the Six Models

According to the present 'engineering,' 'systems' or 'behavioral-objectives' approaches to evaluation, we would remind ourselves that each model has its own goals (Table no. 10.1), and that progress towards these is what we should evaluate, as follows.

(a) *Technique-shaping*. List of specified techniques; each technique is defined by scaled sample, against which the child's work is compared, like the old Ayers handwriting scale.

(b) *Appreciation-shaping*. List of specified items of information and attitudes. Measured by achievement tests, essays and teacher judgment of 'sincerity' during discussion.

(c) *Self-esteem* (personality-releasing). Interview, getting at self-concept. Could also use projectives, sociometrics and free-choice situations (to assess risk-taking).

(d) *Competence* (personality releasing). Critical appraisal of products and of how student talks about his involvement with them — especially in reference to the development of artistic 'discipline.'

(e) *Communication* (transactional). Judgment of products and of the reactions of others to them; assessment of shift towards the style of whatever artistic 'school' was chosen for emulation (i.e. as the 'norm').

(f) *Social action* (transactional). Judgment of the child's performance in the roles of sensitive individual, group member, technician, citizen, etc. Underneath these judgments, and to be retrieved through them, is a sense of the child's 'adequacy' or adaptive skill.

In order to evaluate one classroom, we would ask what its objectives were and how well they were achieved. In order to compare two classrooms whose objectives were different, we would have to ask the further question: how educationally worthwhile were their respective objectives? The questions, 'What can we teach effectively?' and 'How worthwhile is it?' generate a surprising array of answers. Thus, the behavior-shapers usually take the position that it is better to do a few things well than to attempt to reach the moon. (Hmmm.) The personality-releasers tend to argue that a highly significant growth experience for a few students, coupled with mild benefits for the others, is preferable to efficiency for all with limited opportunities for growth. The communications people might pull a twist and deny that they are at all concerned about 'educational worthwhileness': everybody knows what an artist does, and these kids shall have a taste of it. The social-action people might develop a wide range of arguments, because they operate the most complex enterprise. Perhaps the unique point they could make is that they have an image of a decent or humane society, and each child is to learn what he needs to in order to participate and maintain it effectively. In this case, some children would have a great deal to learn and others much less.

We have defined art education as the refinement of adaptive pattern-seeking processes (as exemplified in five functional categories of behavior). I suspect that teachers of the six models would agree 'in principle' with this definition, even though they might be a mite unsure of what it means. Further, it would not surprise me if our teachers felt that they in fact really do help children adapt to themselves and the world — and that what I have called their 'goals' are merely reasonable expectations of what the child will accomplish in a set of already-decided, time-tested activities. In this case, differences among the models would be as differences among means towards the same generally accepted ends. And the agreements needed to settle the differences — if that be the intention — would have to do with teaching methods and principles much more than with moral precepts and principles of value.

In any case, having asserted that the rationale for art education is to encourage — and refine — the pattern-seeking processes of adaptation, our task is quite clear: to compare the six models of art education with respect to the extent and manner of their attending to the adaptive processes. These processes, we recall, were identified as starting, orienting, assimilating, symbolizing and completing.

Table 10.2 presents the comparisons. Obviously, there is no way to list specific behaviors that would be found in specifiable quantities within the six settings. On the other hand, one can look back on the specific behaviors (such as those listed at the beginning of this article) to *functions* that they implement, and one may then ask about the centrality of each of these functions.

Thus, starting behavior is a symptom of stimulation by the situation. It translates into the question: what are the pressures that students are forced to respond to? Or, what are the demands or 'challenges' they have to do something about? Perhaps the most interesting comparison among the six models is that the two shaping models make definite but trivial demands that can be met by imita-

Table 10.2: Adaptive Behaviors Consistent with Five Varieties of Art Education

Behaviors	(B) SHAPING		(P) RELEASING		(E) TRANSACTING	
	Technique	Appreciation	Self-esteem	Competence	Communication	Action
Starting	Demand for competing in objective performance Skill challenge	Demand for participation in discussion Decide + or – response to artifacts	Unstructured expectations about use of time, product criteria, etc.	Unstructured expectations in regard to what to try to discover	Demand for personally meaningful and feasible 'subject'	Demand for social action
Orienting	Skill level 'Place' in competition Standards to set oneself	'Place' in regard to knowledge. participation. values of content	Awareness of own impulses in coping with lack of structure	Develop alternatives consider values and costs Set new goals	Set own expectations for performance and for responses of others	Hunt for situation to which there is motivating affect
Assimilating	Practice-feedback-practice cycles	(Minimal) fitting together ideas about men, art, society	Decisions about what impulses to follow up and how	Purposive behaviour evaluate own approach	Product-response evaluation-product cycle	Participate in action-strategy as person. artist, citizen
Symbolizing	(Possibly) practice piece as exemplification	(Possibly) a term paper	Informal, in psyche-group discussion (sensitivity-labeling?)	Practice pieces as evidence of quest	Efforts to 'explain' effort to others	Making own suggestions and actions explicit so others can cooperate
Completing	End of unit Achieved level of mastery	Conformity to expected obeisances	Topic attrition—go on to next	Finished product Tested hypothesis New angle	Get audience response	Action completed (Go to new project)

tion of the teacher's performance. The releasing models confront the student with what is usually a severe stress: to operate within a deliberately unstructured situation. The transacting models demand that the student relate to a larger interactive context. Thus, the demand stimuli are respectively for imitation, for coping with lack of structure and for developing one's interests and abilities within an interactive group.

The orienting behavioral possibilities include comparisons of self with others on one or two dimensions (skill and knowledge and attitude toward competition) in the shaping models; awareness of one's internal complexity (flux of impulses) or outward opportunities (action alternatives) in the releasing models; and finally, in the transactional models, orientation in one case emphasizes clarifying expectations of self and others, whereas in the other case it emphasizes development of a rationale for action to which one can subscribe.

With respect to assimilation and symbolization, these are intertwined in the same sense as doing and thinking. Symbolization is the basis of transfer and significance of whatever is assimilated. In the technique-oriented model, the student is engaged in cycles of practice-feedback-practice, and there is little place for symbolizing because technical practice does not transfer; it has little meaning beyond itself. In appreciation, assimilation clearly requires conceptual interconnectedness; the job is to pull ideas together. Each student has to do this in ways that make sense to him; and, since the process involves language, a written paper would be the most appropriate product. Assimilation in the case of 'releasing, self-esteem' would presumably be of new perceptions and conceptions of self, with one's feelings about his own art production the ostensible focus and with continual emotional support and interest expressed by the teacher. Symbolization would include putting self-concerns into words which probably would be taken as expressions of feeling rather than as assertion of facts. With regard to the competence model, assimilation symbolization would be guided by ideas of experimental or developmental methods. The student's work would be purposive and easy to evaluate, and the means-ends relationships among art performance, personal aspiration and product quality would be matters for continuous inquiry by the student. The situation with respect to the transactional-communication model is a richer version of the technique-shaping model. The eliciting of satisfying responses from other students, and perhaps the art community as a whole, may take the place of teacher approval. A complete piece of art, rather than practised exercises, is the product. The possible variety of reactions from many people is much more stimulating and thought-provoking (especially when there is disagreement) than is feedback from only the teacher. By addressing a larger, more pluralistic public, the student has access to a wider range of sensitivities and apprecia-tions. Finally, assimilation symbolization in the environmental action situation is the richest of all in multidimensional meanings, because the student is simultaneously taking the role of learner, citizen, designer, executor, cooperator and possibly manager. He is 'in on' a total effort, and in this effort are reflected practically all the problems of society — including, I may add, the 'place' of the aesthetic in everyday life. The considerable dialogue required in this model enriches it very substantially and invites the widest range of discovery about art, society and self.

Finally, completing, however subtle at the microscopic level of the individual making twenty or more choices an hour, is quite clear at the macroscopic level of a class. The more nearly the experience of the learner approaches that of a can of peas in a Salinas, California, packing plant, the less meaning, short of the ultimate completion, does the idea of completing have. Accordingly, the shaping tech-niques, in which the student simply 'processes' a stream of inputs from the teacher, would have neither beginning nor end in any psy-chological sense; beginnings would be each period at 2.05 p.m. and endings would be at 2.50 p.m. Of course, if the students had planned any of the work, so that they did have the concept of a series of defined tasks, then there would be from time to time a sense of winding up one thing and starting another. I conclude that, in the shaping pattern, the student does not get the sense of beginnings and endings beyond being told when to leave the activity and when to resume it.

In the releasing-self-esteem variation, the subject matter — oneself — is preoccupying, and tends to move readily from figure to ground; but, with the exception of occasional, hard-to-come-by insights, there is little drama, few disjunctions. Concerns do change; one emerges as the other subsides, and attrition may be a more precise name for it than completion. In the competence model, there is a clear ending for activity, and it is clear because there are at least some explicit purposes whose accomplishment brings some aspects of activity to an end. The competence model, like the self-esteem one, also includes private purposes of the learner and, with respect to these, there are no clear beginnings and endings. But activity is in the public world, and it is ostensibly guided by publicly assertable purposes. Drama is signalled by events that occur, not by changes in intensity of preoccupation.

In the two 'transacting' models, events occur, and they have beginnings, middle, and ends. The activities of the learner follow a sequence of decisions, and each decision is both the culmination of a transition and the commencement of a new action. In the action model, there are at least several dozen decisions that would have to be made from first to last, and these decisions are made by individuals, subgroups and class; they are about policy, prohibitions, specific details; and they differentiate and specify values, friendships, interests, status levels, etc. The 'culminations' or completions are rich in number, content and reward-possibilities; and, when studied as interesting processes in their own right, they make the experience of social action a significant foundation for adaptive behavior for years to come. The communication model has some of the same features as the social-action model, but to a lesser degree.

How shall we evaluate these six varieties of art education? It seems to me that the logic of our discussion so far shrieks for the giving out of report cards. But, before attempting it, perhaps we had better be clear about just what can be evaluated on the basis of the 'evidence' above. We are confined — are we not? — to a discussion of *opportunities* for the five functions to be actualized, but we cannot say anything about whether they *will* be or, for that matter, whether they *could* be. Further, I suspect that each teacher would insist that, in *his* hands, what I have called technique-shaping (for example) is a rich experience which encompasses all the goodies I have reserved for the other methods. Nevertheless, sticking to the bare bones of the six models, I would draw up a report card as in Table 10.3, in which rank 1 is best and 6 is worst. I find the ranks rather interesting and quite

Table 10.3: Report Card. Opportunities for the Realization of Five Functions in Six Varieties of Art Education

Function	Technique	Appreciation	Self-esteem	Competence	Communication	Social action
Starting	4	5	1	2	6	3
Orienting	5	6	4	2	3	1
Assimilating	5	6	3	1	4	2
Symoblizing	6	5	2	3	4	1
Completing	4	5	6	3	2	1
Overall rank	5	6	3	2	4	1

revealing of principles worth making explicit. (The overall ranks, however, are exceedingly dubious — like overall grades — and are included mostly for fun.) Consider the features of rank 1 for these are the strong points of the models, and we may well want to incorporate them into any improved future model.

For *starting*, I choose the personality-releasing self-esteem model; the unstructured situation compels reaction. I rate self-esteem over competence because of the greater opportunity for students to recognize, and deal with, their personal ideas and feelings.

For *orienting*, I choose the transactional social-action model. The dialogue in the group provides rich opportunities for the child to 'locate' himself as a unique person, a member, a leader, a producer, a bright-ideas man, etc. During discussion, the child can see whose views are similar and different from his own and where he fits along almost any dimension to which he is sensitive.

For *assimilating*, I choose the personality-releasing competence model. The student is expected to set his own goals, assess his own work, garner his own learnings, try out his own ideas for betterment. The purpose of present experience is to revise outcomes from the past and create anticipations for the future.

For *symbolizing*, I choose the transactional social-action model. The rich dialogue mentioned under the orienting function above means that many aspects of experience are put into words. Moreover, the fact that much of the talk is salient to decision-making means that it will use the rhetoric of persuasion, and this in turn means that it will invoke cultural values, expectations and traditions.

Finally, for *completing*, I choose the social-action model. Certainly here it is most obvious when the job is done!

The explanation of the features of rank 6 is less instructive, but may suggest things to avoid in pedagogical methods.

For *starting*, I put the communication model last, because the demand to 'paint a picture for others to react to' strikes me as a bad motive for art and a turn-off, tune-out kind of gambit for most kids. (Let the prospect of communication come up *after* someone has developed something worth sharing.)

For *orienting*, I put the appreciation model last because, in most courses organized around informational subject matter, the child has little or no idea why the stuff should be studied, what will come next and how to tell by himself how well he is doing. (Dependence on the teacher is substituted for orientation.)

For *assimilating*, I put the appreciation model last because of the strong possibility that the content will be compartmentalized; it will be seen as foreign to the kid's own lifestyle and will not be assimilated.

For *symbolizing*, I put the technique model last because developing techniques is an end in itself, opens no conceptual doors and invites nothing beyond itself.

For *completing*, I put the self-esteem model last because there is no end. Dealing with one's own self — without externalization of purposes — is like listening to a never-ending piece of music. It has its ups and downs and its intermissions, but no finale.

An Exemplary Scenario for Art Education

The above analysis serves as a fine overture to the construction of an inquiry-oriented scenario along the lines suggested in Chapter 9. Let us now walk through a model sequence of possible art activities.

I begin by passing out to each child a bundle of wires and telling them all to 'make something.' This task arrests attention, evokes emotion and generates or stimulates ideas — it is a 'confrontation' and it elicits 'starting' behaviors.

After the children have tried to be self-consciously creative for a little while (ten minutes), I invite them to form small groups with others they choose, to talk about their experience with the wires and to swap views on what they have found out about why creation-on-demand is so difficult. (Note that the question is not what makes this sort of thing so difficult in general but rather about each child's own partially buried reactions.)

These 'orienting' behaviors, well started in the experience-swapping of the small groups, continue in the whole class as I list their various (volunteered) ideas on the board. I invite the class to look at *our* shared list and see what questions it raises. (There are several ways, such as developing classificatory categories, that would help pull the items together, but my strong preference is to see if we can arrive at an intuitive 'sense of meeting,' articulated as a purpose to which we can all be committed. (Such a purpose would signal the end of diffuse permissiveness and would usher in more focused means-ends planning.)

In order to develop this communal sense of meeting, I invite the group to look behind the list of items on the board. 'Would you say that we have here 22 different items, or that we have the same item expressed in 22 individual ways?' If the latter can be demonstrated, then we may assume that there is some common underlying stress to which each person responds in his own way but which nevertheless can be dealt with as a circumstance in the common environment. Class diagnosis of common concern is a rich and complex process. It is 'orienting' in that alternative interpretations can be compared as an aid to emergence into awareness of each student's thoughts and feelings. It is 'assimilating' to the extent that there is effort to reconcile or relate the just-experienced activities to the residuum of past experiences. It is 'symbolizing' in that the language and concepts employed at this point are strongly expressive of one's internalized, habituated culture. In short, this diagnostic period is functionally heterogeneous; it has not yet 'shaken down' to a focused action-oriented course of action. It is a period of transition from diverse individual reactions to a sense of common purpose, from a collection of individuals to a cohesive group and from the authority of the teacher as master of ceremonies to the authority of shared work expectations and goals.

With so much riding on the success of this transition, the teacher is well advised not to leave everything to chance (or to 'faith in the students'). The teacher has a role to take, and his special contribution is not at all likely to be generated by the students, no matter how patiently he waits. The teacher's contribution stems from his insight into the discipline of art, both as a field of study and as a field of productive activity. The discipline of art is a body of ideas, skills and lore organized around a few basic and everlasting questions to which answers are sought and continually reinterpreted through aesthetic experience. The teacher should know such questions and should have a profound sense of their significance to man. And, if the questions get at universal concerns, then they are going to crop up wherever art is being done or thought about. This means that even within the suggestions of the class there will be some that the disciplined and open-minded teacher can recognize as primitive or naïve variants of the deeper questions. These primitive suggestions are the cues the teacher needs, and they stimulate him to encourage their further pursuit.

As a nonartist and nonteacher of art, I do not hold myself responsible for knowledge of 'the' questions (if any there be) that organize the discipline of art. But I want to illustrate the sort of question I think would make sense for the class to identify following their confrontation by the demand 'to create something.' I shall leave it to the experts to decide how universal and fruitful questions such as these may be for guiding the study of art.

(1) What social experiences in the past make it hard for a person to just go ahead and 'create something'?

(2) What features distinguish 'art' products from 'nonart' products? (How can you tell when you have created something? What do we mean by 'being creative'?)

(3) What sorts of discoveries does the child make as he creates art that are hard to come by in more ordinary activities?

(4) What relationships are there between making one's own art and appreciating art made by others? (How does each contribute to growth?)

(5) How, through art, might a person's individual feelings or intuitions become important to society?

(6) Et cetera.

Once the common concern has been identified, vigorously reinforced by the teacher and accepted by the students as something to work on, the next step is to break it down into a variety of projects which can be investigated in a variety of ways. The 'breakdown' calls for an analysis of alternatives and possible combinations. Thus, any question about 'art' can be investigated with respect to a specific art: water-colour, oil, abstract, folk-song, computer patterns, etc. Any question about meaning or interpretation of art can only be investigated within a specified culture: past, rural, affluent, traditional, etc. Any question about people can only be answered with certain persons in mind: the artist, the housewife, the child, the political leader, etc. Any question about expressiveness requires one to be aware of possible emotions; and for communicativeness, one needs to think of levels of sophistication. The questions I listed above are broad and general; they can be talked about in broad and general terms, but they cannot be investigated until they are made operational by specifying *who* you are talking about, *what* he is doing, *who else* is on the scene and *where* all this is going on. The formulation of subquestions that could be investigated, and the rehearsal in one's mind of what would be involved in the inquiries if they were to be carried out, is a very effective kind of 'anticipatory' assimilation; it makes the actual experience later far more meaningful because it is enriched by anticipations of all sorts.

Following planning and selection of subquestions by individuals, work begins. The teacher moves into the role of consultant. From time to time, individuals may report and show progress to a review committee, which offers feedback, criticism, appreciation and suggestions of further resources available from other students within the class.

Finally, the time comes for putting it all together, for reflecting all the individual investigations back on to the initiating common concern and for deciding 'where we stand now.' One might, of course, ask each individual to show or report on his project, and this would be consonant with the tradition that the proper outcome of individual work is competitive display. That, however, misses the point of what learning is for: to develop resource understandings and skills in the students so that they can be first-citizens and members of a concerned and enlightened community. Thus, instead of show and tell, what is required is a further class activity in which each individual's role is a consequence of the fact that he has conducted his own investigation. The appropriate activity should be complex enough and big enough to require a wide range of contributions; it should invite both bright ideas and hard work; and it should enable the students to experience some qualities of artistic enterprise even though they are not expected to be 'artists.' Possible examples of such further 'consummatory activity' might be: humanizing a city block; planning and executing a series of posters or dioramas for planned communication; compiling and pooling a long list of bright ideas (with drawings and photos) for improving the home environment; tutoring a group of younger children in skills that were learned through the individual projects; experimenting with crossmedia, crosscultural, and/or cross situational variations of whatever the projects studied, using the whole class to consider the principles involved in making such transitions. What we seek in such activities is, of course, the 'completing' or winding up of a period of personally involving and hard work.

Steps in Curriculum Construction

After so much detail, it may be useful to recapitulate our steps. They were as follows.

(1) To identify naturally occurring, universally distributed (culture-free), important (adaptive) behaviors and explain why art education should be concerned with these.

The five categories — starting, orienting, assimilating, symbolizing and completing — seem to me to be as good as any other five and better than most. Anyone who assumes, as I do, that education can only improve behaviors that already exist would probably point to the same phenomena, even if he imposed a different scheme of classification.

The reason why art education should be concerned with these behaviors is that they are the ones through which man develops his intuitive 'structures' of comprehension, awareness, openness and emotion. These structures mediate all his transactions with the objective world; they express his orientation to the world; and they organize his responses as an adaptive or effective person.

It seems to me that these effects are the functions of art, and that its concern with such structural properties as stability, form, universality and complexity should greatly assist the student's quest.

(2) To identify the various models of art education and compare them with each other and with the five functions that they should, presumably, facilitate.

I found that emphasis may be placed on variations of behavior-shaping and personality-releasing, or on transactions with the environment. I found that the unstructured situation for personality-releasing will be most likely to 'start' the student; that the sharing of reactions and setting of purposes in the social action model would be most usefully 'orienting'; that the competence model should maximize meaningful 'assimilation'; that the social-action model would stimulate most 'symbolization' and would also have the most marked 'completion.'

I also found (although I did not mention it before) that the six objectives — technique, appreciation, self-esteem, competence, communication and action — are all desirable and contributory to the five functions to be improved. This leads me to see the six existing models as partial rather than as wrong and to anticipate a better model which is more comprehensive than the present models.

(3) To present a better model which preserves the best features of existing models, but goes beyond them in its rationale. (The point I emphasized was not behavior, personality or action, but rather *common purpose*, to which each individual is commited and to which he contributes.)

The model views teaching as the supervised movement of the class among six major activities:

(1) alone: being confronted;
(2) alone: investigating own project;

(3) small groups: getting hold of thoughts and feelings after being confronted;

(4) small groups: reviewing project work of individuals and trying to facilitate it;

(5) class: listing alternative reactions, developing sense of purpose, planning activities;

(6) class: pooling the project learnings of class members in a single integrative activity; meditation together on the whole unit: meanings, ways to improve, etc.

Every activity arises out of readinesses that develop as the preceding activity runs its course, and every activity develops imperatives for the next. The art of teaching (in this view) is to get the feedback that enables teacher and class to see what activity shift is appropriate and how best to accomplish it.

I do not allege that this is the 'best' model. I think that it does identify much of what goes on in classrooms that one would consider well-taught. I shall be pleased if the reader feels that these activities (or something equivalent to them) are already parts of good teaching. In that case, the 'model' is only a systematization and, hopefully, a conceptual clarification.

(4) To encourage rapprochement between artists, pedagogues and behavioral scientists; to invite them to dig beneath their own lingos to the common experience of human adaptation, artistic production, and effective learning. I suggest that all three are concerned with variations of the same human drama: the beginning in individual, semiprivate impulse; the legitimization of individual concern through its merging in group purposes and societal goals; the development of individual competence along with the differentiation of a classroom culture that makes it meaningful; and, finally, the translation of individual effort, however modest, into concepts of growth of the humane community of the classroom and larger society.

Summary

So far, our study has paid little attention to school subjects. We have seen the teacher responding to the group, to individuals, to growth processes, to value questions, to diagnostic needs, etc. When we shift our concern from classroom dynamics to school subjects, we enter the field of curriculum. In the present chapter we attempt to show what sort of analytical thinking is involved in curriculum construction — using art as an example.

We first ask what distinctive special capability to the subject may help the student develop. What does a student do when he is 'doing art'? Five activities are identified: starting, orienting, assimilating, symbolizing and completing. We interpret these processes as vehicles for 'structure-seeking'; and we define the qualities of this seeking when it is in the field of art.

We offer six types of scenarios that may inform and guide classroom art education: we see that curriculum-makers can try to shape the child's techniques or tastes, can try to release individual growth in self-esteem or competence or can try to help students use art in the service of communication or environmental improvement.

We compare the ability of the six scenarios to facilitate the five processes and we see that each has its special strengths and weaknesses. Building both on this analysis and on Chapter 9, we offer a brief scenario for educative art education. We close by summarizing the steps through which our analysis of curriculum has taken us.

Notes

1. A preliminary version of this chapter was presented to the Conference on the Supervision of Art Education (Atlanta, Georgia, 21 January 1970). An earlier version of this chapter was published as 'From Individual Behaviour to Classroom Activity: An Inquiry into Art Education,' *Journal of Curriculum Studies*, vol. 3, no. 2 (1971), pp. 135-57.

2. Jerome J. Hausman (ed.), *Report of the Commission on Art Education* (National Art Education Association, Washington DC, 1965).

3. Kenneth Marantz, New Dimensions for Citizenship: Visual Responsibility.' (Graduate School of Education, University of Chicago, mimeographed, 1967).

11 The Enterprise Come to Judgment

Youngsters may judge a course to be a drag and the teacher a drip. Teachers try to judge how well the lesson went. Principals have to judge how good a teacher Mr Jinks is. The school authorities want to judge the 'success' of the reading program that they spent $289,672.46 (or the equivalent in Sterling or lire) on last year. Reporters and reformers judge how badly the school has failed to meet their romantic fantasies. Legislators judge what 'educational' problems are politically hot and therefore should be prodded with money. Funding agencies want to judge whether they got their money's worth.

These are often fateful judgments because peoples' lives, opportunities and reputations ride on them. Whether to promote Johnny, fire Ms Schmaltz, raise school taxes, purchase the 'new mathematics,' admit Henry to the University — these are serious God-like matters. Mere impressions are not good enough. We want evidence. We want to know not only what the judgment is, but also how trustworthy it is. We want to know what data were used, how the data were turned into evidence and how the evidence was considered in reaching the judgment. The word 'evaluation' refers to this sequence of consciously designed and contrived operations.

Evaluation can get tricky, because it is done by people who have a stake in what conclusions are reached. Those who benefit from a judgment think the evaluation was great; those who suffer are likely to think it unfair, inadequate, discriminatory, etc. No matter how the evaluation is conducted, skeptics and theorists can and should raise hard questions: do 'reading' tests measure reading? Are the things we measure really significant for educational purposes? Does a B grade in algebra mean that the student's algebraic ability is comfortably above the average of the class or of some national sample? Or does it mean that the student learned more and tried harder than most — even though he still isn't much good in algebra? If the student is judged to have become a superior writer will he ever utilize this ability or will he hate and avoid literate writing for the rest of his life? If you give a student a D will be give up or will he try harder? If you judge teaching by what the students learn, is the better teacher one who gets everybody to learn a little something or one who gets a few to learn a lot while the rest learn little? And if you give no pretests to see what the student knows at the beginning of the course, can the final examination be taken as evidence that the student learned anything?

These are run-of-the-mill questions and doubts about 'evaluation.' A great deal of effort has gone into developing the 'art' and more will be required to resolve the doubts.[1] But if it be the case that the doubts are by their nature inevitable and unresolvable, then it seems to me to be time to ask whether further efforts along these lines make much sense. Maybe we are asking the wrong questions. Perhaps we ought to stop and rethink the whole matter. A good place to start would be by developing a coherent conception of the educational enterprise and then seeing what follows from *that*. Since this book attempts to develop just such a coherent conception, let us accept the challenge to see what follows with regard to evaluation.

What to Evaluate

The hope of 'evaluating the educational enterprise' is as vague as it is well-intentioned. The first problem is what to include. We have five possibilities: first, there are the individual students engaged in their inquiries in the classroom; second, there is the classroom as a community in which students learn and teachers teach; third, there are the schools, School Board, administrative offices and possibly affiliated parent groups which constitute a local school system; fourth, there is the educational enterprise of a nation — the societal system — which includes the organized school systems in relationship to 'nationalizing influences'; finally, there is the conceived educational system, including all the people and acts that influence the child's education and, in so doing, monitor society's intentions for 'education.' In this conception, 'the educational system' is coordinate with 'the political system,' 'the economic system,' etc.

Let us see what sorts of questions tend to be asked about these first four parts and then the overall conceived system.

The Students' Learning

With respect to the student, he is presumably the client for whom the educational enterprise is run. In that case the enterprise is a success if it 'educates' him and a failure if it does not. As to which it is, you can have it any way you want; by picking a suitable definition of 'education.' If educating the child is equivalent to getting him to attend and stay in school for many years and then graduate, the contemporary educational enterprise is probably the greatest success story in history — even though it still discriminates against some groups. If educating the child means getting him into college or university, then the overall picture is that most middle-class children who want to do so make it to some institution or other. If educating the child means getting him to pass tests of character, creativity, critical thinking, etc., then we can say how he compares with the others who take the test, but we have little idea of what threshold level for each test would correspond to 'being educated.' We also have no idea how the various test competencies may be integrated and utilized within the child's character and coping style: *that* would come a lot closer to what education is all about. If becoming educated means developing a repertoire of effective roles in society, then the art of evaluation is not well enough advanced to handle the question. Finally, if getting educated means personal growth, self-realization and nourishment of potentials, then we have little more to go on than the wise and compassionate guesses of an occasional humane teacher.

Insofar as this book is concerned, there is one clear and fundamental question; is the student moving toward a more educated — adaptive, participative, transcendent — way of life? I do not think this question can be fully and completely answered, if only because nobody sees enough of students' lives to make an overall judgment. But teachers can testify to the ways of life in their classes; and their different descriptions can be combined into impressions that are at least worth talking over with the student and his parents. We shall, therefore, consider this evaluation within classrooms. (We shall see that in certain classrooms — communities — this evaluation is easy to conduct, whereas in other classrooms — collectivities — it is virtually impossible. I should say that the former class is supportive of the student's inquiries, whereas the latter is only concerned about his overt performance.)

To examine a way of life it must be engaged in some activity vital to the person. That is, a way of life is judged by how it inquires into its own experience as it copes with some challenge, be it an intellectual puzzle, a set of unreasonable requirements, an experiment in the real world or a problem of social conduct. It is impractical to try to deal with all the inquiries of a student. There are, however, some confrontations that are essential and knowable and to which reactions are interpretable. These confronting situations I call *prototypes*.

Prototypes represent the fundamental activities of the course. The reason they are prototypes is that they continually recur, not only in the course but metaphorically, as internalized forms, in the rest of life. To put the matter too simply, let us imagine that in the coping or educated life certain basic confrontations occur over and over. The individual must make and reply to interpersonal demands; he must handle himself in hate- and love-arousing situations; he must weigh evidence and form reasoned judgments; he must seek awareness of his own motives and decide on courses of action. How many such prototypical situations comprise the art of living? I do not know — the matter cries out for serious investigation. But I do know that within the narrower confines of a classroom, at least some prototypical situations can be identified. They can be identified because they are the cardinal activities through which the discipline of knowledge is developed, and applied to human affairs. Thus the prototypes I was aware of in teaching high-school chemistry include: (a) identifying an 'unknown' chemical (diagnosis); (b) figuring out what will happen to other variables when the pressure, temperature, volume or amount of a gas is changed (predicting on the basis of known lawful relationships); (c) predicting, on the basis of solubility and ionization, other properties such as electrical conductivity, completeness of reaction, boiling-point elevations, etc. (application of reaction principles or tendencies); (d) symbolizing, through chemical notation, a host of observed and imagined chemical phenomena, and figuring out the relative amounts of chemicals involved in these reactions (use of symbolic system and its relation to real-world events), etc.

I was also aware of other prototypes that one might not consider part of 'chemistry' but that were certainly part of an educative course in chemistry: (a) teacher-pupil planning of experiments — making suggestions, judging relevance to purpose, assessing practicality, imagining what would happen if particular courses of action were adopted, discriminating between what could be planned in advance and what would have to be decided as the experiment went along; (b) carrying out a project as a member of a small team of students; (c) performing a demonstration in front of the class; (d) making use of time left over from activities while waiting for the next one to begin; (e) reacting to disappointing or pleasing feedback from tests, teacher and other students; etc.

There are two points to be made about such prototypes: first, a great deal of my course was organized around these activities and they recurred over and over at increasingly higher levels of sophistication and complexity; and second, they can be 'taught' in such a way that they 'transfer' — that is, give the student power to cope with similar demand structures outside of chemistry. In this sense, they are internalized as part of 'character' or way of life. This is the proper contribution of 'chemistry' to the 'general education of the citizen.'

From the technical standpoint, the big advantage to evaluation through prototypes is that their structure is relatively clear; their purposes or demands are known to and accepted by the students; they can be reacted to in different ways; and the reactions of a student may be fairly typical of his behavior in a wide range of more or less similar situations. Some procedures for the evaluation of such students responses are: to describe what the child is observed to do in significant prototypical confrontations; to talk with him about what he was observed to do and ask him to correct, explain and comment on the description; to help him see how to develop his capabilities further in such a way that they can compensate for or even overcome his disabilities. Such discussion is basically counseling: identifying talent and thinking about possible careers; figuring out ways the child can use course opportunities to increase capabilities and achieve newly exciting purposes; suggesting ways to cope with the situations that embarrass or trouble him; agreeing on special help the teacher can give in whatever special efforts the student commits himself to undertake.

The evaluation record includes: (a) a list of the prototypes he copes with well; (b) a list of the prototypes he has trouble with; (c) a statement of goals the child sets for himself in the remainder of the course; (d) a memorandum of agreement on what the child expects from the teacher and the teacher from the child during the next period of the course. Cooperative preparation and periodic revision of this record is the aspect of evaluation that contributes most to education.

The reader may have noted that I have substituted the concept of prototypes for the typical list of things that every child is 'supposed' to learn: the facts and abilities so dear to curriculum committees.[2] In terms of individual growth and development, the purpose of education is to enable each child to develop an effective style of coping with whatever he must cope with.[3] The belief that all personally effective ways of coping involve the same bits of information that must be learned, specific skills that must be mastered, specific performances that must be displayed, etc. has some plausibility, but it too often blinds us to the rich pattern of each child's singular real life, and it thus destroys our capability for compassionately meeting each person in ways helpful to him. Moreover, if the child is engaged in genuine inquiry, he will inevitably run across the principles and concepts demanded by the logic of his inquiry — and, if he does not, the claim of the principle to universality would seem to be a mite shaky.

Our regard for the child as educatee generalizes to a similar, although less central, regard for every individual in all the groups in the enterprise: administrative staff, faculty committees, student clubs, special-interest associations. I think it is fair to say that the vitality of each part of the system depends on the opportunities afforded to each person for educative growth.

The Classroom as Educative Milieu

There are several things one might want to evaluate as one moves to the classroom; these correspond to different ways of characterizing its functions. In the first place, the classroom lies between two extremes: either the instrument for making the child learn what he is supposed to, or the setting which offers him the opportunity to learn if he is ready and willing. The typical classroom 'provides opportunity' and then makes sure the child uses it — thus jumbling its theories into a pragmatic mish-mash. From the point of view of 'opportunity to learn' or 'exposure to learning,' the need to evaluate the classroom setting (as well as the students) depends on how important it is to be 'fair' to the child. If he has not learned much, one might say that he should not go on; he's incompetent. On the other hand, one might be less hasty and ask what sort of opportunity he had to learn. If he had a good opportunity and yet did badly, then there seems little point in his continuing in the same kind of classrooms or school, and one asks what different educational environment might be more effective. On the other hand, if his opportunities were poor and his learning was poor we find ourselves in a very sticky but, unfortunately, common situation. It seems unfair to deny further opportunities, because it presumably was not the child's 'fault'; but to let him go on requires either a lot of remedial work (which may be rejected) or a double standard which debases the achievements of others and leaves him ill-prepared for the world — even though he might have a diploma.

The present conventional wisdom with respect to evaluating opportunity tends to substitute sociological assumptions for observations of actual learning; it takes for granted that opportunity depends primarily on the socioeconomic status of the students. If they are all lower-status (poor), then their opportunities must be poor. If they are all middle-class, then their opportunities are said to be good.

A second kind of evaluation of opportunity to learn is based on the proposition that opportunity depends on how 'good' the teaching is. Since in this view all the teaching is done by the teacher, this boils down to evaluating the teacher. Since studies of what traits make a good teacher have been generally inconclusive, the evaluators have had a hard time. But it is not hard to define incompetence from the standpoint of a smooth-running school: teachers who cannot keep order or who infuriate parents or who make trouble for the staff are 'incompetent.' For the most part, what is evaluated has little to do with the effectiveness of the teacher in the classroom.

Another sort of evaluation in the classroom is for the purpose of improving the management of 'learning systems.' A learning system is a set of instructional materials and procedures. It assumes certain capabilities, interests, docilities, etc. on the part of students. Since there are always students who do not fit the specifications, the learning system has to be 'individualized' or 'flexible'; or the children who do not fit have to be separated from those who do; or remedial measures must be taken. There is great concern about how well each child does in the system, and virtually no concern about why the system is worth doing well in.

The reasoning of this book arrives at somewhat different ideas about what to evaluate in classrooms, namely the development of each class both as an interactive milieu of individual inquiry and growth and as a quasiautonomous, purposive small society maintained within the larger school organization. As these two aspects mutually enrich and stimulate each other the classroom develops into a community with its own distinctive culture and ethos. Culture-building is a major responsibility of leadership, whether it be by a teacher, team, chairman or committee of the whole. It is up to the teacher to nurture the class's growth toward being an educative community: one that increasingly expects and facilitates each child's efforts to learn the use of its invitations and resources as he acts more and more like an educated person. The teacher sets and enforces norms and standards, brings in materials, reflects on student behavior and acts as expert, guide, friend, group leader, mature adult, curriculum constructor and master of ceremonies. The educative teacher does not set up a different curriculum for each child. Instead he sets up the most open and inquiring community he can, and then helps each child use it to advance his own inquiries. He needs his students' cooperation and participation to build this sort of community.

The aim of our second mode of evaluation, then, is to chart the progress of the classroom (or any other group) from an accidental collection of people in a situation structured only by their varying, mostly undefined, expectations to an orderly community whose expectations are known, whose operation is involving, whose work 'feels' significant. It is a growth from dependence on the teacher to call the shots, plan the work, encourage students and set the tone or affective mood to dependence on the tested experience of the children, the authority of the subject-discipline, the cooperatively developed norms of behavior and the encouragement by students of each other. It is the movement from uncertainty as to one's adequacy and one's place — along with the various individual ways of reacting to these painful stresses — to security, a sense of autonomy and feelings of capability, adequacy and effectiveness. It is a shift from apprehension, docility and reliance on general civility to a sense of adventure, initiative and reliance on one's own and the class's resources.[4]

Progress is charted and evaluated through changes in whatever operations are responsible for the state of *authenticity*, *legitimacy* and *productivity* of the classroom community (Chapter 6). The state of authenticity is probably best indexed by the location of the boundary between public and private: what the child can express about his feelings, interests and private theories, while ruminating on and planning for classroom activities. It is reflected in his making suggestions that he is personally interested in; in his voluntary citing of personal experience and fantasy in order to show what he means by ideas; in the way that the children respond to each other's ideas; in the freedom with which children take the risk of trying to behave differently; in the expansion of the range of resources the children muster as they participate in classroom activities — whether alone, in small groups or in the formal assembly; it is in the fluid formation of partnerships with anyone who can help in the business at hand.

The state of *legitimacy* is more complex because the legitimating authorities are more abstract. As compared with authenticity, in which one can almost count the children who are out of it or really with it, legitimacy cannot be judged against concrete persons. Legitimacy is an idea. Ideas are made known in dialogue, whether spoken or written. The ideational content of legitimacy is the rationale for activity, the 'fundamental reasons serving to account for something.' The 'somethings' to be accounted for are of the order of, 'Why do we have to do it? From what point of view or line of reasoning does this make sense? On what basis can we determine the truth, morality or value of our ideas and behaviors? To what extent and in what ways is our activity a prototype for other activities? How does our experience connect to that of other people in other situations, other institutions, other places and times?'

To me, the basic themes of legitimacy are authority and universality. By authority I mean the ideas, whether in subject matter, tradition, common experience or logical construction, that one turns to as *decisive* in selecting or creating new alternatives. After all the smoke clears away, what is it that *really* settles the argument? By universality, I mean the middle-level policy, theory or understanding of the world that enables present experience to be reorganized as an aid to better further experience; that enables every experience to have meaning as an instance of things more universal, enduring and valuable than the immediate experience itself.

The most obvious signs of development of the class's insight into legitimacy are such as the following: a shift from, 'What do you want us to do?' to, 'What is the "logical" thing to do next?'; a shift from, 'Is this idea of mine right?' to, 'Under what conditions or in what situations would this idea of mine make sense?'; a shift from, 'I don't want to do that so you shouldn't make me,' to, 'That doesn't sound enjoyable to me, but I can see that it needs to be done'; a shift from, 'Let's vote,' to, 'Let's look at the pros and cons'; a shift from, 'This is the way nice people behave,' to, 'This is what this particular situation would seem to call for'; a shift from psyching out the teacher and the tests to following the logic of a variety of methods of investigation.

The state of *productivity* is easy to assess when the purposes of activity are stated and understood; and it is practically impossible when they are not. So perhaps the most fundamental thing to look for is simply how well the class knows what it is attempting to accomplish through each of its activities. Sometimes, of course, there are 'transitional' periods during which about all that can be said is that we are expressing highly individual reactions and hoping to arrive soon at some purposive 'sense of the meeting.' But even here, *that* should be understood to be the 'purpose': to find a purpose. The signs of productivity are absence of aimlessness, awareness of each step as part of a strategic sequence of steps, reorganization of the class (alone, small groups, etc.) as necessary to facilitate work; knowing when the job is done; proceeding skillfully; etc.

These three concerns are not independent of each other. The teacher's aim is not to maximize each, but to optimize their blend. Trade-offs are always involved. One concern may dominate at one time, another at another. Thus the pressure for formally disciplined argument or for skilful performance (in the name of productivity) may stifle personal interest and creativity (authenticity). The pressure for grinding out the work (in the name of productivity) may move its legitimacy from reasons to threats. The allowing or encouraging of too much 'permissiveness' (in the name of authenticity) can rob the child of the security (legitimating of warranting authority) which he needs in order to use the 'freedom.' Having each child go off and do his thing destroys the legitimacy of the class purposes, but having all the children do the same thing at the same time destroys authenticity. And so it goes. If the most basic concerns for culture-building are authenticity, legitimacy and productivity, then the most basic educational assumptions are the understandings through which the three concerns are adjudicated in each situation.

The evaluation of teaching in the terms just outlined can be systematized and made practical in three ways, all of which should probably be used. First, the teacher can simply record in his notebook the comments which he recalls that seem to be most clear indicators of the state of the three concerns. Second, the teacher can hold class discussions, as during the planning or follow-up discussion of activities, in which he systematically probes (hopefully tactfully and indirectly) the dimensions of the three concepts as understood by the children. Third, tests such as our ALP-ethos instrument (Chapters 1 and 6) can be given toward the beginning and end of the year. Such tests have the virtue that they are systematic and interpretable, but they can only chart overall changes; they cannot give the feedback from each activity that a teacher needs to keep an on-going professional inquiry in full swing. Summarizing class averages on such tests and then asking the class to interpret them and say what they 'mean' not only helps validate the test results but adds further dimensions and makes up for some of the deficiencies that are inevitable in any 'ready-made' test.

The Local Educational System

The organized educational system is a bureaucracy manned by

employees who are paid to undertake the specified duties and responsibilities that define their jobs. Job specifications are usually a mixed bag of procedures to be followed, attitudes to be 'shown' and judgments to be exercised. In each job a modicum of judiciousness is expected; and this is supposed to adapt the system to more or less routine variations in circumstances and performance. It is generally supposed that if each person does his job properly the system will operate correctly.

Obviously all this is very rational and systematic. But it also produces results that at times are either laughable or infuriating. For example, a certain experimental school was set up in a large city. Its goals were enlightened, its procedures were flexible and its reception by the public was excellent. The assistant superintendent in whose department the school was located was fired because he was too careless about meeting the specifications of his job — specifications which had no provision for treating different schools differently. A new man was brought in and he followed the specifications to the letter; he was the darling of the higher echelons. But what looked to the bosses like punctiliousness and responsibility amounted, in the experience of the experimental school, to intolerable harassment. Morale dropped, procedures reverted to the norm and the school lost everything that had made it exciting, experimental and important.

The district superintendent I most admire was a man of sprightly humor and flexibility. His retirement banquet was attended by subordinates, superiors and community leaders; and they came because they really wanted to. The key to this man's outstanding success was that he knew which specifications to ignore; and he knew how to ignore them in such a way that it was not worth trying to catch him. It helped, too, that his office was several miles from downtown, so that he was able to make himself relatively invisible; he didn't run into bureaucrats every time he went down the hall! His freewheeling style was a great boon to his superiors, who were constantly confronted with annoying problems from other district superintendents who followed to the letter the job prescriptions, which had not anticipated emerging, urgent and real problems. For these, the superiors routed memos back and forth, hoping that the problems would go away. When they did reply to the petition from below, it was usually to set up a ceremonial conference to exchange mutual vows of cooperation with the district superintendent — and to cite one or more regulations and tell the underling that he would be held responsible for his handling of the problem. The moral of all this seems to be that job specifications ought to be rewritten in terms of authentic systems criteria rather than be seen as technical and managerial rites to be produced by each job-holder.

Thus, to evaluate a system, one must define each of its several major functional components or subsystems.[5] Each subsystem comprises all the specific acts — regardless of actor — through which the function is implemented. One may then ask how well specific projects and problems are coped with by the subsystem. If this evaluation is gratifying further probing will not add much. On the other hand, as is usually the case, one or more functions may be in trouble, meaning that some kinds of problems are being handled badly; and then a more thorough examination is called for. What policies seem to govern the deficient operations and what assumptions about values and costs legitimate these policies? How, in each office, are policies translated into procedures that are supposedly adaptive and self-correcting? Where are the bottlenecks, breakdowns and ambiguities that make certain procedures unsatisfactory? And finally, after serious efforts to see the questionable function holistically, one has the right to ask what part of the difficulties can be properly attributed to particular individuals; and should such individuals be helped, shifted to a job more congruent with their capabilities, fired or promoted?

When the purpose of evaluation is to improve the system, then the participants who will have to mend their ways should help to evaluate their own processes and procedures. In the course of these self-studies, many small changes tend to be made voluntarily and unobtrusively as a result of better morale, new or confirmed insight, or more caring; threatening confrontations by 'outside evaluators' are avoided. But if awareness and better understanding of how we are operating is enough to bring about adaptive changes, then why not build such self-scrutiny into the normal operations of each unit? This sounds like a small, almost trivial question, but it is in fact quite profound, for its changes the whole conception of the system from that of a machine to be checked and occasionally repaired by outsiders to a self-regenerating inquiring system operated by multi-dimensional human beings, and not by job-holders. With this shift, the problem of the 'guarantor' becomes salient; some higher authority than making the machine run smoothly or meeting job-specifications has to be found.

We have proposed that this higher guarantee must come ultimately from basic concerns for authenticitly, legitimacy and productivity

(Chapter 6). Thus, in evaluating a real system, the evaluator's first task is to construct a model against which this real system is to be judged. Let us consider what is involved in a rather simple case, the use of parents as tutors within the school. Let us say that parents are invited to visit classes and to tutor certain pupils. The parents are to be brought in from 'outside' and made part of the instructional sub-system of the school. The school is uncertain how large the parents' role should be and what it should entail beyond following the teacher's instructions. The teachers want to include the parents in the work of the classroom; and they must show the parents what to do, help them do it and try to make the work satisfying enough that the parents will continue to come. The teachers realize that they will need to get acquainted with the parents, feel easy in talking with them and bring about a trusting, mutually confident relationship. The parents see that the new activity may provide opportunities for expanding their horizons, for helping their children develop skills and self-esteem, for exploring career possibilities, for contributing to the community and so on. Parents may hope to include teachers and some or all of the children within their circle of friends; incorporate tutoring within their repertoire of capabilities; and assimilate the school's educational ideology within their internalized culture.

Reflecting on all this, the evaluator sees that his overall model consists of the relationships between: (a) the ideal goal of getting enough help of the right kind to all the students who need it; (b) the practical goal of helping the students who need help most and are also most likely to profit from the kind of help that will be available; (c) the process goal of institutionalizing the operation; (d) the transcendent goal of managing affairs in such a way that the growing resources of competence, involvement and concern continually improve the program's effectiveness and aspirations. Putting these goals together we see that the overall model is that of an educative system in which getting adequate help to students who need it is the test of the performance of the system as a whole[6]; developing and maintaining trust, productivity and shared aims are interrelated parts of the system's management and functioning; and engagement in dialectical processes of growth and emergence of new goals is the underlying process which produces the other two outcomes.

Nationalizing Influences and National Goals

The major source of funds for experimentation and school improve-

ment is the national Government. In the United States, funds have
been made available to ensure the 'right to read,' for Head Start,
Follow Through, Career Education and counseling, for the development of performance objectives, programs for the handicapped and
so on. These funds are appropriated by Congress, and are intended to
help or induce schools to meet 'national goals' for education. We may
anticipate that Congress would have its own notions of what it means
by 'national goals' and would also have its own political reasons for
formulating them. At the same time, educators would also have their
own somewhat different understandings of the nature of a national
goal. We further anticipate that these two views would differ in
important respects and that Congress and the educators must operate
from somewhat different assumptions, about what to do, what it
means to do it and how to react to whatever occurs as a result. Clearly,
an important aim of evaluation within the larger system is to clarify
the differing or conflicting basic assumptions held by the various
partners in the enterprise.

Consider, for example, the case of 'the right to read,' a national
educational goal identified by Congress. During the early to middle
1960s, a great many varieties of social unrest converged in the
development of Black Power. Public (and political) attention was
focussed on the many ways in which black populations are discriminated against by the dominant society. These discriminations were
made illegal, by establishing that they were denials of various consti-
tutional 'rights.' The success of the Brown case in 1954 dramatically
confirmed a long-standing contention of the NAACP: that to secure
his rights, an individual must be able to utilize the courts and other
available recourses. Congress acceded to the position that if blacks
are to achieve their proper rights, then discrimination must be
reduced in the main society and blacks must become literate. And so
it came to pass that much of the affect of Black Power and a nation-
wide concern about civil rights got channeled by Congress into a
'national goal for education': that of giving every child the 'right to
read.' Put this way, attention was diverted from discrimination in
other parts of society; and black equality could be postponed until the
present youngsters, made literate, had grown up. The Office of
Education was given funds to recruit several consulting, research and
training agencies which would work with schools to improve instruction in reading.

Campbell and Bunnel[7] characterize such agencies as 'nationalizing
influences on education'; they are transmitters of national policies

and goals to the schools. These agencies identify with the same politico-technical-corporate complex that speaks through Congress. It is obvious to them that schools could indeed develop better procedures and techniques of instruction; and, of course, they just happen to have such to suggest.

Teachers can agree that many children do not learn to read very well. They would be happy to have some sure-fire techniques with results guaranteed. But they do not expect to find them. Moreover, teachers know or suspect something else: that how well students learn from techniques has little to do with the techniques. What matters more is the student's family and community 'background.' Regardless of classroom techniques, the successful students come from literate homes. Their parents read and discuss current issues and problems; books and magazines abound. And that is not all: the parents, more likely than not, started reading stories to the child while he was still a baby, and now they regularly invite him to show how well he can read and they give him encouragement and approval.

In this view, teachers consider it unrealistic to expect 'poor' children to read — regardless of teaching techniques. On the other hand, maybe techniques could be found to solve the teacher's 'real' problem: that the 'poor' children are apathetic or rebellious; they are hard to manage and control. What is really needed is some 'reading' procedures that will make classroom management effective. And so a new 'learning system' is installed. It is likely to be heavy with drill and repetition and so long as 'evaluation' is confined to the drilled-on performances there may be marked 'improvement.' The improvement results because 'reading' has been redefined and reduced to what the new techniques can accomplish.

Comparison of this technical operation with an educative dialectical model suggests that at first there are probably more benefits than costs but that in the long run the costs of missed opportunities may turn out to be very great. Although the teacher's concern for reading and the educator's concern for literacy led them to the verge of the same insight, that parents would have to be deeply involved to improve the childrens' reading, there was no way that this insight could filter back to the level of national policy and goal-setting.

Now let us return to the national goal and see how a systems educator would think about it. He would surely agree that one appropriate response to the plight of discriminated-against minorities is indeed to help them increase their literacy. But he would locate the responsibility for such efforts in society, not soley in the schools. The question therefore would not be, 'What can we get the schools to do about it?' but rather, 'How can the schools participate along with other enterprises to help improve the literacy of minorities?' This would call for analysis of the total situation and for setting of priorities.

One might start by testing the announced rationale of the program. Are there, in fact, people who cannot get jobs (even though jobs are available) because they cannot read — but are otherwise qualified? How can we identify them? How many are there? In what setting can they be found? Who are they in contact with? How can we get these 'contacts' to teach them to read or to steer them to someone else who will teach them to read? What are the ways bus lines, supermarkets, churches, police courts, ball games, TV, etc. might contribute to skills of reading or to the readiness to learn? Is there some place where people could turn in their magazines when they were through with them? Would that be helpful? How? Didn't our experts make some wonderful films that significantly helped reduce illiteracy in developing nations? Could similar films work here — possibly with free admission and entertainment at their weekly showing in local movie houses?

Thus, to the educator a national goal would be a concrete outcome sought through the coordination of all the efforts in the nation that can help achieve it. These activities would interlock within a newly conceived 'literacy system' of society. As the educator reflected on all the meanings and values that could be enhanced in the creation of, and operation of, such a system, he might begin to feel that the benefits would be so great in comparison to the few millions or billions it would cost that we cannot afford not to get busy on it.

Perhaps the biggest difference between the system-wide dialetical approach to 'problem-solving' and the technical-procedures approach is that the former is always reaching out to make more connections and to include more goal-salient activities within the system. Within the classroom, reading techniques could be enlarged to make room for pupil teams which would function like small support systems. If the notion of improving parental literacy as a way of supporting the child's efforts were taken seriously, the question would arise as to how to develop the support system for the parents. This would lead into a further examination of what adult literacy means.

If literacy is to help the learner lead a better life then it will be most effectively developed in connection with ongoing efforts of many sorts to create a better life in the community. In this all-out conception, the distinction between technical learning systems and support systems would disappear and be replaced by the concept of the inquiring, humane or dialectical community; and 'education' would become a lifelong aspect of the human quest.

We learn, then, that a campaign to help schools to get lower-status children to read has to be embedded in the larger quest for literate communities. Limited functional technical programs, like 'right to read,' are spawned by the society, but the support systems are communal. When schools upgrade techniques and downgrade dialogue, however, they erode their own communal aspects and therefore have to rely more and more on outside support systems.

At the present time, a good case can be made for regarding families, not youngsters, as the primary client of inner-city education. The time has come for us to try to figure out what this more or less staggering truth means for education. In the meanwhile, the most hopeful, properly modest, Federal effort that I know of at present is to help communities set up learning-resource centers for the use of any person or group engaged in any kind of educational effort within the community.

The Conceived Educative System

In this chapter we have considered the individual learner-inquirer, interacting with materials and activities; the classroom, developing toward a more educative community; the local school organization, held together by interdependent functioning of its parts; and the 'nationalizing influences' which act on schools through special agencies. In order to evaluate these levels of the educational enterprise, we must set up models against which to compare them. Over and over, on all levels, we find the same two basic philosophically rationalized models: one oriented to techniques, rationality, problem-solving, and impersonal interactions; the other oriented to dialectics, intentionality, emergent principles and humane interaction.

It cannot be denied that our societies are dominated by a 'technicist orientation,' whose underlying faith is that human-social ills can be rationalized and recast as 'problems' of such a nature that they can be 'solved' through the development of more efficient techniques and procedures. Moreover, ills that cannot be processed through rational technology are to be ignored, smothered in a barrage of verbal image-making or denigrated to the status of 'mere' individual whim, neurosis or lack of patriotism. The new moral authority of this orientation is the principle of the technical imperative: that every new technological capability must be immediately developed and incorporated within our lives regardless of the human-social consequences.

These assumptions have placed the improvement of education within the ethos of research and development — R & D. But 25 years of experience with heavily financed R & D efforts have led to a clear conclusion: these efforts have largely failed to improve the educational system. Not only were the specific goals of R & D programs *not* met except, occasionally, by accident, but the dominance of such programs by partial or false premises about the nature of educational effort has tended to corrupt the enterprise, turning teachers into technicians rather than professionals, politicians into middle-men rather than leaders, government agencies into supervisors rather than expediters and researchers into entrepreneurs rather than inquirers. Any semblance of dialectical processes ends with the receipt of grant money. Yet nobody wanted these things to happen.

The most fundamental false premise of our society is that the meaning and value of interdependence among men is given by their respective relationships to the technical-political 'productive' efforts of societal subsystems rather than by their common fellowship as human beings. The price we have paid in education and elsewhere for the most productive system in the world is the sacrifice of the humane community to the functional-distributive society. Our futures both as nations and as human beings depends on our ability to get them back together.

As we try to identify constructive possibilities it might be useful to remember the two bricklayers at work on a large wall. They are asked, 'What are you doing?' The first replies, 'I am laying bricks.' The second says, 'I am building a cathedral.' The first is a technician or tradesman; the other has the soul of an artist or professional. The difference is in the meaning of the activity to its participants. It is not in how expertly or skilfully they daub mortar on to brick; it is not in the number of hours of supervised practice they have had: it is not in how much information they have about the job; it is not in their loyalty to the boss. It is in how they savor and feel about what they are doing, in their sensing of relationships between their work and that of others, in their appreciation of potentialities, in their sense of form, in their need for and enjoyment of significance, in their identification of self with civilized aspirations, in their whole outlook on life. It is in their sense of *vocation*.

Can we find a generic term for the kind of vocation exemplified by the cathedral-builder? Adjectives like humane, transcendent, compassionate, and integrative come to mind, but they do not capture the full pattern of the lifestyle to which we want to refer. In the 1890s, however, there was a precise word for it. That word was 'professional' as applied to the man and 'profession' as designating his vocation. In these days when kitchen cleanser is peddled on TV by a 'professional' dishwasher, the term no longer evokes the aspiration for the highest and finest that civilization has to offer. But at the turn of the century, the word expressed very well the way of life for which doctors, lawyers and ministers should be trained.

Discussing the United States, Borrowman[8] has written that as early as 1827 the concept of teaching as a profession was close to the surface, and that it probably expressed the consensus of educators when it was made official in the charter of the National Education Association in 1870. The paraphernalia of the education profession was developed piecemeal: normal schools and university-type programs; state and local certification; research and professional associations. The special knowledge, characteristic of professions, was located first in 'standard works on moral and mental philosophy' and later in the pedagogical systems of Herbart and Pestalozzi. In the 1890s, during the soul-stirring flowering of intellect in America, the new social sciences emerging in universities were connected to pedagogy and the new 'scientific study of education' offered the prospect of continuous and systematic growth of the special knowledge that would give substance to the profession.

But even these new social institutions and vistas of knowledge would not, by themselves, make teaching a profession. A third element, a sense of vocation — a commitment to an ideal, spirit or ethos — was needed. And it was found in the great movement toward social reforms that swept all aspects of American life. By 1895 (according to Cremin[9]) the school was seen no longer to be merely a device for training citizens; it was to become an instrument of social reform. This idea galvanized education, pulled together the various elements and generated the archetype of teaching as a profession.

The vision of the professional archetype in education was but a moment in history, a coincidence of political-economic reform, stimulation of philosophy by the new sciences, expansion of public education and commitment to traditional religious and humane values. The passing of the moment was also the passing of what the moment meant: that schools could be genuinely educative and that people could build a society more 'worthy, lovely and harmonious.'

I do not suppose that anyone seriously thinks the moment and the meanings could occur again. But may there be other moments — moments of shared inspiration that can 'galvanize' education into better realizing its potentialities for the humane person and society, and for helping make the great American Dream a reality?

It is to this hope and possibility that this book is dedicated.

Summary

In order to evaluate the educational enterprise we have to see it whole; we must be clear about the concepts that organize its parts in relation to each other and the overarching system. We see that for the purposes of evaluation it is useful to regard the educational enterprise as four component 'nested' systems: the individual inquirer and his quest for educational growth defined as improved effectiveness for coping with demanding prototypical problems; the class group and its ability to grow itself into an increasingly effective educational community; the organized educational system with its many functions, each of which may be evaluated by means of comparison models; the national influences on the role of the school *vis-à-vis* other national subsystems.

Generally speaking, we find on all four levels the same restless conflict between two conceptions of education. The first is oriented to techniques, rationality, problem-solving and impersonal interaction — as assumed within the cultural archetype. The second revolves around dialectics, emergent principles and humane interaction — as assumed in an ideal professional archetype. We see that the task ahead is to redress the balance between these images, and to that hope this book is dedicated.

Notes

1. B. S. Bloom, J. J. Hastings and G. F. Madaus (eds.), *Handbook of Formative and Summative Evaluation of Student Learning* (McGraw-Hill, New York, 1971).

2. H. A. Thelen, 'Programmed Material Today: Critique and Proposal,' *Elementary School Journal*, vol. 63, no. 4 (1963), pp. 189-96.

3. H. A. Thelen, 'Testing by Means of Filmstrips with Synchronized Recorded Sound,' *Educational and Psychological Measurement*, vol. 5, no. 1 (1945), pp. 33-48.

4. H. A. Thelen, 'Evaluation of Group Instruction,' in *Educational Evaluation: New Roles, New Means*, Sixty-eighth Yearbook of the National Society for the Study of Education (University of Chicago, Press, Chicago, 1969), pp. 115-55.

5. C. West Churchman, *The Systems Approach* (Dell, New York, 1968).

6. Churchman, *Systems*.

7. R. F. Campbell and R. A. Bunnel, *Nationalizing Influences on Secondary Education* (Midwest Administration Center, University of Chicago, 1963) See also Grace Graham, *The Public School in the New Society* (Harper and Row, New York, 1969).

8. M. L. Borrowman, 'Teacher Education: History,' in *The Encyclopedia of Education* (Macmillan, New York, 1971), vol. 9, pp. 71-9.

9. L. A. Cremin, *The Transformation of the Schools* (Random House, New York, 1961), pp. 168-176.

Index

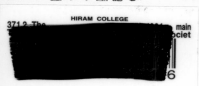